Blues Before **Sunrise 3**

MUSIC IN AMERICAN LIFE

The Music in American Life series documents and celebrates the dynamic and multifaceted relationship between music and American culture. From its first publication in 1972 through its half-century mark and beyond, the series has embraced a wide variety of methodologies, from biography and memoir to history and musical analysis, and spans the full range of musical forms, from classical through all types of vernacular music. The series showcases the wealth of musical practice and expression that characterizes American music, as well as the rich diversity of its stylistic, regional, racial, ethnic, and gendered contexts. Characterized by a firm grounding in material culture, whether archival or ethnographic, and by work that honors the musical activities of ordinary people and their communities, Music in American Life continually redefines and expands the very definition of what constitutes music in American culture, whose voices are heard, and how music and musical practices are understood and valued.

For a list of books in the series, please see our website at www.press.uillinois.edu.

Steve Cushing

Blues Before **Sunrise 3**

GUITAR SLINGERS AND BACKBEATERS

INTRODUCTION BY
WAYNE EVERETT GOINS

UNIVERSITY OF
ILLINOIS PRESS
Urbana, Chicago, and Springfield

Manufactured in the United States of America
1 2 3 4 5 C P 5 4 3 2 1
♾ This book is printed on acid-free paper.

Library of Congress Cataloging-in-Publication Data
Names: Cushing, Steve, author. | Cushing, Steve, interviewer. | Goins, Wayne E., writer of introduction.
Title: Blues before sunrise 3 : guitar slingers and backbeaters / Steve Cushing ; introduction by Wayne Everett Goins. Other titles: Blues before sunrise (Radio program) Description: Urbana : University of Illinois press, 2025. | Series: Music in American life | Includes index.
Identifiers: LCCN 2024044808 (print) | LCCN 2024044809 (ebook) | ISBN 9780252046605 (cloth) | ISBN 9780252088711 (paperback) | ISBN 9780252047916 (ebook)
Subjects: LCSH: Blues musicians—United States—Biography. | Guitarists—United States—Biography. | Drummers (Musicians)—United States—Biography. | Blues (Music)—History and criticism. | Blues musicians—United States—Interviews. | Guitarists—United States—Interviews. | Drummers (Musicians)—United States—Interviews. | LCGFT: Interviews.
Classification: LCC ML394.B6475 2025 (print) | LCC ML394 (ebook) | DDC 781.643092/273 [B]—dc23/eng/20240924
LC record available at https://lccn.loc.gov/2024044808
LC ebook record available at https://lccn.loc.gov/2024044809

Contents

Introduction

Chicago Blues: The Movement, Musicians, Monuments, and Makers

WAYNE EVERETT GOINS

The Movement

In what has come to be known as The Great Migration, Black Mississippians who had been both collectively and uniformly subjugated to an inferior status initiated an exit *en masse* in hopes of bettering themselves as they sought a higher quality of life. The tainted legacy of The Deep South, with its Jim Crow laws and unfair practices of one-sided benefits to the sharecropping industry—essentially the sole manner of income for Blacks throughout that entire region of the country—was more than enough reason to escape the poverty-stricken lifestyle that plagued minorities both during and after the end of slavery in 1865.

Fast-forward several decades to the early 1900s and you still find that the history of oppression and conditions for African Americans had scarcely improved. In what started as a trickle, minorities began looking North for a way to escape. As early as 1916, both the Illinois Central and M&O rail lines brought them to Chicago as a result of job vacancies created by the First World War. By the time World War II had ended, thousands more found an opening as a result of a significant need in America for industrial workers to fill the void caused by men who never returned home. More specifically, urban cities—including New York, Detroit, Chicago, Cleveland, Pittsburgh, and Philadelphia, among others—flung their gates open to receive the underclass who sought better wages and were willing to work for it. Indeed, the trickle became a flood. According to liner notes written by Studs Turkel on the back panel of the 1958 Chess LP, *The Best of Muddy Waters*, "The National Opinion Research Center of the University of Chicago estimates an increase of 250,000 Negroes since 1947."

Just as African Americans carried along their physical possessions, both gospel and blues traditions were also exported from the southern territories of Mississippi, Alabama, Louisiana, Texas, and Tennessee; these travelers sought to find fertile ground in the concrete and steel environments that awaited them. They sought relief in both churches and nightclubs from the rigors of long work hours. The musical works of Chicago's own "Georgia Tom" Dorsey represent a perfect example of balancing the sacred and profane to satisfy the needs of the ever-increasing Black population who turned to music to soothe their souls as they dragged their weary bodies home from the stockyards and steel mills after working both day and night shifts to earn a more decent living.

During the mass migration, the highly transportable acoustic instruments of drums, harmonica, and guitar gained popularity and prominence in the inner city, marking the beginnings of what ultimately became a sonic transfusion. Black sounds of rural Mississippi porch music burst forth in the more modern form of urban electric blues, as ambitious entertainers slowly became frontrunners in the burgeoning market for what we now know as "the Chicago blues sound." Indeed, early South Side migrant musicians like harp player Sonny Boy Williamson, guitarist Muddy Waters, and drummer Earl Phillips emerged as instrumental leaders among those who would forge this new sound. A second wave of artists included even younger artists like Little Walter on harmonica, Fred Below on drums, and Buddy Guy on guitar, who also sought work as musicians.

These newcomers joined the network of already-established musicians—an older generation of Deep South blues transplants who were willing to lend a hand in providing them access to house parties, blues bars, and nightclubs of Chicago. Tom Dorsey was, in essence, Chicago's musical embodiment of a multitasking blues producer, composer, and performing entrepreneur—he was Willie Dixon *before* Willie Dixon arrived. Muddy Waters readily admitted to leaning on his personal contacts, which included not only guitar/harp ace Robert Nighthawk, his mentor (and Dorsey cohort) Tampa Red, and guitarist/vocalist Big Bill Broonzy, who served as the staunchest advocate of all for Waters. Even the Chicago harp legend John Lee Williamson (the *original* "Sonny Boy"—not to be confused with Alex "Rice" Miller) had guitarist Sleepy John Estes and harmonica player Hammie Nixon as influences when he arrived in Chicago during the twenties. This tight brotherhood and sharing of ideas between musicians of similar instruments on guitar, harmonica, or piano is relatively easily documented.

The history of blues drumming, however, is not so clear cut.

The Musicians—Drummers

Unlike the well-documented history of blues guitar, the actual performance style of *blues* drumming did not yet exist within the genre. One only has to examine the musical evolution of legendary Chicago drummer Fred Below to discover that the category of what we nowadays readily acknowledge as "blues drumming" was yet to be crystallized by the time Elgin Evans introduced him to Tampa Red around 1946. Although the quintessential Chicago blues band during the embryonic period between 1945–1960 consisted of the essential elements of bass, drums, piano, guitar(s), harmonica, and vocals, the very specific role of the blues drummer found its stylistic evolution not in the genre of blues, but of *jazz* origins. When asked to speak on their biggest and earliest musical influences, the majority of interviewees for this book responded in unison when the subject arose concerning the drumming prowess and big band exploits of these prominent *jazz* percussionists: Gene Krupa, Buddy Rich, Cozy Cole, Chick Webb, Max Roach, and Art Blakey.

Cushing's interviews reveal the common denominator that binds these drummers together—the outward passion for their predecessors who ruled the roost in the world of big band jazz during the Golden Era of Swing. Over a span of roughly about twenty years, each of these artists who formed the crux of Chicago blues drumming would collectively shape what became the style itself. Serious blues fans who closely follow the arc of these musicians might easily recognize the trademarks that identify them as blues drummers: The unique floor tom pattern of Earl Phillips, and his snare technique he learned from Chick Webb; Clifton James's influence of Webb's big bass drum; S.P. Leary's patented brush work that he borrowed from Count Basie's drummer Jo Jones and stick work he learned from Art Blakey; Odie Payne's unparalleled fast kick drum work; Willie "Big Eyes" Smith's "pocket" groove—deliberately played very far on the *back* end of the beat; the classic bebop-era cymbal work of Fred Below, and the "dropping bombs" technique he learned from Muddy's previous drummer Elgin Evans during those early "Headcutter" years with Waters.

When these drummers were striving both night and day to find their way, they all crossed paths like streetcars in the night, traveling from one hotspot to another—making the gig, subbing for each other, setting up and breaking down. Odie Payne first served under Tampa Red before branching out with numerous Chess Records artists; Earl Phillips, upon Muddy's specific recommendation, became the longtime drummer for Howlin' Wolf; S.P. Leary got his first experience with Sonny Boy II; Fred Below played with damn near *everybody*—and became the most frequently recorded session drummer in Chess history; Willie "Big Eyes" Smith became Muddy's longtime drummer during later stages of Muddy's career. And, of course, this entire drum legacy was handed down to the youngest member of the generation included in this book, Casey Jones.

He was only seventeen years old when he first came to Chicago in 1956—just after the tradition was being established, and blues drumming was an actual *thing* the world could wrap their hands around. He followed in their footsteps, doing stints with Howlin' Wolf, Otis Rush, Magic Sam, and a host of others as he rose to the top and became a first-call blues drummer.

There was among them a high level of networking that furthered their cause while simultaneously perpetuating the art form. Being a member of the blues drum fraternity represented a club *within* a club. They belonged to a subspecies that existed on its own terms. Their shared stories usually involved tales of first-hand accounts of events only witnessed from a unique vantage point that only comes from being behind the drum set on the bandstand. Their challenges and obstacles ranged from equipment failures, tempo dilemmas, and any number of extraneous issues related to the sound-space continuum.

Blues Drumming—An Analysis

The concept or definition of "swing" has many interpretations, but the simple truth is this: Almost *any* style of music can "swing" if the drummer maintains a steady groove. In the jazz genre, the component of the drums that determines the swing is primarily the responsibility of the ride cymbal; but for blues drummers, the patented *shuffle* groove is related to the overall coordination and syncopated rhythm of the entire band: The kick drum pattern locked into the bass player's quarter-note pulse; the snare locked in with guitar's rhythmic shuffle gallop; and, presiding over all of it, the *spang-a-lang* rhythmic pattern of the cymbal. Each component of the drum set plays its own individual role.

For a blues drummer to establish himself as legitimate, he must be able to properly execute this essential shuffle pattern, which is based on four beats per measure. All drummers must contend with exactly where the center of the beat is placed related to the *overall* tempo. There are three general time zones that drummers either deliberately target—or unconsciously vacillate between—when trying to establish a steady pace. All three of these tempo placements have a direct impact on the degree to which the entire band has a "groove" or what most drummers refer to as the "pocket."

There are recordings where drummers inadvertently or gradually play more "on the front end" of the beat, which tends to make the entire combo's groove *lean forward* sonically speaking, or "rush." The opposite is also true: If the drummer gradually pulls back the tempo, the tendency is to *drag* the tempo, thus losing the groove. A perfect example of a non-wavering "pocket" is Fred Below's performance on the Jimmy Rogers recording of "Walkin' By Myself" from the *Chicago Bound* album by Chess [LP407]. The groove is *so* deep that it no doubt inspired "Big Walter" Horton to blow one of the strongest solos of his career. Then there's the ultimate example of Below delivering his patented "dropping bombs" during the harp solo on "You're the One" on that same album—the first LP in Jimmy's career, which influenced several generations of blues guitarists since its release in 1970.

This concept of placing the "two-and-four" at the front, center, or back of the beat also applies to non-triplet swing groove. The *straight* eighth-note groove is what we hear when we listen to a song like Chuck Berry's classic "Johnny B. Goode" [Chess 1691]. Listen to the straight-eighth feel Odie Payne plays on the 1964 Chess [1884] recording of Berry's "Nadine"—the drums propel the entire band. On the other hand, almost nothing beats a medium-tempo, hard-backbeat shuffle when it comes to finding a drum groove meant for Black folks dancing in the late-night clubs. Listen to the infectious groove that occurs as a result of the heavy downbeat Willie "Big Eyes" Smith delivers on the Muddy Waters 1981 [Blue Sky JZ 37064] version of "King Bee." Smith uses his signature triplet figure at the end of each chorus for what is known as the "turnaround."

Then there is the *combination* of the 4/4 time played in sets of triplets—as in Earl Phillips's groove on Jimmy Reed's 1959 Vee Jay recording, "Baby What You Want Me to Do" [VJ 333]. It creates a totally different feel than the dotted-rhythm pattern he delivers on "Found Love." Phillips never *needs* to crash the cymbals or use heavy kick drum patterns—the snap of the snare and the hi-hat on beats two and four are the only ingredients needed to make the tune swing. However, on the 1959 Vee Jay 45 release of "Goin' To New York" [VJ 326], he actually *does* use the crash cymbal to great effect, gradually increasing the tension on the first beat of every measure until he finally unleashes a torrent with his patented, thunderous triplet punctuations on the floor tom.

There is the superb playing of S.P. Leary on the 1964 Chess label recording of "You Can't Lose What You Ain't Never Had" using a 6/8 light ride cymbal pattern while laying down snare drum hits on beats two and four. Willie Dixon supplies solid quarter notes on bass while Pee Wee Madison delivers a dotted eighth-note rhythm guitar pattern that locks in perfect sync with both Leary's left-hand snare and Dixon's right-hand bass pluck.

In Muddy's first "greatest hits" album, the 1958 Chess release of *The Best of Muddy Waters* [LP 1427] is a collection of all his 45s released between 1947–53. Listen to Fred Below's groove on "I'm Ready" to hear an example of pure unadulterated jazz drumming: the swing ride cymbal sizzling throughout the chorus; the stop time on the verses; the triplet snare figures leading into the killer solo by Little Walter; the four on the floor kick drum; and "bomb" crash cymbal that sets up the squalling solo by Walter.

Over time, stylistic shifts in drum grooves paved the way for several new directions in popular music. The blues shuffle associated with the 1950s eventually gave way to the straight-eighth grooves of rock n' roll made popular by Chuck Berry, along with the jungle-like rhumba grooves played by Clifton James for Bo Diddley. The advent of the hippie culture—the incoming era of go-go boots, mini-skirts, bell bottoms and Afros—slowly made its way into the mid-'60s as the decline of popular blues gave way to the psychedelic "boogaloo" grooves that permeated American culture. So powerful was this movement that even the jazz genre was not immune to its effects.

Witness the shift in approach by the tag team of Buddy Guy and Junior Wells, who began playing boogaloo grooves for the club audiences, as well as on their recordings. A perfect example comes in the form of "Snatch It Back and Hold It," one of the "hip" grooves on the seminal *Hoodoo Man Blues* released by Delmark [DS-612]. On that same album, Junior's version of Big Mama Thornton's "Hound Dog" also has a brisk, up-tempo go-go beat.

The drum grooves shifted yet again as the "funky" drumming style emerged—Chicago blues guitarists openly embraced psychedelic beats borrowed from soul/R&B artists like James Brown, Wilson Pickett, and Sam & Dave. Harp players like Junior Wells teamed with Buddy Guy (listen to "Out of Sight" from their joint live album in 1984 at the Chicago Blues Festival, *The Original Blues Brothers*) to incorporate the stylistic changes that influenced the new direction of blues drumming. It was during this period when the youngest drummer among these Cushing interviews rose to prominence. Casey Jones became a "first-call" recording session player and joined the bands of so many legendary Chicago guitarists, including Howlin' Wolf, Earl Hooker, Fenton Robinson, Jimmy Johnson, Eddie Clearwater, and Freddie King. He also played with Magic Sam at the Tay-May on Loomis and Roosevelt, Otis Rush at Pepper's Lounge, and he even had a recording session with Muddy Waters at the Chess Studios.

Having said all that, these patented drum grooves haven't evolved very much over time; it is, in fact, the very absence of drastic change that has established these drum styles as tradition. Adding too much—or taking away too much—loses the authenticity of what can *truly* be called a shuffle. In similar fashion, erratically rushing or dragging leads to the immediate destruction of the beloved "pocket." The entire reputation of drummers can be determined by the consistency with which a pocket can be established and maintained. One can listen to any number of the most popular Chicago blues recordings and, after homing in on the drum track, you can hear almost immediately why those songs *swing*—it's usually based on the drummer's ability to consistently carry that groove throughout from start to finish.

The Musicians—West Side Guitar

When examining the role of the electric guitar, the importance of the instrument and its significance in the evolution of Chicago blues cannot be overestimated. Indeed, when one thinks about what exactly constitutes a "classic" blues band sound, the essential ingredients almost always include the guitar and harmonica. Add a solid drummer, bass, and piano to round out the group, and there you have it—the full-throttle blues band. No insult intended to horn players such as Abb Locke, A.C. Reed, Eddie Shaw, J.T. Brown or "Little Bobby" Neely—they made contributions as well to the history of Chicago blues—but brass and wind instruments such as trumpets, trombones, or tenor saxes were never necessary ingredients for this specific genre.

Since the mid to late '40s, the tag-team sound of electric guitar and harmonica reigned supreme over the previous presentation of unamplified piano, acoustic bass, and vocals—the impact of Muddy Waters teaming up with Little Walter cannot be overestimated. When Phil and Leonard Chess released "Juke" as a single [Checker 758] in May of 1952, they changed the game not only for harp players but also for blues bands in general. Although Snooky Pryor may have been the pioneer of playing with a Shure model 520 "Green Bullet" microphone in Chicago during the '40s, it was Little Walter's amplified overdrive that grabbed listeners' attention both on vinyl and in live performances. By the mid to late '60s, what people clamored for *most* was the electric surge of the deliberately distorted Marine Band harmonica blowing heavy through a 10" Blackface Fender Princeton Reverb amplifier and a microphone, co-mingled with the razors-edge sting from the guitar tone of either single-coil or humbucker pickups.

Most diehard Chicago blues fans instantly recognize it when they hear it, but what exactly defines the classic Chicago West Side guitar sound? During the late '50s, a convergence of guitar styles manifested when Magic Sam, Buddy Guy, and Otis Rush led the charge in what became known as the "West Side Sound." In general, these elements were present during their performances: a stinging guitar tone; some degree of either tremolo or reverb added to enhance the tone; a high degree of string-bending notes incorporated in their solos; a wicked left-hand vibrato in their single-note phrases; and an upper-register, *pleading-and-moaning* vocal style whenever they sang.

But what else makes the Chicago blues sound so special? The double-stop rhythm guitar shuffle pattern—referred to as either *lump de lump*, *lumpty-lump*, or simply *lump*—is a revered staple of Chicago blues guitar. Upon closer examination, we discover that on many of the legendary recordings, there is not only one guitar but *two*. The intertwining dual-guitar approach of Jimmy Rogers and Muddy Waters was established as early as 1947, with Rogers playing in tandem with Waters on so many of the biggest hits of Muddy's career from 1947–54, including "Hoochie Coochie Man," "I'm Ready," "I Just Want to Make Love to You," and so many others.

Robert Jr. Lockwood and Luther Tucker's tag-team work on the 1958 Checker Records [833] release of the Sonny Boy Williamson's tune "Ninety-Nine" offers a perfect example of the classic *lumpty-lump* groove. Tucker plays a steady lump while Lockwood plays tasty single-note guitar runs. Sonny Boy's harp is burning with a signature piercing tone, while the drums of Fred Below are pumping with a hard backbeat to drive Willie Dixon's bass and Otis Spann's piano. The song never stops galloping—it's two minutes and thirty-five seconds of sheer ecstasy.

You can also hear dual guitars in Jimmy Reed's music with Eddie Taylor on several classic Vee-Jay recordings—it's a sound that's impossible to replicate without the delicate dance of twin guitars. Listen, for example, to the interwoven guitar work for the December 1959 Vee-Jay recording of "Found Love" [VJ 347], which finds the two guitars of Lefty Bates and Eddie Taylor executing their lines to perfection while being supported by Earl Phillips on drums—the absence of an actual bass goes practically *unnoticed*. The March 26, 1959, recording of "Take Out Some Insurance" [VJ 314] is equally compelling—the groove created by the dual guitars is hypnotic, as is the November 1956 "You Got Me Dizzy" [VJ 226]. The slower, medium-tempo groove of "Baby What You Want Me to Do?" [VJ 333] also finds the twin guitars weaving their magic, with the loping groove being locked in place by Phillips's patented backbeat. It is also worth noting that in the last two measures of every twelve bars, there is a recurring fourteen-note phrase that has become the standard "lick" when executing the proper style. Guitarists who play Jimmy Reed's particular brand of blues are practically *required* to master this riff when trying to play legitimate Chicago-style blues—their arsenal of licks just wouldn't be complete without it.

It's almost impossible to have a thorough discussion on the subject of Chicago blues without mentioning the tune that has become practically a universal anthem for guitarists everywhere—"Dust My Broom." Robert Johnson penned the tune and recorded it in 1936 for Columbia Records, though it became more popularized by Elmore James, who recorded it numerous times over his brilliant but short career.

The song has a lengthy and diverse history of recordings and renditions—James originally recorded the song with Rice Miller (Sonny Boy Williamson II) in 1951 for Trumpet Records in Mississippi. As it relates to Chicago blues lore, "Dust My Broom" has a bit of deceptive documentation that warrants discussion. Elmore James recorded a second version of the tune (the session can be heard on the LP *Whose Muddy Shoes*) at Universal Recording Studios for Chess Records [LP 1537] on January 17, 1953, with bassist Ransom Knowling, pianist Johnny Jones, tenor saxophonist J.T. Brown, and none other than Odie Payne on drums. The song title is familiar; it is not, however, the rendition that most people might expect it to be—it's a version with a different tempo and an alternate set of lyrics.

The third, *definitive* version that Chicago blues guitarists copied note-for-note was actually recorded more than ten years later in New York City when James delivered a highly charged version in April 1960 for a small independent label (located at 125th St. & 8th Ave.) at a Harlem record shop owned by producer Bobby Robinson. The 45 release [Enjoy 2027] is sonically superior to the earlier 1951 Trumpet monaural release—this particular February 1963 Enjoy recording session was released in stereo in 1965. More importantly, Elmore James sings with the fire and passion of the characteristic West Side Chicago sound of the '60s—it is by far the most memorable and mimicked rendition among guitarists.

There is, however, a song on the *Muddy Shoes* album that sounds much closer in style to the "Broom" that listeners are accustomed to being swept away with. Listen to "Talk to Me Baby (I Can't Hold Out)" and you can hear a prime example of the patented *lumpty-lump* guitar groove, as well as the shimmering double-stop triplets heard on "Dust My Broom." The monaural issue of this stellar recording was released by Chess in 1969 on the same *Whose Muddy Shoes* album mentioned earlier.

By the end of the '60s, the blues movement slowly migrated to Chicago's North Side, marked by the increased participation and popularity of white musicians like harmonica player Charlie Musselwhite, and guitarists Mike Bloomfield and Elvin Bishop—three artists who were already fully entrenched in the West and South Side blues. In 1963, the South Side Chicago-born harmonica player Paul Butterfield got asked to start a band to play four nights a week at Big John's, a North Side club. Butterfield got Howlin' Wolf's main rhythm section men—bassist Jerome Arnold and drummer Sam Lay—to join him. He then added Bishop and Bloomfield; it was the beginning for white North Siders to merge with Black blues artists. The band was an immediate hit—Bob Dylan used Butterfield, Bloomfield, Lay, and Arnold as his backing band for the 1965 Newport Folk Festival. By the time the '70s had arrived, numerous taverns on the North Side were fully immersed in blues music.

The Monuments—South, West, and North Side Venues

As early as 1943, Albert Luandrew ("Sunnyland Slim") was playing at Club 21 (21 N. Western Ave.) when Muddy arrived in Chicago. Guitarist and vocalist Eddie Boyd had a gig at the Blue Flame, but Sunnyland soon took over the gig and helped advance Muddy's career. The West Side had The Triangle Inn at the intersection of Racine and Blue Island Ave. where Sonny Boy Williamson played with Memphis Slim. Between 1946–48, Little Walter, Muddy, Jimmy, and Baby Face Leroy roamed the streets and were known as the Headcutters. They got their first gig at The Chicken Shack located at Polk and Ogden. Jimmy Rogers played with Tampa Red at the Purple Cat on 2119 W. Madison Street. Little Walter was there too, casually dropping by to sit in and "play for the kitty" (the money jar that garnered tips from the patrons).

Around the time of Muddy's first recordings for Chess, they played on the South Side at Docie's Lounge located at 5114 and Prairie; other "hot spots" included the 708 Club at 47th and Cottage Grove and Club de Lisa at 47th and South Park. On the West Side there was Zanzibar at 13th and Ashland Ave.; the Dew Drop Inn at 36th and Wentworth; and Howlin' Wolf and Elmore James played regularly at Silvio's on 2254 W. Lake. In the late '40s and early '50s, Big Bill Broonzy played at Ruby Gatewood's Tavern at the corner of Lake and Artesian Street, which is where Muddy first met Broonzy—it's also where Memphis Minnie regularly hosted the infamous "Blue Monday" house parties.

During the '50s there was the Club Claremont at 39th and Indiana; Pepper's Lounge at 503 E. 43rd St.; and Big Walter Horton played harmonica at the Cozy Inn on 43rd and State. Late in the decade, the Blue Flame held a legendary "battle of the bands" that included a showdown between none other than Otis Rush, Buddy Guy, and Magic Sam. Smitty's Corner at 3456 S. Indiana was Muddy's mainstay gig for more than a decade.

In 1966, the North Side had the Butterfield Blues Band at Big John's (Mike Bloomfield played there as early as 1964). The West Side had Big Duke's Lounge at 2755 W. Madison Ave. On the South Side there was Theresa's at 4801 S. Indiana where just about *every* serious Black blues musician played (the list too long to mention here). There was Florence's at 5443 S. Shields, and Pepper's Lounge would soon relocate to 1321 S. Michigan. By the '70s, the North Side had Wise Fool's Pub at 2270 N. Lincoln with the Bob Reidy Band (Jimmy Rogers played there frequently); Alice's Revisited at 950 W. Wrightwood; and Ma Bea's 3001 W. Madison where Jimmy "Fast Fingers" Dawkins regularly held court.

The Music—Sounds of Chicago

How do we measure any great blues guitarist? We not only examine their playing skills, but we also consider their readily identifiable sound qualities. So where do we begin? The wicked, wide-vibrato slide guitar sound from Muddy's trusty candy apple red 1958 Fender Telecaster is as good as any place to start. His urban sound represented a significant departure from the acoustic blues he'd been raised on as he listened to his guitar heroes in Mississippi. He used a glass finger slide from a Coke bottle (eventually upgrading to metal) to craft a signature sound that was honed and perfected over the years. Those specific characteristics that became his "trademark" sound made him recognizable with a matter of relatively few notes—those unique traits associated with all legendary blues personalities.

Other signature styles that further enhanced the blues tradition: Magic Sam, who often played his snow-white Fender Stratocaster using his fingers and nails to get the cutting tone for his rhythm and lead guitar lines that typified the West Side guitar sound (he recorded his two best solo albums for Delmark, *West Side Soul* and *Black Magic*); Freddie King's fat tone from his cherry red 1960 Gibson ES-345 guitar with humbucking pickups on legendary classics like "Hideaway" and "San Ho Zay"; and the tremolo-laden guitar shimmer of Otis Rush using his reverse-stringed, upside-down, left-handed 1954 Sunburst Fender Stratocaster on his classic Cobra recordings from 1956–58. Then there's Hubert Sumlin's unique tone using his Bartolini model guitar on Howlin' Wolf's classic 1965 Chess Recordings—he produced an amazing vocal-like quality on "Love Me Darlin'," [CH-1911] (not to mention his guitar tone on "My Country Sugar Mama" on Side B) or his killer tone on "Louise" [CH-1923]. He influenced multiple generations, including Stevie Ray Vaughan who played a note-for-note Hubert Sumlin solo on "Love Me Darlin'" on his 1989 album, *In Step* [Epic EK 45024]. On that same album, Vaughan also covered Buddy Guy's 1961 recording of "Let Me Love You Baby" [Chess 1784]. A fine representation of Guy's West Side Chicago stinging guitar tone using his 1957 Fender Stratocaster can be best heard on the 1960 release of the single "The First Time I Met the Blues" [Chess 1743] that features Fred Below playing drums on the session. You can clearly hear the direct influence of B.B. King in Buddy's vocal style and guitar phrases.

Beyond the Boundaries of Chicago

There are other stories being told by worthy musicians whose reach extends well beyond the confines of the Chicagoland area. Indeed, Texan Roy Gaines was a disciple of T-Bone Walker, and one of the few remaining artists alive who can speak from first-hand experience about the legendary "Stormy Monday" performer who paved the way for so many jazz and blues guitarists alike, ranging from B.B. King to Stevie Ray Vaughan. Roy's interview about his upstart career—including a rare encounter when he was invited by Walker to join him on the stage—is a story well-worth reading.

David Kearney, *aka* Guitar Shorty, has quite a unique story of his own to tell, including his musical background that involved mastering several classic jazz standards. He migrated to Chicago to record under the auspices of none other than producer Willie Dixon. Guitar Shorty recorded "You Don't Treat Me Right"/"Irma Lee" in 1957—with none other than veteran Otis Rush playing rhythm. It was his very first 45 released on Cobra [5017]. He later worked under the umbrella of Chicago's own Alligator Records pioneer Bruce Iglauer who distributed and released the LP *Watch Your Back* in 2004, *We The People* in 2006, and *Bare Knuckle* in 2008.

Then there's Floyd Murphy, the lesser-known younger sibling to the guitarist of the *Blues Brothers* film Matt "Guitar" Murphy. A Memphis-born native, he and his band (The Blue Flames) eventually made their way to Chicago and later returned to record for Sam Phillips on Sun Records in Memphis. As the backing band for Junior Parker, Floyd performed on Parker's classic Sun recordings and eventually Don Roby's Peacock and Duke labels. West Coast Oakland Johnny Heartsman worked for the legendary Bihari Brothers who operated Modern Records (the label for B.B. King's early career). With jazz guitar influences that include Charlie Christian, T-Bone Walker, Barney Kessel, and Kenny Burrell, Heartsman tells Cushing of chance encounters with legends like Lowell Fulsom and Guitar Slim.

Finally, the highlight of Cushing's collection is the inclusion of the extended interview with Honeyboy Edwards, who survived The Great Depression while living in Mississippi. He alone was the rarest of blues veterans who could proudly attest that he knew all the veteran Chicago players *before* the migration. Names such as Big Joe Williams, Muddy Waters, Son House, Charley Patton, Sonny Boy Williamson (Alex "Rice" Miller), and—yes—even Robert Johnson. He caught the train from St. Louis with Little Walter and came directly to Maxwell Street in May of 1945, where he immediately met Jimmy Rogers, Floyd Jones, Moody Jones, Snooky Pryor, Robert Nighthawk, and Elgin Evans. His memory is astounding; his entire life story is illuminating.

For Chicago blues lovers everywhere, it is good to know that the decades-old tradition of promoting the highest quality of blues guitar remains intact, as evidenced by the recent releases by the home-grown institution of Bruce Iglauer's exalted Alligator Records, which boasts the likes of Christone "Kingfish" Ingram, Ronnie Baker Brooks, Coco Montoya, Selwyn Birchwood, Shemekia Copeland, and several dozens more. Equally important is the resurgence of Delmark—the oldest and most venerable Chicago blues record label—which continues to keep alive the legacy and memory of Bob Koester with guitarists like John Primer, Mike Wheeler, Nick Moss, Billy Flynn, Breezy Rodio, Corey Dennison, and a host of others.

Blues Before Sunrise

In today's current socially divided and politically charged climate in America, the issue of "white privilege" is an often-discussed topic regarding certain opportunities systematically afforded to some while being denied to others. It is, historically speaking, a very real issue in our country, and, as such, should come as no surprise to anyone that the nature of such conversation usually touches on sensitive nerves. As the subject relates to this particular manuscript, there are those—rightly or wrongly—who might find reason to take exception to Cushing's position as "the voice" and authoritative figure on the airwaves representing Black blues music in Chicago.

As for the body of work of the author, let it be said that the more than forty years of excellence in broadcasting is no small feat. Since his start in 1980 working at WBEZ, Cushing has dedicated countless hours to the pursuit of gathering interviews as host producer and DJ of *Blues Before Sunrise*. His late Saturday night shift has earned a stellar reputation that extends far and wide to listeners across the country. In a world where "AI" permeates our culture—making us question what is actually *real*—radio programming is dominated by computer-generated algorithms that produce automated set lists. Yet Cushing's *human* presence as a member and friend of the blues community seems more important now than ever before.

The five-hour show (which got its start on the NPR affiliate WBEZ radio in Chi-Town) consistently offers his best collection of not just Post-War blues, but R&B, gospel, and jazz. The depth and breadth of his knowledge is insurmountable, culled from more than ten thousand albums. He has also paid his dues as a blues musician, logging late-night hours in areas of both the South and West Side, at a place and time in our country's history when most whites wouldn't *dare* venture in a predominantly Black neighborhood where blues music thrived. During that period, he played drums with Magic Slim, Smokey Smothers, Eddie Taylor, Sunnyland Slim, and a host of others. His "street cred" is legit, and his *bona fides* have long since been confirmed by those elite members of the urban blues community. Regardless of whatever position anyone might take in this current climate, his history and place among active supporters of the musical culture of African Americans cannot be denied.

Part One **The Drummers**

Blues Drummers' Round Table

This transcription of the Chicago Blues Drummers' Round Table presents an extended conversation with the best blues drummers in Chicago during the 1950s. I organized and staged this event in September of 1984, for the specific purpose of taking a group photo. Fortunately, all the best and best-known drummers were still alive and relatively healthy at this late date. What was then the Chicago Historical Society, now the Chicago History Museum, agreed to host the event. But they insisted that in addition to the group photo, the event include a round-table interview which I conducted. Included in our round-table discussion was Fred Below: Fred was the first-call blues drummer in Chicago and the house drummer at the famed Chess label. He played and recorded behind most everybody who's anybody—Little Walter, Muddy Waters, Jimmy Rogers, Buddy Guy, Chuck Berry, Sonny Boy Williamson II, and many others: Odie Payne, a close second-call, the house drummer at the famed Cobra label and who played behind Tampa Red, Elmore James, Otis Rush, Magic Sam, Jr. Wells, Chuck Berry, etc.: Earl Phillips, who worked most notably with Howlin' Wolf and then became the house drummer at the famous Vee-Jay Label, where he worked behind Jimmy Reed, Billy Boy Arnold, Snooky Pryor, Floyd Jones, and John Lee Hooker among others: S.P. Leary—S.P. (nobody knows but there are many profane guesses) played and recorded with Howlin' Wolf, Muddy Waters, Sunnyland Slim, and T-Bone Walker; Completing our round-table line-up was Clifton James who worked with Bo Diddley and Willie Dixon.

■ ■ ■

We're at the Chicago Historical Society, September 16th, 1984, and with me are the cream of the crop of the Chicago blues drummers during the postwar years. They're all still here, they're with us today. Let's go around the table—everybody state your name, the date you were born, and where . . .

O.P.: Odie Payne Jr., born Chicago, Illinois, August 27th, 1926—the 300 block east of Cottage Grove.

S.P.: My name is S.P. Leary. I was born in Dallas, Texas, June 6th, 1930.

And just for the record—what does S.P. stand for?

S.P.: Well, I can't tell you that . . . [*Everybody laughs.*]

C.J.: My name is Clifton James. I was born October 7th, 1936, in Chicago, Illinois, at 26 East 44th Street.

F.B.: My name is Fred Below Jr., I was born in Chicago September 6th, 1926.

E.P.: I am Earl Phillips, I was born in New York City, New York, in Harlem Hospital on April 25th, 1920.

For those of you who weren't born in Chicago, how and when did you come to Chicago?

S.P., how did you come to Chicago?

S.P.: On a train! [*Laughter all around.*] 1949.

Were you playing by that point?

S.P.: No, I was in the service when I first came to Chicago. I fell in love with Chicago and after I got discharged, I went back home. I went to school for two years—and I came back to Chicago to make it my home in 1954.

Earl—how about you?

E.P.: I came to Chicago on a train, at the Polk Street station in 1940. I started playing music out on South Park at 39th Street. The same night I came in, one of my buddies from Nashville, Tennessee—I finished school in Nashville, Tennessee. My buddy was playing there. When I was in Nashville, I had my own little band, and he was in my band. But when he came to Chicago, I had no idea I was going to run into him. But I ran into him December 1940—December 12th. I started playing with him—I was playing swing then. That's when I first got here.

Odie—How about you? When did you start playing?

O.P.: It's been so long I've almost forgot. It started in DuSable High School, I was in the band there. Then I was drafted—in the service. I started playing in the service. And when I first came out my first job—my first strongest gig was playing with Tampa Red. So, we're talking about 1949 or 1950—professionally I started playing . . .

Weren't you an alumni of that famous instructor over there at DuSable?

O.P.: Yeah—Captain Walter Dyett . . .

Who else was over there with you at the time?

O.P.: A fellow by the name of Crutcher—a long, tall, lean fellow.

F.B.: Jay Crutcher?

O.P.: Probably so—yeah. Crutcher and you had another fine drummer there, Wesley Landers.

A fine drummer. You had a girl there, too. She was an instructor—her name was Mattie. I thought she was very mean. When she would talk, she would talk out of the side of her mouth, "Alright, Odie Payne . . . " She was an instructor . . .

Were there other famous players on different instruments?

O.P.: In that class was Johnny Griffin . . .

F.B.: Also, Marshall Thompson

O.P.: I didn't know him. In that class also was—a fine drummer, he plays at Andy's. I can't think of his name but he plays all the time. We were in concert band together—Oh well, it'll come to me . . . [Wilbur Campbell]

How did the thing with Tampa Red Happen?

O.P.: At the time, I was playing with Johnny Jones. Before we got together with Tampa Red, we were playing together on 1300 West on Twelfth Street. I can't recall the name of the place. The thing is, I was with Cool Breeze first—You remember Cool Breeze? [*Moans and laughter all around.*] Yeah, the bass player. He told nice jokes. And from there to Johnny Jones—because I didn't know Tampa Red. I only knew he did a tune called Let Me Play With Your Poodle. I was going to school. At that time at the Met Record Shop at 46th Street and South Park, and there was a loudspeaker out there. They sold records there and that particular record was playing, "Let Me Play With Your Poodle." Every day I would sit and listen and laugh at the record—not knowing a few years later I'd wind up working with the man. That's how I met Tampa Red—through Johnny Jones. So, he would always call us Little Odie and Little Johnny because he was our senior—a very nice fellow to work with. I think that lasted about four or five months. Then I worked with Memphis Minnie about four or five months, then Memphis Slim.

What was Minnie like to work with? I heard she was a rough character.

Aaahh yes! She and Son Joe, that was her husband. There were just three of us. He would play rhythm guitar—play it like a bass. He'd sit there and play and say "Yes, Honey." And like you say, Minnie was quite rough. [*Laughs all around.*] But I would take both of them home from the gig because they wouldn't drive. That brings back quite a few memories. We would stop and eat at a restaurant, and they would be eating chili and they had a bowl of hot stuff and Minnie would just take spoons full and put it in her chili—and eat and sweat [*laughs all around*]. I'd just sit there and shake my head. How could you eat that hot stuff like that?

You had a story that I heard one time about Johnny and Tampa in the car . . .

I was driving, because I used to pick both of them up—Boy, I picked up so many musicians. Neither one of them drove and Tampa stayed on 35th and State. Johnny Jones stayed on the Westside. I stayed farther south so on the way to the gig I would always pick up Tampa Red first, and then Johnny Jones. It was interesting—Johnny Jones, I never will forget, was in the back seat and he was smoking—I'd see the little red light from the cigarette back there—and all of a sudden I had to let the windows down because . . . [*Laughs.*] I said, "Johnny, what are you smoking?" [*Laughs.*] I had to hang my head out the door—I couldn't take it. I said, "Don't ever do that in the car." He said, "Aw—shucks." You know what it was. It was a lotta fun but he was doing the wrong thing in my car . . .

S.P.—How about you. How did you start playing?

S.P.: When I was in high school, I played the snare drum in the marching band. This was in Texas. I had a hard time getting in there because I had a rough time getting the drum. My sister was doing domestic work and she bought me a snare drum. That's the way I got started by playing the snare drum. I was working odd jobs, saved my little money, because Papa wasn't able to buy me one at that time. And I eventually worked up to have enough money to buy me a set of drums. Back in those days, the first set I had cost me $124—it costs you that much today for a snare drum—if you could get one for that price, and that would be a used one. I started playing in the high school band, the marching band. I was sitting up in my Spanish class one day and I saw this guy by the name of Fred Cooper. He was playing Gene Krupa's number "Elk's Parade." And that's when I decided I wanted to become a drummer. Then after I started playing drums in the high school band—along with David "Fathead" Newman and Leroy Cooper, they were my real close friends—then Newman and I got into the union. In Texas, I was fourteen years old, I joined the Junior Local there in Dallas, Texas. We had a union card for Juniors, but we had to have a tutor to take us back and forth from the clubs. They'd take us home, bring us out and take us back. At that time, I was playing with Buster Smith—and Newman was playing with Lloyd Jefferson. After that, T-Bone Walker, that was the first big name that I ever worked with—the second was Lowell Fulson. T-Bone Walker used to come to my home and pick me up. Lowell Fulson was living in Fort Worth, Texas. T-Bone Walker was living in Dallas, in Oak Cliff. I worked with T-Bone for about five years, until I came out of high school. Then when I came out of high school I went into the service, at 18. I was in the Third Armored Division Band in Fort Knox, Kentucky. I had the opportunity of playing in the band with Cannonball Adderley, his brother, Nathaniel Adderley, and also

Junior Mance—all of us were in the same band together. We had a ball—you better believe me.

Jr. Mance—the piano player—in a marching band?

S.P.: No, we had a dance band. They'd pick the dance band out of the marching band. In special services were the guys that played in the dance band. That's why I never did have to go overseas.

When you played with T-Bone, was that all in the Oak Cliff, Dallas, Fort Worth area?

S.P.: I never went any further with T-Bone than Oklahoma. That's as far as I was able to go. That's as far as my Mom and Dad would let me go—or wanted me to go. Not that I didn't want to go but that's the way it was. Rules were rules. You had to obey rules—back then. It ain't like it is now.

When you came to Chicago, who was the first person you played with here?

S.P.: Sonny Boy Williamson—in Argo, Illinois. I was practicing over at my sister's house. She lives in Maywood. I was packing up, getting ready to go back to Dallas, and Sonny Boy heard me practicing downstairs. So, he came across the street and that's when I first met Sonny Boy . . .

We're talking about Rice Miller now?

S.P.: That's the only Sonny Boy I knew . . .

F.B.: Who were you playing with that time when I saw you down there in Mississippi?

S.P.: I think that was old Bigfoot—The Wolf.

O.P.: Oh, that's the Big Foot—I've been reading about this other Big Foot—you know, the one in the snow . . .

(laughs and groans all around)

S.P.: I was playing with Wolf then—Howlin' Wolf. I met you in Mississippi, in Jackson, at the fairgrounds. Those were some times, man. I thank Mr. Earl Phillips for giving me a break . . .

Clifton, let's start with you. How did you get involved in drums, who did you play with first? How did the whole thing come about?

C.J.: I got inspired to play drums by watching the parades going up and down the streets. I didn't have any drums or sticks either back then. I used to take my mother's knives and forks and beat on chairs, tin cans—and everything, playing those parade beats . . .

S.P.: How many whuppings did you get?

C.J.: Oh about 9,985—a day! [*Laughs.*] I was just beating on anything. I had knives and forks and tree branches. After that, going to school I met up with

Eddie King, the teacher at Moseley School, and I got in the drum and bugle corp. I started playing in Bud Billiken's Parade. Some evenings after I'd get out of school I was sitting in the house, just messing around, beating on something. Mr. King gave me a pair of sticks. My brother was a maintenance man. He was around the corner, working in the building. He told me a fellow had some drums around there, but he didn't know how to play them. So, he took me around there and introduced me to him—and lo and behold—you can just about guess who that was—it was Little Willie—Popped-Eyed Willie—Smith, Muddy's drummer now. During the time, he was really trying to play harmonica a little bit. So, we hooked up there together and he would be playing the harmonica and I would be beating on the drums. We met another friend, named Bobby Lee. He played guitar. So, we decided we were going to go out and get a gig. Our first job was out in Robbins, Illinois. We first went to The Apex. The man let us do auditions for him—and he had about a 13- or 14-piece band sitting there—and they were laughing at us playing, you dig? You know how big The Apex used to be but he didn't hire us. So, we were standing outside looking around and happen to look down the street at those little old joints down there at a place they call The Hollow. We went in there and asked the fellow if we could give him an audition. He said, "Yeah." So, we played a little bit for him and he hired us, told us to come back Friday night to play. Friday, we played and at the end of the night, he gave us four dollars apiece. We came back the next night—the same thing on that weekend. The following weekend we came back out to play and it was raining hard. We were in there jamming and there were people outside, trying to get in. The Little Hollow wasn't too much larger than the washroom. We drew people down from The Apex—The Apex didn't have nobody—that's the truth. They didn't have anybody down there. Everybody was standing out on top of cars—you know how Robbins used to flood. The water would be up to your waistline down there. [*Laughs.*] At the end of the night, old Bob raised us, we got $4.50 then—and a pint of whiskey! [*Laughs.*] We were doing good! So, we got together and we put on a show. The first person I met that had a big name was J.B. Lenoir. We asked him if he would come out and put on a show out there. He agreed and he didn't charge the man a whole lot of money or anything. He came on out to help us out. We had it jam-packed—you couldn't get another mosquito in there nowhere. We stayed like that for a couple of weeks and then we decided to go different ways. My big job after that was with Lee Jackson, I played with him. Next came Sunnyland Slim. After that I was playing behind one big name after another . . .

How did you playing with Bo Diddley happen?

C.J.: Bo was playing out on the streets and he met my sister-in-law. She told him about me, and he came by the house. We got to playing and a couple of nights we went out and played on the streets. I'd bring a little old drum, and I'd beat on it. We'd be out on the streets—Bo, Roosevelt and Jerome Greene, who played the maracas. We started getting jobs and working around different places. Do you remember the 430 Club, on 43rd Street? That was the joint. We used to go and sit-in sometimes at the 708 Club.

Did you bring the Bo beat to the group—or was it already there?

C.J.: Well, the beat that I played behind him, I brought it out—and he's been playing it ever since . . .

Fred, how about you? What's your story?

F.B.: I went to DuSable—and I tried to play trombone but me and trombone didn't get along at all. So, I hurried up and put that down and picked up on the drums. I figured that was much easier than the trombone. But I found out a little different later on—playing drums was very hard, when you really get down to it. I graduated from high school and by that time I was ready for the army. I went into the army and I stayed until 1946. I came out December 13th, 1946. Then I met Elgy Edmond [Elgin Evans] at the union hall, and he introduced me to Tampa Red, Sunnyland Slim and a lot of the other blues guys—because he was playing blues then. Elgy was working with Muddy Waters—and Tampa Red, too. He was working with both of the bands. I wasn't playing with anybody, so I was just around listening and just playing little gigs with younger musicians that were around. Then I re-enlisted and went to Germany. I came back in 1951 and met Elgy again. This time he introduced me to David and Louis Myers, along with Junior Wells. And they were the ones that taught me how to play the blues . . .

What were you playing up to this time?

F.B.: I was playing swing and jazz.

I read somewhere that you had a run-in with a famous jazz man while you were in the army?

F.B.: There were a lot of good jazz men there. Frank Williams, tenor man. I ran across Lester Young during my first stint in the army. I met him down in Fort McClellen, Alabama. I used to sit-in with them.

For the folks unfamiliar with the story of you and the Myers Brothers, can you tell us how that all happened?

F.B.: I was introduced to Louis and Dave and Junior Wells. I worked with them for a while. During that same time, Little Walter came out with a record called Juke. Dave, Louis, and myself had formed a band and so we switched over and got with Little Walter because Little Walter had the name—We didn't have any name. He could get the jobs, where we couldn't. That's the way that happened . . .

Can you explain—you said the Myers Brothers taught you to play blues. You said you were playing swing. What was the problem with what you were playing initially, and what did you have to learn to play blues?

F.B.: The first time I played the blues, I told Dave and Louis that I was going to quit, because I couldn't understand what they were playing. And they told me "Man, Elgy already told us that you play drums—and you went to school." I said, "Yeah—but what you're playing is not in the books." And I was really having trouble trying to fit my beats to what they were playing. So, what I did was—not to be outdone—I said, "I'm going to learn this." And I fit my beats to what they were playing, which was off-time music. Instead of playing three and four bars, they'd play five and six and in-between the bars—things like that. I never heard anything like that before. When I did get right down to paying attention to what they were doing, I found out what they were doing and then I fit my beat to what they were playing. Therefore, it came out a little different and I put a little swing into it anyway to fill out the rest of the measure.

C.J.: That's very interesting, but it's the strangest thing. If you notice, most all blues drummers can play jazz, or anything—but a jazz musician cannot play blues . . .

O.P.: But when you break it down to just plain facts—it's the simplest beat in the world to play, but it's the hardest . . .

F.R.: That's right . . .

C.J.: It sure is . . .

O.P.: It's as basic as you can get . . .

C.J.: It's the foundation . . .

Fred, when you were playing jazz and converting to blues—when you were playing backbeats, or were you playing swing with bombs (accents)? [Backbeats are generally a single beat on the snare drum.]

F.B.: Well, I was dropping bombs—but not the kind of bombs you're familiar with. I was dropping bombs to make phrases, that's what I was dropping bombs with. I wasn't dropping bombs which you were speaking of. I would drop bombs at the end of eight bars—"BAM!" It was to let them know they'd finished that phrase and now to move on to the next phrase. Right—I was the punctuation at the end of the sentence.

When you began to play with the Myers Brothers, did you incorporate a backbeat?

F.B: I did . . .

And was that tough to learn?

F.B.: Yes, it was. It became more than I had anticipated. I hadn't anticipated doing what I was doing—but to make the music come out round and whole, I had to make these beats. If you try to write them down on your sheet, it won't come out right. Sometime I play in-between. Sometimes I have to stop. Sometime I have to phrase to pick up the harp player—and push him into another phrase. You see, he's breathing in and breathing out . . .

Earl, tell us how your story with drums and drumming began.

I was still in Nashville. When I finished high school, I was one credit short, and I decided to take music. I flunked French so I switched over. I went into music hall to sign up for music. I had a lady professor. She wanted to know what instrument I wanted. I looked. I had never played any instrument since I was a little-bitty kid. My mother and father gave up on me on that. My mother wanted me to play a violin—and I tore it up on another kid's head. My daddy wanted me to play the saxophone. He came home and found me blowing bubbles—so they gave up on me on that. So, I didn't bother with any more music until I got to high school. I was looking around and another little boy said, "Why don't you take the drums? Try the drums!" So, I picked up a drum and it felt kind of good—and I started whamming away on it. After three months in the class, the drum seemed to be a part of me—and I was a part of it. I got kind of good with it. One afternoon the teacher was late getting into the classroom and we were playing The Double Eagle March. It got good to me and I got carried away with it. The teacher walked in on me and I got suspended for that. Then, the next suspension I got I was playing this song "Monkey wrapped his tail around the flagpole." Anyway, I was swinging away on that—and I got suspended for three months. I turned around and bought my own set of drums and started rehearsing at home. I went to my professor one afternoon. A bunch of us boys were getting together out of the band. So, I asked the professor to have her hear us. She listened to us and said, "My goodness. I didn't know I had such students. Who's leading the band?" I said, "I am. I formed it." She said to me, "You have a mighty fast left hand." I said, "Thank you." I didn't think I did. So, after that she said, "We can't get a band to play for the Junior/Senior Prom. What about you and your boys?" I said, "Okay." So, we played the Junior/Senior Prom. The Governor's daughter was at the Junior/Senior Prom, so Governor Hill McAllister heard us. He liked the way we played and he said, "I want you all to play on my boat for my anniversary." I started inching out from there. A lady on Church Street down in Tennessee said, "How would you like to start teaching some of my little students how to play drums?" I didn't know I was getting that good. She said, "I'll give you five dollars a week." I said, "Maam?" [*Laughs.*] Then, I was teaching the little kids how to play drums. One day Bill Reedus—he had a band—he said, "I heard about you—I'd like to use you." I was working part-time at the railroad. I said, "Well, I'll see what I can do about it." My uncle, being in good with president of the L&N railroad, told me I could take off when I got ready. So, I went with Bill Reedus, and made these little small towns. I was playing and he started giving me solos. The funny thing about it, the first solo he gave me—we were playing on the boat that evening. There were two bands playing. Our band was the second band. When we came on he asked me "Do you want a bottle of pop?" I said, "Yeah." I was drinking orange pop—I liked orange pop. He said, "I'll give you one before we go on." So, he gave me an orange pop—I didn't realize what was going on. He was the one who introduced me to drinking. It was spiked, and I got up there and got to playing, and he said to me "I'm going to turn you loose." I said, "Okay, I'm ready." I played a solo—everybody left the bandstand. When I left that bandstand I was soaking wet. When I came down everybody was hugging me and everything—what's going on? Man, I was out of it. [*Laughs.*] And this other guy from this other band, he came over to me, he looked at my hands. He said, "Man—where'd you get a hand like that?" "What kind of hand? I ain't got but two hands." He said, "No-no-no-no-no. We tried to watch your beat and we couldn't keep up with it." I just said, "Thank you . . . " So, after a while, I decided I was going to come to Chicago. But one of the boys, I told you a moment ago, his name was Richard, he had formed a band in 1940 here in Chicago. This was a female impersonation show—it was on the corner of 39th Street and South Park, which became King Drive. I happened to walk in there that night. I was trying to locate my mother's sister. So, I stopped there to get me a drink and try to figure out her address. I knew I was in the vicinity but whereabouts, I didn't know. While I was sitting there, Richard spied me at the bar. I had my little suitcase—never found nowhere to stay. Richard came down off the bandstand and he said, "Man—you're the answer." I said, "Answer, what kind of answer are you talking about?" He said, "Man, I need a drummer. That drummer I got ain't from shit!" [*Laughs.*] He said, "You wanna work?" I said, "Yeah—I just got here . . . " He called the boss, and the boss said, "Whatever you do Richard—it's your band." He put me to work that same night, before I even had a place to stay. And I worked with Richard five or six weeks. During that time, Al Benson had been on the air, announcing that I was looking for my people, so they all came to the club one night. That's the way they found me. After that I went to work for the railroad here in Chicago, part-time. I met a man out on the job, Brown—Payne knows Brown. Anyway, Brown didn't drive anything but Cadillacs. They could be ragged as I don't know what—he'd buy himself an old piece of Cadillac. I started playing music with Brown. Do you remember Brown?

O.P.: J.T.?

E.P.: J.T. Brown—Yeah

O.P.: Yeah, I was on his records . . .

E.P.: Yeah, he had awful records . . . [*Laughs.*] I played with him for a while. I decided to get my own little old band. I was playing around on 14th Street, 16th Street. Yeah, over where you stayed drunk all the time . . .

S.P.: Don't worry about it . . .

C.J: Him and a thousand others . . . [*Laughs.*]

E.P.: I played with Little Walter a little while, until he got in a lot of trouble—got us all in trouble, rather. But before I played with him, I played with Cool Breeze over on Madison Street. Brown was usually the MC. I played all up and down Madison Street. Then I used to play with Charlie Jones, over on 16th and Pulaski. I used to play over there with him. I was at this club on Paulina right off Madison—between Paulina and Ashland. It was a strip joint. I was playing there one evening and Muddy came by when we were in there. Muddy said to me, "How about getting with my man—and help him. You might go somewhere"—just like that, Muddy said that. I said, "Yeah—where is he?" Muddy told me where to go. Wolf lived on Green Street. So, I went on Green Street to see Howlin' Wolf. This was 1954. I went over to see him and we got to talking and Wolf wanted me to work with him. I had been playing swing and jazz—in and out, in and out—none of it seemed hard to me. We were rehearsing in Howlin' Wolf's basement—sometimes we rehearsed in Muddy's basement, too—because Otis Spann was with us until we got Hosea. We had to send back to Memphis to get Hosea Lee Kennard. "That No Place To Go"—that was my beat, and Wolf was crazy about it. We were just sitting, bullshitting around and I gave him that beat. [*Sings:*] "Boom, b-boom-boom-boom—Boom, b-boom-boom-boom" Oh, he fell in love with it! He got on that little piece of harp of his and I thought he was going to swallow it." [*Laughs.*] After I got hooked up with Wolf, I just stayed with him a long time—until he made me mad then I said, "No man, I gotta go!"—and that's when you got a chance [*talking to S.P.*]

Can you fellows remember who it was you were listening to—and you tried to emulate when you first started out playing? Odie, who were you listening to?

O.P.: At that time Gene Krupa was considered one of the world's great drummers—at that time. But then again, Buddy Rich—I could feel what that man was doing. And then, you had Cozy Cole. It was between those two basically—Cozy Cole or Buddy Rich.

Nobody was listening to Jo Jones?

O.P.: Jo Jones, Cozy Cole . . .

Wasn't Cozy with Cab Calloway?

O.P.: Yeah, you're right . . .

How about you S.P.? Who were you listening to?

S.P.: Art Blakey, he was drumming at that time with Billy Eckstine 1944/45. Like I told you, I didn't start playing until I was 14, and I was influenced by Art Blakey . . .

O.P.: I think you're right because when that band came through the Regal Theater I went to see that band and Blakey was the man! [*Spoken drums accents:*] "A-Kloom! A-Kloom!"

S.P.: I patterned myself after Art Blakey all my life. I liked his style then and I love his style now.

How about you, Clifton?

C.J.: I had several. I had a lot of old records at the house. One, in particular, was Chick Webb. I liked Max Roach, and I liked Gene Krupa . . .

Fred, how about you?

F.B.: Gene Krupa and Art Blakey. Those were the two that I really did like. I paid attention to a lot of things they were doing . . .

Earl, how about you?

E.P.: Chick Webb—I actually met him—and he used to show me things. I think he made me convert my left hand the way I did . . .

When you say he helped convert your left hand, were you using an underhand or overhand grip? [An underhand grip holds the drumstick with the palm up/stick on top of the hand—an overhand grip with the palm down/stick under the hand.]

E.P.: I used an underhand grip—but it wasn't as limber as he wanted it to be. He used to hold me and do this [*uses his finger to play rhythm:*] "Th-th-th-th-thump." He'd say "Like that—just keep doing that." Use the wrist, as opposed to the whole arm . . .

C.J: Yeah, Chick Webb was the one . . .

F.B.: I saw him "once" and that was in the movies. I never saw him live.

O.P.: He was about the best around though . . .

C.J.: His foot was just as fast as his hands . . .

O.P.: Was he a big fella?

C.J: Big around—he was chubby.

F.B.: With a hump on his back . . .

C.J.: I'll tell you one thing that really inspired me a lot, was a friend of mine—a friend of Freddy's and mine. Do you remember Cornelius Cross? He used to live across the street from me and he played some hell of a drums . . .

F.B.: Odie knows Cross. He knows him . . .

C.J.: Cross used to show me a lotta things. He was bad and I learned a lot of things. He and I used to run together. One night me and Cross went out to the old Tick-Tock. Below was playing up there—and I saw Below. I hadn't played with any real professionals then. And I saw Below and I said, "Oh-oh—there it is!" I'm coming to get him, uh-huh . . . Yeah, old Below was a hell of a drummer . . .

From what I've heard around the table, it seems most of you—before you came here and started playing with fellas with guitars from Mississippi, you were actually into swing and jazz. That there really wasn't too much of a blues beat going?

F.B.: There was no Blues drumming. Nobody that had a big name

How about Judge Riley? Did you fellows know Judge Riley? He worked with Cruddup on all those Blue Bird records?

O.P.: Yeah, I think I met him. Just slightly—that's all

I think he switched over to bass later on. He and Ransom Knowling were playing bass . . .

O.P.: Yeah, and Ransom was playing on Tampa Red's records, Yeah, Ransom Knowling and myself . . .

All you guys came out of swing—and I take it that when you listened to the records, you didn't listen to the tenor men—you listened to the drummers, you listened to the rhythm sections? Is that a correct guess?

C.J.: Yeah.

E.P.: Always rhythm.

O.P.: Well, playing drums yourself . . .

C.J.: Yeah, right . . .

F.B.: You pay attention to the drums but you're listening to the whole thing.

C.J.: You're concentrating on the drums, the foundation, in other words

O.P.: I'd go to burlesque shows and watch the drummer in the burlesque shows.

You?

O.P.: Shoot, yeah [*general laughter*].

C.J.: You sure you were watching the drummer?

O.P.: I'd sit right down, because it's only three pieces . . .

C.J.: You were really watching the drummer now?

O.P.: Piano, drummer, and a trumpet player. I would watch them more than the girls. What the heck.

C.J.: Oh-oh.

O.P.: Because I wound up working in Calumet City where you had to give the girls what they wanted—the bumps and grinds.

F.B.: . . . and the punch line.

C.J.: Yeah, the punch line . . . [*Laughs.*]

F.B.: Yeah—I worked there myself. [*Laughs.*] You couldn't take your drums home.

C.J.: No, sir!

When you say you couldn't take your drums home, what do you mean?

F.B.: If you wanted to rehearse or run something down, you ran it down in the club . . .

While you were working?

F.B.: No, no—you come a little earlier. Just like you say—you've got a recording session to do, or something like that, well then you had to go rent some drums—because they didn't allow you to take any drums out of the place—and there's no such thing as "You're going to quit."

C.J.: No-no . . .

F.B.: When you brought your drums in, they were there for a while—until the job closes.

O.P.: Is that right? Well, well . . .

C.J.: Yes sir! The syndicate operated those things

O.P.: In the burlesque?

C.J.: No—in Calumet City . . .

F.B: At Franks . . .

C.J.: Yeah—at Frank's. Yeah, it was rough out there . . .

O.P.: I don't know what it was but this one girl had her bust insured for $25,000! Well that was the drawing card—so and so and so and so, bust insured for $25,000 . . .

F.B.: . . . and all the waitresses sang songs to entertain the customers . . .

O.P.: And the band was behind the curtain, you know.

F.B.: I worked in another club and you worked behind a screen—you worked behind the screen and people in the audience couldn't see you.

S.P.: You could only have so many players up front, and a lot of times the guitar players had to get behind the screen.

C.J.: I worked out there with L.C. McKinley . . .

[*Everybody groans—then laughs all around.*]

F.B.: I was out there with Lacy Gibson

Let's go back to the year 1950. How much did a pair of drumsticks cost?

O.P.: Fifty cents.

F.B.: About fifty cents . . .

C.J: Yeah . . .

O.P.: You could get some clubs for fifty cents.

C.J.: War clubs!

O.P.: Great big ones—Bam!

Back then it seems you didn't have as much amplification, so you didn't really have to go out there and bang like these guys are banging today . . .

F.B.: No—you didn't play as loud.

C.J.: No

O.P.: No

F.B.: . . . and music was more blended.

C.J.: You get a better contrast the softer you play, anyway.

S.P.: You can hear the next man . . .

And I take it—everybody here at the table was a brush man as well?

E.P.: Oh yeah.

C.J.: Yeah

You couldn't get by without brushes in those days?

F.B.: Uh-uh.

C.J.: No

O.P.: No way

S.P.: Not in those days . . .

C.J.: No way.

And what about drumheads? Did you have adjustable heads? You see pictures of big bands and the tom-tom heads are nailed on. Did you have those kinds of sets?

[*Everybody at once . . .*]

O.P.: I saw one.

F.B.: I had one.

C.J.: I had one like that.

O.P.: I had an Indian drum like that, but not to play on. But before they had the second head, they had the bottom heads was nailed onto all of them. They had the heads nailed on the bottom, before they had adjustable heads on both top and bottom.

So, you could adjust the top, but the bottom one was nailed in place?

O.P.: Yeah, I had one.

C.J.: You had to put a little play in it, but it'd tighten up.

S.P.: I don't know anything about that.

C.J.: You don't?

S.P.: No.

C.J.: Are you kidding?

F.B.: I had a set of collapsible drums. I bought them down at Frank's Drum Shop.

C.J.: That's where I first saw them.

E.P.: I've seen lots of things at Frank's, but I didn't see that.

O.P.: Plastic man.

C.J.: He helped make them! The first drums.

S.P.: Sure did.

F.B.: But see they built collapsible drums. You put them up on a ring and then you set them up. Sooner or later they were going to collapse on you. [*Laughter all around.*] You'd be up there playing and all of a sudden they're going to do this [*demonstrates to laughter*] . . .

O.P.: That must not have lasted very long, did it?

E.P.: No, it couldn't.

F.B.: Yeah, I tell you, never again. I took the drums back to Frank and Frank just stood up there and laughed at me.

Also, back in the days we're talking about, you had to go through headaches that a modern-day drummer doesn't face with natural skin drumheads. You all had to take care of the skin heads more than the plastic heads.

F.B.: Oh, yeah. You had to put your own heads on.

S.P.: Tough

F.B.: And then you have a spoon—just an ordinary spoon—to start tucking them.

C.J.: If you knew how. Then you get you a little heat or something and you tighten it up. Set it out in the sun. If it was winter time you couldn't do it.

C.J.: You wet it [the drum head]. Yeah. Then let it dry.

E.P.: The skin would draw. Uh-huh

Didn't you have to be careful that you didn't draw it too tight?

C.J.: Oh, yeah. Sometimes if you were in a hurry you put it in the sun and let it tighten up a little bit, you know, fast

F.B.: You had to tuck them even, because you'd be sitting up there playing and one side of your drum would be coming loose

C.J.: And when you tighten them [*demonstrates*] you tighten here and over there, here and over there, here and over there. Then here and over there. [*In each case "here and there" were directly opposite each other, like positions on a clock-12 & 6, 9 & 3, etc.*]

F.B.: That's why they tell you you're supposed to tighten two, you know, five then across to ten, two then across to eight . . .

Directly across from each other?

C.J.: You never go all the way around. You go from one side to the other until you've got them all even. And put the same amount of turns on each one.

When did you fellows meet each other? You've talked about meeting Fred Below for the first time. When did you guys all run across each other? How far back?

O.P.: I was playing with Willie Dixon when Below was sitting out there looking up at me, and I was playing something—and he said, "I'm going to get that." And I said, "You get it." He was watching my left hand.

E.P.: Who, Below?

F.B.: He's always had one of those flying hands. That was back in the '50s.

O.P.: Yeah, because we were working, I think, on Wentworth Avenue. And when I met this gentleman here, it was at The 708 Club, over on 47th Street. I never will forget him—Earl Phillips. But that's a story I prefer to keep to myself. [*Laughter.*] I liked his beat and his singing. Good beat. Good singing. I liked it.

F.B.: Well, when I met Phillips the first time, it was on the West Side, over at the Zanzibar.

C.J.: You liked his drum playing better, though, than his singing?

O.P.: No, he played a nice drum and he sang a nice song.

C.J.: Oh, he did?

O.P.: Yeah.

C.J.: Ooohhh! I'd like to hear that.

O.P.: I mean we'll let it go at that. The rest I cannot put on tape. [*Laughter.*]

How about you, S.P.? When did you meet everyone around here? You stepped into Howlin' Wolf's band after Earl left.

O.P.: That's when I met S.P.—he was with Wolf.

S.P.: Well, when I was getting started in Chicago, Below was noted for the hand, and Odie Payne had the reputation for the foot—which still remains today. Odie Payne's got the best foot I ever saw in my life. Ain't it, Below?

F.B.: That's true.

S.P.: That man can roll with his foot, just like a man makes a roll on a snare drum.

C.J.: Chick Webb was the same way.

F.B.: Yeah—he's sure enough got it.

S.P.: I don't know where he got it from, but ever since I've known them, Below had the hands and Odie Payne had the foot. So, that had to be around '55 when I met Odie and Fred. Because I remember when Fred was playing with the Four Aces—right?

F.B.: No—I was playing with Little Walter.

S.P.: Yeah, well you all played over there at that . . .

F.B.: No, I was on the road with Little Walter and then I happened to come in a place where you were playing.

S.P.: Who was I with—Sam, or who?

O.P.: Magic Sam.

S.P.: Yeah. You remember we played at Loomis and Roosevelt. Because, Earl, you were playing with Wolf.

E.P.: That's right.

S.P.: And after you quit, Wolf hired me to play with him.

F.B.: That's right, because you came up here.

S.P.: Yeah.

O.P.: Because I was with Sam and Shakey Jake myself.

F.B.: Because the last time I saw you, I said, "Why don't you come on up to Chicago?"

S.P.: Yeah.

F.B.: And you said, "Yeah, I think I might do that."

Every one of you here was in the Chess recording studios, but, Fred, you were the house drummer.

F.B.: Well, I know I made quite a few records for Chess.

C.J.: Yeah.

S.P.: Oh, yeah, Below, boy. Oh, my goodness.

F.B.: I was making so many records down there that they had to have an extra set of drums put in the studios.

S.P.: You were the one that had them put in there . . .

F.B.: Because I couldn't break my drums down every night. And I told them, I said, "I can't break my drums down every night just to make a session, man." I said, "You ought to get some drums down here."

Can anyone elaborate on the famous stories we hear about how Leonard Chess used to get everybody angry at him so they'd play better?

F.B.: No.

No one will touch this?

O.P.: Well, what he did, he'd tell me to turn the stick over and use this part [not the tip—the blunt end of the stick]. He had you playing so hard—I just didn't believe it. And I just looked at him. You'd be the loudest thing in there and when the record came out, "Bloop, bloop, bloop."

C.J.: Yeah, man, that's what you heard.

O.P.: But that's the way he did it.

F.B: And there was a certain beat that Chess liked.

C.J.: He wouldn't let you get off of it.

F.B.: And once he heard it, that's what you had to play.

O.P.: You sure worked for your money, though. He would wear you out.

S.P.: "Boom-chang!" man. Wasn't that right Earl?

E.P.: That's right.

What about his method of cussing at everybody?

C.J.: That was just natural. He didn't mean it.

F.B.: That didn't mean anything.

O.P.: Well, he talked- you know where he got it from, and he just used it. He's throwing it right back at you.

S.P.: That's what we fell out about.

O.P.: See, if we had been the type of band who had violins and tails and everything, high class, you know, he'd have used a different type of language. But, for us, you know, it was the bottom line. So, naturally he was throwing it right back at you. I didn't like it. But I know why he was doing it, because that's what they understand.

F.B.: And he only used it to people that he was very familiar with. If he's not familiar with you, he wouldn't use that language.

O.P.: See, he would sit up in the studio and do his head like this. [*Shakes his head.*] We'd be playing and I would stop and say, "What's the matter man?" "Keep playing." And I'd say "Why are you doing this?" He said it was a feeling. He had to get the feeling so he would do this [*shakes his head*] instead of this [*nods his head*]. He'd go like this here, you know, and close his eyes. And you thought you were doing something wrong, see. But what he was looking for was that feeling, that drive.

F.B.: It was that certain beat.

E.P.: He loved that drive.

F.B.: And when you got that drive.

O.P.: So, I asked him, "Why do you keep shaking your head like this?" "Man, I got to get the beat, I got to feel the beat, blah blah." [*Manic imitation of Chess:*] I said, "Yeah, but you're going like this, like something's wrong." He said, "Ain't nothin' wrong, that's the way I do it."

C.J.: He'd get excited sometimes.

O.P.: So, we'd just go ahead and accept it, you know. You had to learn the producer's ways, that's all.

Do you think that he had pretty good taste in the beats that he wanted you guys to stick with?

F.B.: Oh. Yeah.

O.P.: You've got to consider the products that came out of that studio. He must have known what he was doing, what he was trying to get by on. He was really being a duplicate of you, actually.

F.B.: He'd come into a session, you know, and certain people he recorded, see he'd bring in two or three quarts and sit it down there on the floor. This is to get the session rolling smooth. And on some of those sessions you had to have it. [*Laughter.*]

O.P.: Arbee Stidham, after he did this thing for Chess, and Chess liked it. When he got to the studio, the man sang himself hoarse and then wound up doing it the way that he had done it in the first place, and Chess liked it. But what Chess did, psychology-wise, he got everything he could out of you—his way—as much as he could. And if nothing would change, he'd say, "Alright, man, go ahead on." But he was going to throw his ideas in there. And if they don't get to you, you wind up doing it your way. That's how it's going to come out. But by that time, the singer got as hoarse as the devil.

S.P.: That's why they had so many takes.

F.B.: I got him on one, though. We went to the studio with Willie Dixon and we made the Walkin' Blues. We got down to the studio and I was doing it with brushes and sticks and everything, trying to get the sound out—the sound wasn't coming. So, I said, "Well, man, why don't you put a board down on the floor and let me walk on it?" [*Demonstrates a triplet on the table with his knuckles.*] And he said, "Do what?" I said, "Put a board on the floor and put the microphone down and then let me walk." Leonard said, "Well, let's try." We did it in two takes. Walkin' the Blues. No drums at all, and here I brought the whole set down to the studio. [*Laughs.*]

From what you're saying, a lot of you were on the bandstand with the musicians you were recording with, but when you got to the studio you never really did record the songs the way they were done on the bandstand. Did that happen very often?

F.B.: Right.

E.P.: Yeah, they changed it when you got there.

O.P.: You're going to change it. You're going to change it to his feelings.

E.P.: That's right.

O.P.: Then after he ran out of ideas, they'd say, "Oh, go ahead on, man, do it." But, by that time you're dead—and you could have done it that way in the first place.

F.B.: You could have done it that way the first time.

O.P.: Johnny Jones did seventeen takes one time, man, seventeen on "Dirty by the Dozens." Seventeen times before they got it right.

Earl, you were the house drummer over at Vee-Jay. What was the situation like over there? How many of you made it to the Vee-Jay studios? How many of you recorded there?

C.J.: All of us, I think.

E.P.: I think all of us did.

F.B.: Everybody did. I did it with Memphis Slim

With Matt Murphy?

F.B.: Yeah.

Earl, you were behind Billy Boy (Arnold), Snooky (Pryor), Eddie (Taylor), and Jimmy (Reed).

E.P.: Jimmy Reed. I was more with Jimmy Reed than any of them. I was on just about all the Jimmy Reeds.

S.P.: That's for sure.

F.B.: When he stopped, then I started.

How about you, Odie? You were sort of the house drummer for the Cobra label, weren't you?

O.P.: In a way, yeah. I did a few. Betty Everett and Magic Sam, of course, and also Otis Rush.

Buddy Guy?

O.P.: Yeah, his first. Junior Wells' first—but it was Atlantic, Junior Wells. And Buddy Guy. I don't know where that one was. I was on Junior Wells' first Who Hoodooed The Hoodoo Man. And then I did a set with Muddy Waters, on Don't Go No Further. And then I think Memphis Slim was overseas a couple of years ago when I was on a session with him. Of course, all overseas trips are made onto records, you know.

F.B.: Yeah.

O.P.: They make albums on that.

Let me ask you a question, Fred. You told me once about breaking a strap on your pedal . . .

F.B.: Oh, man, yeah. I was in a session and I had a leather strap on my foot pedal, and down my foot went and that's it—it didn't come back up no more. The strap broke. Then I had to take the tongue out of my shoe and put it up, and fix it up in there.

O.P.: What a creative mind . . . [*Laughter all around.*]

C.J.: You know one incident happened to me once when I was in Baltimore at the Royal Theater. We were playing out on the stage. The next thing I knew I'm flat on my back; my heels stay up in the air. The best thing I could do there is to make an act out of it. The stool had busted. I got up with my sticks and beat around the platform and I danced around the drums, stood up and started playing.

F.B.: Same thing happened to me at the Apollo Theater in New York. I got down and the seat slipped down in one of the holes on the drumming bandstand. And backwards I went.

O.P.: Well, that's the reason I think I have what I have today—these physical complications. It only happened to me once with Memphis Slim. We were playing at the Playtime. And I don't know what happened. I stood up. I'll tell you one thing . . .

C.J.: Did the stool break, or were you happy? [*Laughter.*]

O.P.: The drums went that way. People thought it was an act. They were actually laughing, you know.

C.J.: Well, I made an act out of mine to cover it up. Oh, when that seat went out from under me, "Boom."

F.B.: Oh, you talk about embarrassed.

C.J.: It doesn't ever happen at the beginning or the end or before you go out there, when you're testing your stuff. It always happens when you're right in the middle of your number.

O.P.: But drums, I think, are about the only instrument that can foul up, because you got a lot of things going on, see. You got this going, you got the foot pedal going, you got the cymbals on stands, this, that, and the other—anything can slip. You know, a horn player—might lose a pad or a reed—can get away with it. But the drums, everything is mechanical. The thing can get loose on the sock cymbal. Like you said, a strap can break on the pedal. You can go to hit your ride cymbal and the stand can fall over . . .

C.J.: That happened to me several times, too.

O.P.: You can break your sticks, you can bust a drum head. A lot of things can happen on a drum set. A piano player can knock out a key, but he'd just go to the next one, you know. But you—the drummer—if anything goes wrong, they will know it.

F.B.: I was playing up in Michigan—Saginaw, Michigan—at one of those big things with Little Walter. And somebody in the audience threw some panties up at Little Walter. And he ducked [*uproarious laughter*] and they landed right dead on my cymbals [*laughter*]. You should have seen me sweep. [*Demonstrates.*]

E.P.: I was in Florida—it was about forty miles out of Miami. The club is indoor and outdoor. He had it so he could close it over and make it an indoor club—open it and it would be a grove. Well, one night the Wolf was just a howling. I'm beating away there and my pegs on that slick floor, they just lost their hold and they started moving. And here I am [*demonstrates to laughter*], skies blowing, and they thought I was part of the show. They tried to start out, "Whoo-woo-woo! Whoo-woo-woo!" [*Loud laughter.*] They go, "Do that number again. Do that number again." Man, I'm hurting all up in here.

C.J.: That made me start carrying a rug with me.

F.B.: You know what I carry? I got a piece of rope that I tied on my bass drum. And just keeps it right up there. From when I get to a place where they got slick floors, or concrete or something like that, I take that rope out and tie it around my seat.

E.P.: That's what I had to do.

Let's go around the table—How many sets of drums have you lost—had stolen, had burned . . .

F.B.: I had one set of drums burned—burned up in a fire on 39th and Indiana Avenue, leaving them in the club overnight.

C.J.: I did, too.

E.P.: I lost mine, too. Burned up in a club on Madison Street, between Ashland and Paulina.

C.J.: I had a couple of sets stolen—and a lot of cymbals.

O.P.: Two sets stolen—right in front of the house.

Did you leave them in the car?

C.P.: No, these were in the club.

S.P.: One set stolen right in front of the nightclub. We were packing up to leave, right after the job. We brought my drums out and set them down. The guy went to pick up the car and I went back in and helped some of the guys bring their stuff out. I brought a load out and set it down—and mine was gone! It was probably someone who didn't even know how to play.

About the only consolation is that whoever stole them is working hard trying to carry them away.

O.P.: My first set was stolen right in front of the house. I circulated around the neighborhood and offered a five-dollar reward. Parts of the set were found in various garbage cans around the neighborhood.

E.P.: Somebody took a tom-tom from me—and a cymbal!

O.P.: I've always believed in two. I've always kept two sets of drums. I believe in two.

My biggest fear is that my car will break down with the drums in the car. Lose the drums, for sure—and you might lose the car as well.

F.B.: I had that happen, too. On the way to the job. So I had to stay right there. The way I went to the job was the same way Otis Rush traveled, that same route. So I had to sit right there until Otis came. Otis loaded the set in his car.

Let's just pay some tribute here to all the hours that you guys have spent breaking drum sets down, setting drum sets up, carrying them around. No other musician does that kind of work, do they?

F.B.: Ooooh. Man.

C.J.: Horn players pick their horns up and walk out the door.

E.P.: Yeah, walk right out the door. I'm there sweating, right?

S.P.: And you're still taking it down and packing it up.

C.J.: Piano players, he ain't got nothin' to carry. And he's not going to help you, you know. You're the last man out.

F.B.: First one there and the last one to leave.

E.P.: I give credit to Wolf though; he had a young valet. Wolf told him, "You just take care of my man there. That's all you gotta do."

C.J.: Man, I used to hate those clubs where you had to go up on the second floor—no elevator—no nothin'!

O.P.: And nobody wants to help you either [*chorus of "No's"*]. "So long, Odie, so long."

Earl Phillips

When I started my radio program, *Blues Before Sunrise*, in 1980, the first person I interviewed on the show was blues drummer Earl Phillips. I may have contacted Earl through Billy Boy Arnold. Earl had quit blues and joined the church. Our deal was that I would make a donation to his church and he would do the interview. Earl was one of the Big Four, the first-call Chicago Blues drummers—Fred Below, Odie Payne, Earl Phillips, and S.P. Leary. He had a lethal backbeat, and of the Big Four, he was the one who employed the tom-toms in his beats. Tom-toms spell drama and Earl had it to spare. His beats were a major part of the dark, mysterious sound of Howlin' Wolf's original Chicago band. "No Place to Go," "Smokestack Lightning," "Who'll Be Next," "Going Back Home," and many more. I went to Earl's place, a big graystone building at 41st and Prairie. He lived upstairs, and as I came upstairs (burglary gates at both the top and the bottom of his staircase) his wife was sitting up in bed with her hair in curlers(!). Earl took me to his recreation room that had a bar and seven(!!!)TVs—one for each broadcast channel in Chicago at the time. He took particular pride in turning them all on and we watched each channel simultaneously. Earl talked about hooking up with Howlin' Wolf. Also, he always told me that he made jazz records, but I wasn't able to find any with him as drummer until I stumbled across a session from 1946 under Roy Eldridge's name several years later.

■ ■ ■

I was born in New York City, New York, in Harlem. I was born April 25, 1920. I had six years of schooling there in New York. After my mother passed, my uncle came and took me to Nashville, Tennessee. I completed my schooling in Nashville, Tennessee, and I graduated Pearl High in 1940. I went a half a year at Fisk. I wanted music, but the music was so high I couldn't afford to keep up the tuition. I didn't form a band until my next to last year in high school. We started playing, a bunch of us boys, practicing, and we started playing with an old fellow named James Reed, in Nashville, Tennessee. You know, we graduated, we played around, and so this guy was going this way—some of us were able to go to college and they were going to leave. The band kind of split up a little bit. So, I said, "Well, I'll go where my auntie is, that was here in Chicago. So, I just bundled up one night, grabbed the train, and came to Chicago. I came to Chicago in December 1940. And then after I got here—there was a joint, I didn't know exactly where my auntie lived. I was lost, but I know it was on Pershing Road—39th Street. So, I got out of the cab at 39th—Pershing Road, and I heard music. I went right straight there. When I got in there, there was a young man, he was in charge of the band and he spied me when I walked in the door with a suitcase. He came right straight to me. "Are you looking for a job?" I didn't know who it was at first—I hadn't seen him since he graduated from school. I said, "Yeah, I'm looking for a job—and I'm trying to find my auntie, too." He said, "Man, come here . . . " He went to the boss of the club there. He said, "I'm going to let this other drummer go. Here's my man right here. He just got here." Just like that—like he sent for me. [*Laughs.*] Sure enough, I went to work that same night—at that club right there on that corner. I didn't know what was going on. It was a [female] impersonation club. They looked like girls—I thought they were girls. But there wasn't any blues—blues wasn't in there anywhere—you're still dealing with jazz, swing, and pop.

I moved to the Westside and I ran into Jody Williams. And how that happened, I was going to what we call a Blue Monday party. And that's where I met all these guys that were all on this blues kick, you know. The cat says, "The blues, man, is what's happening. You better get with it." So, I said, "Well I'll go to a Blue Monday party." So, I'd go to the Blue Monday parties and started sitting in on sets—and it looked to me like it just come to me when I sit down and just pick up sticks and started listening, because I never did read no music. It is something that just came to me naturally, like you sit down, between a knife and a fork and you know what you're supposed to do with it. And that's when I decided to form a little band then—Jody and I decided to form a little band together. And we were playing all over the Westside. Yeah, we go out with Elmore James. Elmore James, he used to get us—just hooked us up with him and away we go. The same way with Sunnyland Slim and Sonny Boy Williamson. He'd pick up my band, if he liked my group he'd say, "Well I'm the leader on this engagement because see my name is here in the contract—you're all the sidemen." Alright—Okay with us because it's an awfully good buck, you know, a little bit more than our old stand-by place was playing. So, we'd jump on the road and go with him. And like JT Brown, he's old but he was a jazz man—mostly.

I was playing at 35th and Indiana. That's where Muddy worked—Muddy had it sewed up. I went to work with Muddy and Muddy loved the way I played. So, I hooked up with him and Little Junior [Wells]. Junior was playing with Muddy before Cotton came in. But then [Fred] Below and Muddy made up. And Howlin' Wolf was coming to town. Muddy introduced me to Wolf. Muddy said, "I want you to hook up with this man. He's coming to town and he needs some good musicians, and I know what you and Jody Williams can do. I want you to hook up with him." So, Wolf says, "Come out to my house." We went out to his house and had a rehearsal out there. And, sure enough, Wolf was just crazy about us. When Wolf come to town, he came in one of those big, long limousines. He didn't have a band—and we were his first band, Jody and myself—and another kid who was playing piano—not Hosea Lee Kennard, because Hosea hadn't come here yet. And after our rehearsal it seemed like he just took confidence in me right off the bat. He told me to come in his other little old room. He opened a foot locker and it was loaded—all the way from top to bottom with quarters, dimes, half-dollars. He asked me to help him count it out. We counted out two hundred and some dollars in change. We put it in the bag, took it down to the train station, and we sent for Hubert [Sumlin]—and Hubert's the one who stayed with him until Wolf died. Then he opened his trunk, he had a little foot trunk—it was full of one-dollar bills! This man had hauled all this jive from Memphis in his limousine—I mean, he didn't have nothing but money!" [*Laughs.*] And he didn't trust nobody but me. I started being his bookkeeper. I kept all his books—and believe me, I kept them straight. The government never did have to come back on him. Later, Leonard Chess said, "I'm gonna get you an accountant." I'd keep his records on the road and when we come home, the accountants took them over and straightened them out. I used to take the boys some money out, write it down in the book. I was his secretary as well as his drummer on the road.

You got to record in the Chess studios. What was that like?

It was fun to me. Leonard Chess, he was temperamental sometimes. And Wolf—he was slow to get mad—but when he got mad it was hard for him to cool off. Sometimes we didn't complete a session. He and Leonard would get into it and say some of those fantastic words. [*Laughs.*] And so, sometimes we'd have to come back the next day—to complete one session. Wolf would tell him right quick, "I don't have to make this session. I'm not begging to make this session!" And then Leonard would call him into the office—and Wolf would come back out. "Well, you all take it easy. We'll come back tomorrow. Chess is going to pay for it tomorrow—I paid for it today." [*Laughs.*]

I told him myself, "You know, you have to spend a dollar to make a dollar." Now when we had to buy uniforms, he ran me all over everywhere trying to get a real cut-rate price. We went all out north, two or three places, I don't remember, I can't recall the name of the places. But the uniforms didn't look like anything. I said, "If we have these cleaned one time, people will swear we've had them a year. It's better to pay a good price and then we've got something to go with." So that's what we did. And then later on, he said [*imitating Wolf's voice:*], "You know what?" "What?" "You were right!" "I know I was right!" He'd call and ask me things, call me off to himself, just us two, you know. "Phil—what you think about this?" and he'd go into detail, and I'd say, "You got to put out some money . . . " "How much?" [*Laughs.*]

I've always heard that if you messed up the music on the bandstand, he'd literally take you into the alley.

He would! He did—Hubert got so many whippings it wasn't funny. I got mad with Wolf one time. I said, "Alright Wolf, you do it one more time, I'm gonna take the whole band and leave you here!" He did—he really did—yes, indeed. If you messed up in rehearsal he'd say, "We're gonna stay right here until you get it right. And you mess up on the bandstand, he ain't gonna say nothing but he'd turn around and look at you. And if he got his head feeling good, he'd just cuss you out on the bandstand. "Now you know that ain't right." He wanted everything down pat! He didn't want you to have to read it—he wanted it up in your head. We were playing at Sylvio's—Sylvio's was our home base. We'd stay out on the road six, eight, maybe ten weeks at a time. He bought a brand-new station wagon. He traded his limousine in for this station wagon and we did all our traveling in that station wagon. We'd take turns driving. I'd drive a while, Hubert would drive—we all could drive. We went to New York—that was something. We went through the Holland Tunnel. Wolf had never been in the Holland Tunnel. We came to the tunnel and I said, "Wolf, you'd better let one of us drive. You got to stay in your lane, you got to stay in that lane—and you have to keep up your speed. There's a man standing up there on the wall." "What's he doin' up there?" [*Laughs.*] "He's there to make sure you keep moving . . . " "Yeah—you better take the wheel . . . " We went through the Holland Tunnel and Wolf didn't sleep at all. A lot of times when I drove, he'd just fall asleep. He just sat up there looking. We went to the Apollo Theater and the man said, "Yes, we've been expecting you." He showed us our dressing room and everything. They had a schedule on the board there. It listed the time for our rehearsal and everything. Wolf said, "Well, you're from New York—you gotta show us around." I said, "Okay—I'll show you everything I know . . . " That was the first time I'd been back to New York since I was nine years old, but I was saved by the bell, because Small, who was sponsoring this Rock & Roll show, sent his man up to the hotel where we were staying. And James Brown came over. You know James Brown? That hollering guy [*laughs*]. He came over—and Little Richard came over. Bobby Blue Bland was on the outskirts of New York and he heard about Wolf. He knew Wolf—Wolf knew him when he was just a little boy. And B.B. King—he was playing somewhere. They all knew Wolf, you know. Wolf was just like a daddy—they called him Big Daddy. And Sonny Boy Williamson II—they used to call him Foots but when B.B. showed up, he called Wolf Foots. We were all saying, "Why is he calling Wolf Foots? Sonny Boy is named Foots." And that's when Wolf told us they used to call him Foots back in Memphis.

At the Apollo we upset the house—just Wolf and I. I opened up playing my tom-toms. We're going "Doo-do-doo-doo-doo" [*sings "No Place to Go"*] and then Wolf opens up with his harp. He's soloing on harp and I've got that same steady beat on the tom-toms. I'd switch over to the snare drum then crash on the cymbal. That's when Wolf would howl at your door. And we played "I Wore My Forty-Four So Long" and I played that in sort of a marching style until I swung out into a straight-on blues beat. That was another one they went crazy about. Then Hubert would come out and it would sound like his guitar was talking because he had it all keyed up. And as we went back offstage, Ed Sullivan came in the room. He talked to Wolf, and then he came to me. "How would you all like to go on the *Ed Sullivan Show*?" It was 1958 and I don't know why it was, but we just couldn't get Wolf to go on.

Wolf and I had a misunderstanding—and Wolf said, "Well, I'll get S.P. [Leary]." I said, "Well—that's your business. You get who you want"—and I cut on out. So then Billy Boy Arnold said, "You quit Wolf?' I said, "Yeah . . . " So, I went to work with Billy Boy. And all of them were reaching for me when they heard I had put Wolf down, Eddie Taylor—all of them were calling me. And during that time, I didn't have a night off all week. Then I went back to Wolf because he couldn't get along with the other guys. I can't use the words he said but he said, "They're alright but Phil—you gotta come on back." So, I said, "Alright Wolf, I'll come on back . . . " and I played until 1960.

I'm going to tell you this—that alcohol can be the worst enemy you ever had. The pores of your skin open up. That alcohol opens them up when you're drinking. Then you jump off the stage and you're messing around and that cold—that chill gets into your muscles. You don't feel it then. You may not feel it for four or five years. Every time you get an ache you take a drink—and your ache is gone! So, my muscular reactions began to slow down. Finally, I had to tell him, "Wolf, I just can't give you the service I should." And he even asked me, "When do you think you might want to come back? Let me know . . . " I was playing for Atlantic and some guy in the studio approached me. He said, "You are one hell of a drummer. I'd love to use you for our studio whenever we need a drummer. How would you like to do that?" I said, "Fine!" Jimmy [Bracken], on this session, he wanted to try a blues number. They told him to go ahead and try it. This guy, he was sitting in there talking to Albert King that day—and he was surprised how I fit right in when he turned it into a blues number. He called me over when the session was over and he said, "You are versa-TILE!" "Well, when you play it, I hear it—and that's the way it comes out." He said, "How'd you like to be a studio drummer?" "Yeah!" Just before the session, they called me at home and asked me to come down to the record store. When I got down there, they said, "Yep—he's the one." "We heard you the other night—we were over on 18th Street. You had your own little band over there. We were out in the audience and I was telling Vivian [Carter] that you had the kind of 'oomph!' that Jimmy Reed needed." He said, "We got a session and you're going to be playing for Jimmy Reed." And when the Vee-Jay label called me to that first session—that's when I met Jimmy Reed. I came to that first session to play with him and I knew the blues—but Jimmy hadn't heard of me! And from then on, every time Jimmy had a session, he wouldn't call anybody but me. And Billy Boy—he was crazy about me. Billy said, "When I get ready to cut, I'm going to use you for my drummer." Eddie Taylor used to play on all the Jimmy Reed sides for Vee-Jay, and Eddie said, "When I get ready to cut, I want you to play drums for me." Jimmy Rogers—same way—yeah, I got a record with Jimmy. Once he played with me, he said, "Man, you hold us." I didn't play to play notes—I played from my heart.

I can hear things. Just like we were rehearsing with Wolf, at his house, rehearsing "No Place to Go." We couldn't get anything straight on it. I just started hitting something on the drums and Wolf looked over at me, and Hubert, he listened. Now these are people in the same category I'm in—we didn't use any notes—we used our ears! So, I started something—that Boom de Boom Boom Boom, and Wolf started howling [*howls like Wolf*] and Hubert starts ding-ding—and the first thing you know, we got it—"No Place to Go!" And the same way with Billy Boy—Billy played certain chords—they just vibrate through me, and I got it. I've never tried to play like anybody. Guys used to try and show me how to throw up my sticks while I was playing a solo—and all that kind of stuff. I said, "Yep—um-hmm . . . " I played it my way. It was just something that was given to me—and it was just meant to last a certain amount of time, I guess. I looked at notes—and studied them a while, and I could tell you paradiddle, triple paradiddle, that staff hit soft, this staff hit loud—I do all that but it didn't move me none. It dawned on me—I guess it was from way back training. I was raised up in the church and I had these peculiar dreams that stayed with me all the time. I had just about quit playing music and in my dreams, it said, "It's time for you to go back where you first started." I never could figure that out. I got sick—very sick—and went into the hospital. The doctors just about gave me up—and that dream came back to me again. I said, "Alright, I know what it is." The Lord wants me to get back and do the work I'm supposed to do. He let me do this other work long enough. And to tell you the truth, it looks like it all just vanished away from me. Now at church, I see a little boy playing the drums, you know, and I want to get up there and teach him—and I do! Maybe I should feel ashamed because I was out there playing worldly music. But I read it in my Bible now. It says play all instruments, play them all—but play them in a religious way—not in a way that's serving Satan, you know. I kind of answered my own questions when I read it. I had someone ask me the other evening, a boy that was working up on the northside, he wanted me to come over there and sit in a session with him—just sit in on his show. I just told him, "I don't think I could even get the feeling of that rhythm anymore." I would come—just to be a guest, but I couldn't play because my life has turned completely around. I don't criticize anybody—do the best you can at whatever you're going to do. If you're going to serve the Devil, serve him the best you can. When you turn around and serve the Lord, serve him the best you can! So that was it. It was my time to put it down and leave it alone . . .

S.P. Leary

Of the Big Four blues drummers—Fred, Odie, Earl, and S.P.—S.P. was the most underrated. He faced the world mostly with a backbeat, a joke, and a smile, but his backbeat was smoother than most in delivery—and farther back "in the pocket" which gave it great feeling. He also had accomplished brush work. He was the youngest of the Big Four but managed to work and record with both Wolf and Muddy. Wherever he went he brought a tremendous thirst with him, which over the years was cause for repeated firings and re-hirings, but when he was "right" he was hard to beat. The Drummer's Roundtable event was my first opportunity to meet and talk with him, and on the strength of that meeting, I asked him to come in for a "one-on-one" interview. For some reason, I came away from this interview with a great sense of disappointment. At that time, I was so disappointed with the interview that I never edited or presented it on the air. It's a pleasant surprise to hear how good and informative it actually is thirty years later . . .

■ ■ ■

Let's start at the beginning. Can you tell me when and where you were born?

Well, I was born in a little rural town by the name of Carthage, Texas—East Texas. June 6, 1930. My daddy was a farmer.

How many brothers and sisters?

There were eleven of us—six girls and five boys.

Where were you in that order?

I was the baby. I was the eleventh child.

What got you interested in music—was anybody in your family a musician?

Now that is one heck of a question, because the first one who became a musician was me. The family sang in the church choirs, my brothers and my sisters, but I was the only one that played an instrument. I had a heck of a time trying to do that, but I guess that I was just musically inclined.

What was your first instrument, a drum?

Yes, it was—made out of a nail can with tire innertubes. Years and years ago, I used to play in a rhythm band in Carthage, Texas—that's my home—that's right. That is my home, Carthage, Texas. My music teacher was Harris Neely—that was her name then—I don't know what her name is now, but she's still living. She lives in Maywood, Illinois, right now, and she's just as beautiful as she can be—yes, indeed.

Well, that's right next door to me—I'm in Forest Park . . .

I've got a whole bunch of nieces and nephews in Maywood. I've got piano players out there, I've got flute players out there—everything out there since I became a musician, they all became musically inclined. Well, you probably heard of my niece, Joy Bell? She's a professional. She plays the cocktail lounges at times and she's been around the country different places, Vegas and places like that. She looks after the old man [me].

Let's talk about the little rhythm band. What age were you in this rhythm band?

I think I was about five or six years old. Then my daddy jumped up and he moved up to Dallas, you know, and I went to Dallas—that's where I was raised, in Dallas. I was born in Carthage, which I call my home, and that is my home. In Dallas, I went to school with David Fathead Newman and—oh boy. I can't think of all the names of all the guys up there. There were some big boys up there—like Leroy Cooper, played bass with Ray Charles—of course, Fathead played with Ray Charles. I was just on a show with Fathead about two months ago down in Texas—man, it was beautiful, boy, to see the kid up close. You know, just the feeling of, you know, he and I, being on the same bandstand together. It was a gas, it was a flabbergaster.

Was this down at Antones?

Yes—that's where I was. I went down to Antones twice. And that is a beautiful place to visit. You better believe it because I think that he got the best blues in the world. They go in and out of his place—you hear me. I'm not jivin'. Antone's place is together. And on top of that, he is a heck of a gardener! He's beautiful people!

When you're talking about Fathead Newman and Leroy Cooper—was that in grade school or high school?

Well, Fathead and I—we went all the way through, you know, for grammar school. Of course, I was a couple of grades ahead of him—know what I'm talking about—because I'm a few years older than Fathead. And, when Fathead joined the Ray Charles organization, they played at our school before we even graduated from grammar school. Fathead was a big night. He came in there and was playing with Ray Charles.

They came in there—and they play down man. And I was so surprised. Just as I saw Fathead, I look up as I thought, well if Fathead can do that, then I can do that too!

When you were playing drums in school? What kind of drum was it? Like a concert band? Were you playing a whole set of drums or a single drum?

No, I used to play the snare drum. I used to play the bass drum. Because during that time I was going to high school, we didn't have no timpanies—timpani drums. I don't know if they got any now in high school. But at that time, I used to have to turn the bass drum over and make a timpani out of it—and use the mallets to try and play.

What inspired you to take up drums?

I was always beating on something—I was *always* beating on something! Mama didn't want me to play no wind instrument. I wanted to blow saxophone. I wanted to blow trombone. I wanted to play trumpet, but I used to suffer with asthma when I was coming up. So, I couldn't play no wind instrument. But I said, "I'm gonna play something." So, I laid back. I started shining shoes. My first set of drums cost me $125. I shined shoes—I saved my little money—and I got that set of drums.

About how old would you say you were when you got that first set?

At the age of fourteen I was a pro . . . Well, I mean, I consider myself a pro because I was playing with my godfather, which was T-Bone Walker, and he hired me, Mr. Lard Jefferson, and Mr. Douglas Fernell. I played with Fathead—Fathead was out there.

This was in Dallas, right?

Yeah. Oh, yeah. Fathead and I were the first two young musicians to join the union—in Dallas, Texas. David Newman—his name is David Newman. That Fathead came from . . . well, I don't have to tell you that . . .

No, I think you better, I think you better tell me.

Well, you know, his mother used to keep his hair cut short all the time, cut really short. So short his head would shine. And do you remember that head boppin' stuff? That's right—"Bam!"—everybody'd bop him on his head—"Nice shine young man . . . " and he was scared to fight [*laughs*]. Whoo boy! [*Laughs.*] I don't know about him now—I wouldn't want to chance it but he still ain't no giant—know what I mean?

So, when you got that set of drums, would you practice at home? Were you still at home with your mom and your dad?

No, I was home. They called me Gene Krupa—until I learned how to play. I'd run across my friends and neighbors and they'd say, "Yeah—that's Gene

Krupa and Buddy Rich over there!" That's what they called me, and I was still practicing and I was getting jobs.

What were you listening to at that time?

Man, at that time, we didn't have anything but a radio. It mostly was up in here [*pointing to his head*]. And then you know, I could walk down the street. I wasn't old enough to go in no taverns but I could stand on the outside of the tavern. I could hear the music and I'd go back home—and I'd play it. I heard the music and I memorized it up in here. Back in those days with Gene Krupa, Buddy Rich, Louis Bellson, Lucky Millinder, we could hear that on the radio—you know what I'm talking about. I never will forget that stuff and I'd play it.

Were you still in high school? Did you finish high school?

Yes, I did. I finished high school. I wasn't able to go to college because my father wasn't able to go to the city. Like I told you, my dad was a farmer. We had moved from the farm to Dallas and I wasn't able to go. I wanted to go to college. I just wasn't able to go. If I had gone to college, I'd have been up there at the same time as Charles Brown. But I wasn't able to go—so I joined the army.

Who were some of the other people you saw in Dallas?

T-Bone Walker, you know played guitar, Doug Fernell, who played trumpet, Buster Smith, who played saxophone. As a matter of fact, he's the one who wrote "One O'Clock Jump," which Count Basie bought from him. I saw Lowell Fulson, also Lionel Hampton, Big Joe Turner, also Illinois Jacquet, and Arnett Cobb. This was all during World War II time. I wasn't in the service during WWII—I was in the Korean War. But the guys I'm mentioning were during WWII, when I was in high school.

When did you get out of high school?

1947.

How long was it between your graduation and going into the service?

One year . . .

And did you do any playing during that time, before you went away to the service?

I used to sit in with them but I think I only played one job—one time with Arnett Cobb in Fort Worth, Texas, out there with Arnett and Big Leroy Cooper, which is a very good friend of mine. And, boy, I just can't recall. All the fellows that I haven't played with . . .

Would you sit in with T-Bone and Lowell Folsom as well?

No—I didn't sit in with him. T-Bone was my godfather—I was working for him.

Tell me, how did T-Bone get to be your godfather?

Because he was the one that used to come to my home and pick me up and bring me back. We'd go to the job. Actually, the way I met T-Bone was through Lard Jefferson, who was a trumpet player. And I can show you right today his name is signed on my street car. Because at the time I was playing with Lloyd Glenn, T-Bone hired Lloyd's band to back him up, you understand? I got to be T-Bone's godson because T-Bone would come to my house, pick me up, and bring me back home.

How old were you?

Man, I was fifteen—I couldn't drive, I couldn't drink—I couldn't even smoke . . .

Fifteen. Fifteen years old. When I first hit the road, I was fifteen years old. I never will forget; T-Bone took me to some little town in Oklahoma. Yeah, Enid, Oklahoma, that was outside Yigaga. With T-Bone wearing a process back in those days, and Lloyd used to put his hand in his hair and say, "Don't you wish you could do this?" [*Laughs.*] That was the best, man. That's why it was so much fun. You know? I never will forget the times that he used to bring me home, and the way that he'd tell Mama and Papa—he'd say, "Well, here's your baby back—he's all right. Give him a month. I've doubled his money." I didn't like that. Yeah, he gave the money to my parents. No, he'd give it to them. I didn't worry about it.

How many pieces in the band?

T-Bone had a big band—and he had a small band, like a combo, okay? When he played certain places, he would go with the big band—fourteen pieces. Sometimes I played with him and it would just be a little band, five pieces. And T-Bone was a blues man. He was a bluesman—he loved the blues—but he could play anything. It didn't matter whether it was jazz or it was blues—if it was music T-Bone would make it fit. In the small group you had the guitar, drums, piano, and bass—sometimes a horn, a sax. Now I'm talking about when I played with him. I don't know what he used on other jobs. I do know he had a big band—fourteen pieces. He had a reed section, a brass section—and you know good and well he's got a rhythm section because he's up there on guitar, with drums, piano, and bass.

What would you guys talk about when you take long trips? Did you talk about music? Did you talk about other stuff?

Yeah, well, you know, naturally that's gonna be discussed. Different things—where he thinks this should go—or that should go, different changes. They'd be talkin' that. The kind of beats he'd tell me to put up in there. That's where that strong backbeat came from—from T-Bone—and Lowell Fulson. That strong backbeat that they got today.

How about brushwork?

That's one thing that I'm glad that you brought up because I was a master at it. I was—I don't know what's going on out here now. They done fired me and all that old kind of stuff. Nobody wants me to work. That's okay—because I put it there. I know I put it there. Ain't but one man I know today that can beat me using brushes, and that's Mr. Jo Jones, that used to play with Count Basie. I copied off of Jo—and I copied off of Art Blakey. Those two—Jo Jones and Art Blakey—are my favorite two drummers. Now I love the stuff that Max Roach writes. The man is terrific. He's out of sight but the man is just too far out for me. I can't catch up with him and where's he's coming from.

I wouldn't think you could use that in blues anyway . . .

No, wait, wait. You're wrong—you are definitely wrong. I did it—I can take jazz beats right today and cross them around and fit it in with some blues. I did it then—I can do it now. Because I copied off of Mr. Roach and Mr. Blakey. You take those two things and put them together and cross them up like this here—you can something out of there. Now you just got to know how to do it. But it takes—it takes time . . .

What was the nature of the gigs you did play? Okay, you're playing with Buster Smith. Was that a jazz gig? I mean, would you just swing?

Buster Smith was one of the greatest musicians you ever would meet in your life, man. He's a saxophone player, he's an arranger. He's just a musician. Period.

Just like Mr. Lard Jefferson and Douglas Fernell—those guys were music, man.

I guess the point I'm trying to understand—were those jazz gigs blowing gigs or whether they were singing blues on them?

It was all mixed up. Music was music in those days, man. I don't know, Steve, you're too young to remember anything about somebody like Lil' Green, because in those days music was music. Of course, somebody was singing, even Billy Eckstine was singing—and Big Joe Turner. All those guys came in and hollered. I'd even holler once in a while if they'd let me, but don't nobody give me a chance.

When you were in the military service, did you get drafted?

No, I did not get drafted. I volunteered 1948—and got discharged in 1952. I stayed in there. I did my time.

So, did you have any musical activity in the army?

All the way. I was in a military band all the time I was in the service. I was in the Third Armored Division at Fort Knox, Kentucky. After I finished my basic training, I went to the Third Armored Division band. I stayed in there until I got transferred to Fort Louis, Washington. I was in the Second Armored Division band in Fort Louis. Music is my life all the way.

This was during the Korean War. Did you actually see any action?

No. I was sent over to Korea. I was in Kunsan, Seoul, in Korea. But I was behind the lines—behind the action. I played for the fellows when they came in. When they marched and did formations, they needed a band to play for those formations and I was in that band. Now I wasn't on the front line but that didn't mean we never got shelled. There were shells falling all around us, I just didn't get hit—and you get as nervous as hell, you know what I'm saying?

What happened when you got out in 1952?

I went back home to Dallas. I went to business college for a while and took a business administration course to be an accountant. But then drums got next to me again. So, I bought another set.

Who was on the local scene in Dallas when you came back from the war?

Buster Smith and Lloyd Glenn were still there. Fathead was still at home. T-Bone and Lowell had both moved to the West Coast—Charles Brown was there too. But I decided to move to Chicago. I first came to Chicago in 1949. I was still in the army and on a seventy-two-hour pass. So, I caught the train to Chicago. My sister lived in Maywood so I went out there to visit her. I had a little girl that I liked in Chicago. When I got discharged in 1952, I went home to Dallas and stayed for a couple of years. Then in 1954, I left Dallas and came to Chicago. I liked it when I came here in 1949 and I still like it today. When I came to Chicago, I stayed with my sister out there in Maywood and Sonny Boy Williamson II lived right across the street from me. He used to hear me practicing down in the basement on my drums. He heard me practicing and came over and asked my sister, "Where's that boy?" I was getting ready to go back home to Dallas. Sonny Boy said, "I think I'm gonna try him out." They had a little club out there in Argo, down in the basement. So, Sonny Boy took me out and put me on the bandstand. Sonny Boy, Johnny Shines, Lee Cooper—we all got together out there and started doing our thing.

I was plugging pretty good—at least I think I was, 'cause I'm still here. I played with Sonny Boy a pretty good little while, and that's where I got started, with Sonny Boy and Johnny Shines—and Lee Cooper, you dig? Then along came Jimmy Rogers.

How did you start in with Jimmy Rogers?

I honestly don't remember—go ask Spann! People used to think Jimmy Rogers and I were brothers because when we were young, we used to favor each other. We just took a liking to each other—me, Jimmy Rogers, Little Walter—that was it! You remember Luther Tucker? We played together a long time. There was another guy used to play along with us—Bob Anderson. Bass wasn't as popular back then as they are today but Bob would play the bass guitar, Jimmy would play the lead, Henry Gray—Little Henry—would play the piano, and me. That was it! I left Maywood and moved to Chicago. I moved in with Johnny Shines. We were on the Westside, somewhere around Washington Blvd. I played with Jimmy Rogers four or five years. After I left Jimmy, Magic Sam came along. I got tied up with Magic Sam. I stayed with Sam a while. He had Odell Campbell, Johnny Jones, Mack Thompson, and me. Then I did nine years with Muddy Waters. I did fourteen years with Wolf.

How did you get in Wolf's band?

Earl Phillips was playing with Wolf—and his legs began to give way so Wolf was looking for another drummer. Earl let me sit in with Wolf and Wolf liked the way I played.

What was it like to play with Wolf?

When you play with Mr. Burnett, it was strictly business. He'd buy you food, pay for your room—you know what I'm talking about? All he wants you to do is—do your job. You can do anything you want to, after you do your job. The man was strictly business. He didn't want you clowning around in that hotel [*laughs*].

Who was in Wolf's band at that time?

Well, let's see—he'd change around musicians. There was Hubert, and Wolf, and I. Henry Grey was there for a long time and after he left Detroit, Jr. took his place. He had the two guitars, Hubert and Sammy Lawhorn. He had Alfred Elkins on bass. He had Smokey Smothers [Otis Smothers] on guitar—just to sit in. He wasn't part of the band but Wolf liked Smokey. He was crazy about Smokey—yes, sir! And his brother, PeeWee [Abe Smothers]—that's what I used to call him—PeeWee. Man, he could play.

Did Wolf ever fire anybody? What would you have to do to get fired?

We probably don't need to talk about that—but, yeah, he'd fire guys. I know because he fired me. He fired me and then he'd hire me back. I'd beg him to hire me back—and then he would. I'd be fired a couple of weeks—sometimes a month. And he'd hire me back because he knew I didn't like that music I was playing with other guys.

After Pops [Wolf] passed away, I started playing with Blind John Davis. I played some with Jimmy Walker but Blind John Davis—that was my man! I was never happier playing music in my life than when I played with Blind John.

And I can tell you why: You know all these old tunes that you're always talking about? Well, all you gotta do is name it—and he's got it! I ain't jivin' you, Steve, he had 'em all. He was the most beautiful man I ever played with—of course, he was blind, but me and that cat went everywhere, I mean we went all across the country—and around the world! I started to bring you one of those pictures today.

Did you ever pick up any beats from the other blues drummers here in Chicago?

No, I never did. I always put my own beats to the music. Below, Earl Phillips, Mr. Payne—I respect them, but I always picked my own beats. I definitely had my own thing all the way. God rest their souls but, I had my own thing. I consider myself one of "The Big Three"—you know, Odie Payne, myself, and Below.

We haven't talked about Muddy. What can you tell me about working with him? How did you start to work in his band?

Ask James Cotton—ask Otis Spann . . .

Well, I'm gonna have a hard time asking Spann . . .

[*Laughs.*] Yeah, you're gonna have to wait until you get down there. When I joined the Muddy Waters band, I was playing with Magic Sam. When I joined Muddy Waters's band, we were playing over there on 43rd Street. James Cotton and Jr. Wells both played with Muddy—and Cotton caught me off one night and came by the house and picked me up and brought me down to Pepper's Lounge—and I sat in with Muddy. That's how I got a chance to talk with Muddy. James Cotton, Otis Spann, and the rest of the guys in the group, they all went for the way I was kickin'—because I was something like they call greased lightning in those days [*laughs*]. They got together and talked and Muddy came by my house one day. Muddy Waters was an interesting guy. When he'd get up there singing that stuff—everything he sang—he meant that. He meant that from his heart—he wasn't jivin'. And he was just like the Wolf was—he wanted you to do your job—and after you do your job you can do what you wanna do. What can you say about a man that has paid his dues? Just like me—I feel like I've paid mine. I spent a long time playing with Muddy. We stayed in Europe for eight weeks one time.

How did you and the band travel when you were in the States?

When I first joined the band traveled in two station wagons. Muddy had two station wagons. Then Muddy bought a van and we traveled in the van. And you remember Bo—the big dude?—that was Muddy's brother [Andrew "Bo" Bolton—Muddy's longtime friend, driver, road manager]. He drove the van. But we all could drive if we had to.

Would you sleep in the town where you had played—or would you load up and head for the next gig?

It would depend on how far away that next gig was. We might just load up and sleep in the van while Bo drove. In the old days, we couldn't even get a motel and we'd stay in the van. I don't think it's like that anymore but I don't know. I haven't done much traveling lately.

How about traveling with Wolf—was it the same thing?

Oh man, we did nothin' *but* travel with Wolf. After we got off a job we'd go straight to that next job—and you know what? He'd be sittin' right up there with us! You're cottonpickin' right—he'd be right with you. Them records were out there, man—you go to jail—I'll go your bail [*laughs*]. And I'll tell you what I'll do—I'll stay outside and I'll wait for you—that's the Wolf—he's gonna pay it! He'll take it out of your pay. We've been through some things together. That's my man! Wherever he is, he's still my man . . .

Odie Payne

Odie Payne and Fred Below were the two best drummers in Chicago Blues and shared much in common; it was almost a symbiotic relationship. They were born within a week of each other in 1926, in the same neighborhood, and both attended DuSable High School starting in 1940—and died within six months of each other. As much as they shared in common, their styles were separate and distinct. Among those differences was their ride cymbal work; Odie displayed classic Swing Era ride work, while Fred displayed a Bop-influenced ride. I got to see and know Fred Below quite well, but despite the fact that I saw him perform many times on the Northside, I didn't meet Odie Payne until the Drummer's Roundtable event in 1984. After we were acquainted, I followed up and asked him to come down and do a one-on-one interview in the radio studio. Odie was quite different from his fellow drummers—he didn't smoke or drink, or do drugs. As he'll tell you here, he was a loner and struggled in school. My guess was that he suffered from attention deficit disorder. It's ironic that despite living a clean life and remaining physically active almost to the end, he died a painful death from bone cancer.

■ ■ ■

I was born on 42nd Street in Chicago. I'm not going to hedge on my age like the girls. August 27, 1926. And the mother was basically a housewife, the father, he worked in the laundry, and also in the garage on the weekend. Plus, I had two brothers at the time, I was the middle one. And I lost my younger brother at an early age. Yeah, just as he graduated from grammar school, I lost my younger brother. I think he had an enlarged heart. Yeah, he died in the hospital from an enlarged heart. That's all I know about it—I don't think he was a sickly child. But just that one incident. And my older brother, I lost about fifteen years ago. And so, I was the middle one. At that time, I was staying at my grandmother's when I was young. She had an old Victrola, where you wind up with the handle. I never will forget, I had to stand up on a box because I was about five or six and just played the records over and over again. It was fascinating. I was like a loner though, most of the time, even coming up. I had two brothers, but it looks like we just had different natures, you know. My older brother, he was very nice and knowledgeable. And my younger brother was in between, but I don't remember too much about that young life because like I said, I was the type will always be tampering with something—tinkering and going on. So therefore, I was always mostly alone, because I was a junk man type—yeah. I built myself a junk wagon. And when I get out of school, the first thing I'd do is I pull out the junk wagon. At that time, it was made like a fish—the body of it was like to store fish in it. So, when you go around to the back of the stores, you see the old box, you take it out, you know, and you drag it home, and you get some wheels and you put on it, put some wooden handles on it, and you got yourself a little junk cart. You know, and I would go picking up different junk. I don't know why I did it. But that's how poor I was because I wasn't getting any allowance. Mostly kids nowadays get allowances. I didn't get an allowance so I had to make my movie fare, because it was sort of tough back in those days. At that time, you had the old coal stove and the coal wagon would go down the alley and drop off some coal. It went wobbling down the alley. I'd get me a little bucket or something, follow and pick up the coal pieces and bring them home for our stove. That's the way I would do. I did wind up getting a job on the vegetable wagon. I'd work all day on the vegetable wagon and make about a dollar and a half—good money. Then I tried carrying ice; that didn't work because that was so heavy. I even worked in the drugstore cleaning up. I think I did everything a poor boy could do to make an honest buck, because I was a hustler, more than a reader or a bookworm. I was out trying to hustle and make that nickel or fifteen cents. So, I wound up getting a job at the age of nine on a milk wagon. From the age of nine years old, to about twelve years old, I was with the same man named Bert Brennan—Bowman Dairy Company. And he was a nice Irishman. I would work about hour and a half before I go to school and then work Saturdays and Sundays all day. Saturday, Sunday, work all day. Saturday make fifty cents, that would be from six in the morning until about one o'clock. Make fifty cents. Then get off the milk wagon and head right for the show. You know, because at that time there was a movie theater called the Harmony, located right across on 43rd Street, right across South Park, right near Prairie. You could pay a nickel to get in, popcorn was three cents. At that time The Three Musketeers was very famous—three beautiful bars of candy. Nowadays it's broken down to one single candy bar but back then you had three bars—a chocolate, a pink, and white. I'm trying to tell you it was delicious! Oh, Three Musketeers. But here you could go into the show, pay a nickel to get in, three cents for popcorn, buy yourself a drink for three cents, get yourself a Three Musketeer for a nickel. And they had three features, a news reel, and a cartoon, you know, all for a quarter you could do this. And that's how I was spending most of my Saturdays when I would work on that wagon, you know. I would sit through the whole show and wait for that musical to come around and see it, you know, before I'd go home. So, I could spend all day in the show alone by myself. So, I saw quite a bit of that. And then that's why I love music so—because it was the one part in that program that was good. I would wait through the whole show just to see that one part, you know. And like Tommy Dorsey, if the band was in the picture, a drama, doing a music segment, I would sit through that whole drama just to catch the music segment. But the point is—I always worked. It looks like I would rather work than go to school. Because it just looked like I was enclosed when I go to school. It looked like I was locked in. I couldn't wait to get out and get the junk wagon and just hustle, you know.

You're making me think back but a lot was going on then. And by sitting here talking to you, you can reflect. It's a good reflection because you forget all that, because it was a long time ago. I never will forget they had the WPA band, it was going around playing, and it came to the school once. I went to Forestville Grammar School, right on 44th and Forestville—St. Lawrence. And it was interesting because I was watching the band play and for some reason that trombone player, he went down to a low note, growl, and I was just fascinated with the low tone, you know, not the drum. And I just don't know what it was but I never will forget that incident. He made a low note, "Arrrr!" a big growl like. I think it was like for novelty reasons, but I caught that, you know. We had an old radio, a big old radio. And we would sit down with our heads in the speakers. And I admired the bass for some reason. I think the radio had a ten or twelve-inch speaker, but my head would be on the floor with my head up against the radio. Those were the early stages radio, so it was fascinating, just to listen. I just loved the sound of pretty music, especially waltzes. And then a particular tune came on I think at that time was the Peanut Vendor—just the baseline. I would always try to imitate the bass with my voice. [*Sings a series of deep tones.*] You know, I'd walk along and I'd add this [*taps a rhythm*]. That's the rhythm. That's the bass. So, you go [*sings bass notes while tapping*] and sort of entertain yourself. Try it sometime [*laughs*].

So, you don't remember any specific radio programs at all?

Oh no, I remember the *Amos & Andy* program—that was funded by Pepsident. And, oh God, we're going back now—*Fibber McGee & Mollie*, *Bob Hope Show*, Eddie Cantor, and also Joe Penner—with that laugh he had [*laughs like*

Joe Penner]. I liked all the novelty stuff—*Great Gildersleeve*. Sure did. I liked him too. I think I can relate before that. Yeah, in grammar school in my last year, eighth grade, I had a habit of using my fingers to play rhythm. At that time, you know the desks where you put your books inside the desk. Well, if you take books outside the desk and beat on the desk, you get a nice round sound. [*"Boom, boom, boom."*] So, the moment the teacher would leave out the room, I started beating on the desk [*beats out a march rhythm on the interview table*] and for some reason the kids would start shuffling their feet. You know? And started saying "yeah, yeah, yeah"—and the next thing you know, with that particular rhythm going, all the kids would be up jumping around like Indians—and hollering and going on [*laughs*]—and so the teacher, she came back and opened the door real fast and everybody headed for their seats. She stood there and she said, "Alright, who was it who was making that noise"? It looked like everything pointed to me. She said, "Odie Payne—get out, go home, don't come back until you bring your mother." [*Laughs.*] I did—I brought Mother up there. But every chance I'd get, I'd beat with my fingers. Even during recess time, they had the round merry-go-round—just like this table, but you hit on it with your fist and it vibrated [*"boing-yong-yong-yong-yong"*], like that. Same thing would happen—the same beat—and the kids just started dancing around. The rhythm looked like it was just syncopated enough for them to feel a certain time, they just got up and started screaming and dancing around. And I would do that every time I got a chance—I would beat every chance I'd get. And when I graduated from there the teacher, she was a music teacher, she wrote in my book, "Someday I hope you will become a drummer." Those were her last words she wrote in my little autograph book that you sign when you get ready to graduate. And before I learned to hold drumsticks, I was using chair rounds. Chair rounds. I'd be on the back porch with a couple of chair rounds, you know, just beating on the wooden porch, just beating like crazy—I don't know what I was beating, but just beat. And then as I grew up, there were the burlesque days—where I would go to the burlesque. You were supposed to be eighteen to get into a burlesque show, but I would put on some dark glasses and pull the cap down on my eyes because I was big for my age. I'd go up there, put up money, so I could go in and sit down in the front seat right by the three-piece band which consists of a piano player, a trumpet, and a drummer. And then they had the girls doing that striptease up there, but I would watch the drummer more than I would the girls. I wanted to see what the drummer was doing. And then all the stage shows we had at the time. We had the Regal Theater on Southside going. We had the Oriental Theater going. And we had the Rialto Theater going, and we had the Chicago Theater going. And I think for two years I didn't miss going to one of those theaters. You know, to catch all orchestras going through town, two years of just solid going, you know, that was my life.

Let's jump to the point where you actually took up the instrument. Where were you?

DuSable High School. I went to Phillips first, Phillips, about one semester, two semesters, then transferred to DuSable, because I wanted to get in the band right away. But after I switched to DuSable I had to wait one semester to get into the beginner's band. And before I got into the beginner's band, we had the instructors—people who were already in band and were advanced players. I had two instructors: One was very nice—Wesley Landers—a fine drummer. And a girl by the name of Maddie—I thought she was so mean. She would be conducting the class and she would look at me and say, "O-D-I-E Payne . . ." She would do her lip a certain way, you know, she looked like she was snarling. But here again, you know, they're a couple years older than you—and advanced. And I was young, I didn't understand, you know, and you'd be a little—a little smart. But they had the advantage on you because they could read—and you were learning. But I had the rhythm, so here again, I had the rhythm but I didn't have the concentration. You could do something and I could copy what you do. But to read it, I would have to stumble along because I just couldn't concentrate. And that same person almost the same way you would have almost a better rhythm—a feel for rhythm than they would—though technically they could read. Technically, they can read—but you just had an inner feeling of expression. You can't really tell why you had it at that age. All you knew—you felt it and you could do it. An example: After I got into the regular band under Captain Walter Dyett, I tell people now, he put me out of band twice. [*Laughs.*] I'll tell you what he would do. All the drummers had drum pads, you know, a little wooden drum pads, and we'd be lined up on a long table, and he'd be sitting there—there were about eight or ten of us, you know, we would have our books in front of us, and so he would take us one at a time. "Okay, play the exercise, bla bla bla bla bla bla bla bla . . ." By the time he got to me, you know, everybody had played the exercise. I heard it really good. So, I would tap out the pattern, you know, not know what I was doing—I couldn't read it. But I could hear it. And so, what Captain Dyett would do, he'd say, "Stop—Okay, hold it. Stop right there. Where are you?" I would say, "Uh-uh-uh-uh-uh . . ." He'd say, "Get out! [*Laughs.*] Get outta here!" But then after class I'd ask him why he put me out. He said, "Because you were faking!" Well, at that time, the word fake, I didn't know what it meant. He said, "Because you were faking . . ." I said, "What do you mean?" He says, "You know you're not reading—you're faking?" I said, "What do you mean faking? I was doing just like the other kids." "Yeah, but—you were copying what you heard, but you weren't actually reading it by sight. Get out of here." I begged my way back in the band. [*Laughs.*] Anyway, one day the band was playing a beautiful piece—I never will forget it—"The Caliph of Baghdad." A beautiful piece of music. The band was going "Chum-chum—chum-chum." Okay. There was a great big old fat twenty-bar tacet sitting there said that there were no drums supposed to play at all. But some reason I was on bass drum, boy, and I came charging through there, you know, sneaking it in. "Odie Payne!" "Yes sir . . ." "What are you doing playing?" I said, "Well, well, well, well . . ." "Get out!" And at the end of the class, I begged my way back in the band. I asked, "Why'd you put me out?" "Because you were back there faking." "What do you mean fake?" And he says, "Well, you weren't supposed to be playing." I said, "But it fit." He says, "I know it fit, but you weren't supposed to be playing"—and it did fit, I made it fit. It blended right in with the music, but that wasn't the point. I wasn't supposed to be playing—that's what he was trying to get through my thick skull. But as a child, I think all children go through this—the teacher knows but as a child you think *you* know, but really, you're taking liberties as a child, which you shouldn't be doing—but you don't know this, you'd be doing this as a feeling—until you get kicked out and cursed out a few times. Then you start realizing what's going on. And that happened to us because Mr. Dyett, he was one of the best teachers, but he would curse the whole band. I heard him make girls cry sometimes because he said, "Get out. Don't you come back until you bring your mama or papa or something." He was hard. Oh, he could shake up the class. I thought he was mean. I thought he was mean. But the man was business but I couldn't see that—you can't see that as a child. But he had the best musicians. Wilbur Campbell came out of the same class. Johnny Griffin came out of the same place. Jug—Gene Ammons. Jug was ahead of me. He was about a couple of years ahead of me. He was graduating when I was coming into the band. Johnny Griffin, we went at the same time. I never will forget because he was small but he was such a good-looking little kid. You know all the girls loved him. Johnny Griffin. He was small, he was cute—and he was smart and he was good. Claude McLin was in that class. Quite a few good ones were in that band. I never did make the booster band which was the dance band. But I was in the marching band. I never did make booster band—I felt like I could but I never got a chance to swing. I was drafted in my last year of high school. Because I fell a grade behind.

I did fall a grade behind because I remember going to evening school. I wasn't the best student. I tell people now if I was a reader I could concentrate—but I couldn't concentrate because I was so busy hustling. I think that took a lot of my concentration away because right now if I read a book, I can read as fast as anybody but I can't maintain. I can't hold even in school, my book reports were bad because I'd read the first page, turn to the middle, then turn to the last page, and then try to write a book report. It would come back an F minus. I'd look at the teacher and want to know why she gave me a mark like that for. She'd say, "Because you didn't read the book. It goes to show you—how did she know you didn't read the book—but she was the teacher. But it's true, you read about six pages, and you're gonna write a book report? But that was my concentration—I didn't read, I didn't like to read. I did not like to read. Here again, I think your teacher has a lot to do with holding your attention to make you really appreciate school. Because I went to electric shop, I went to auto shop. And in those two shops, because like I said, I love to tinker. But I don't think that the teachers gave the attention to the kid that they should. Because I'd be on the project. I know I was trying to get a car started. But the teacher would always be out in the hallway smoking. I never will forget that. And just as I'd get close to get the thing going, for some reason it looked like there was something was missing. I don't know what it was. But I think it was the teacher. Because you get so close to it. And you will never get to do it. Because the class would come to the end and the both of the teachers, I never will forget, the electric teacher and the auto teacher. Yeah. They'd be out in the hall smoking. I can see this as grown up because they would write something real fast on the board, and say, "Copy this." While you're copying it, they're out in the hall smoking, you understand? Well, this went on for about one semester. And I got out because I wasn't learning anything. I wanted to—but it was just something I wasn't getting. I did get a high school diploma, but it was while I was in the service, I had enough points to get it. Actually, what was going on, peacetime came while I was in. About four or five months after I got in peace was declared. I did camp in Fort Leavenworth, Missouri. Basic Training. Yeah. Then went from there to California, from California to Seattle, Washington. And I tell people that basic training is good for you. But I was an ROTC in high school when I was drafted. So, I knew the basic foundation for marching—this, that, and the other wasn't any problem. The problem was you're young and you're away from home for the first time. The first night you can hear a lot of sniffling in the barracks when you're away from home at 18 and 19 for the first time in your life. You've never been away from home before—it affects you, because you didn't want to be away but by law you had to be away. You didn't go to camp on your own and it was a funny feeling. Because the first night you're away, you don't sleep. You lay down and toss and turn, you know, here in the barracks with a lot of boys, all of you away from home, you know, everybody half asleep because they've never been away from home, funny feeling. But it's good training. I went from ROTC right in, so but I didn't care about it. I wasn't the shooting type—I hated guns. But coming up in the neighborhood, we played cowboys and Indians and I kept the whole neighborhood supplied. I gave guns to all the boys, I had about ten guns. You could buy a cap gun for a dime, and I would work on the milk wagon. I was only one working around there so I could buy the pistols. I'd supply guns to all the guys, but I hated guns. And then I finish my time—one year then I reenlisted. I kept reenlisting and I think I reenlisted for the Army Reserves. I stayed in the reserves for fifteen years. Then the National Guard Reserve, so I had a total of twenty years of reserve time—twenty years and nine months of reserve time—because I was in the 354th Army Band, the reserve band, and I was in the National Guard band. That's why I've taken up tuba bass horn in the Army Reserve band because we had drummers but we didn't have a tuba player. So, Mister—I've just forgot his name—he was fine trombone player too. He made me get on the tuba. "Learn that tuba Odie, we need a tuba player. We got a drummer . . ."

Was that a segregated band at that time?

Your point is good. I think it was just very few white ones in the band because we rehearsed at Navy Pier. But first we were on Bryn Mawr, then somewhere out south on Jeffrey somewhere—and then we went to Navy Pier. And then it dissolved, the band eventually dissolved after about twelve or fourteen years it dissolved. I think you would go to rehearsal once every two weeks and you go to camp two weeks out of the year. So, I appreciated it. And even today, with my condition, I still manage to go to a rehearsal once a week, so I can keep my lip in shape on the tuba. We rehearse every Sunday with a gentleman by the name of Mr. Thompson, a fellow that's up in his upper eighties. There's about ten or twelve of us over-the-hill cats, for a couple of hours, you know, we rehearse, be together. So, it's nice just like a person would go down to the pool hall and shoot pool with the boys for relaxation. I call that my relaxation—to go to rehearsal on a Sunday because it's about a mile or so away but it's only about hour and a half—just to keep the old lip up.

So, when I got out of service in 1949, for some reason. While I was in high school, a record came out at the Metropolitan record store located right by the Metropolitan Theatre on South Park. And they had this speaker out there playing this tune, "Let Me Play With Your Poodle." I would listen and I would stand there and just laugh and laugh and laugh because of the words you know. And just laugh and laugh. Now this was Tampa Red. And I was a late teenager—I never knew anything about the man. But I tell people, it's funny—about three years later I wound up working with the man. My first tavern engagement. I wound up working with Tampa Red. When he did that tune on the bandstand, I looked at him and laughed [*laughs*]. He would call us Little Odie and Little Johnny [Johnny Jones] because he was old enough to be our father. So that was about the beginning of it. In fact, I think I met Johnny Jones first—and then we joined Tampa over on Lake Street, I think that was the beginning of it.

Was that a working band with Tampa?

Yeah, we would do Friday and Saturday. Mostly Friday and Saturday, right on Lake Street—Lake and Francisco. During the time we were with him Tampa never played many places, looked like you could count them, because we stayed there for a while, you know, like a month at a time. A few blocks down was a place called Play Time, that's where Memphis Slim was playing. And also, about three or four blocks from us was where Sunnyland Slim was playing. He was also on the piano. So, within that one-mile area, you had those three bands going.

Was Ransom Knowling in the band at the time?

On the records. That's where I met Ransom Knowling. When Tampa recorded, that's when they called him in. We rehearsed at Tampa's house on 31st Street and State. We would rehearse there before going to the studio date. Ransom would come to the rehearsal. Ransom was already with a group called the Three Brown Buddies, who I never met—but they must have been playing in outlying suburb area, but he was the bass man on Tampa Red's records.

Would Lester Melrose be at the rehearsals?

Yes, he would.

Would he would have a lot of input?

I would say yes and no because I think Tampa's wife would write most of his tunes. Tampa was always a laid-back type of a man. He wasn't frisky, he was just laid back and very cool. When he walked, he'd take his time—when he talked, he took his time. That's the type of man he was. He didn't have a lot of flair, a lot of flurry. He had a parrot in the house. There was a parrot, a dog and a pigeon. It was interesting in his house. But Tampa, he was just a cool laid-back guy, you know, I'd just look at him—very laid back and cool. And he rode a bicycle. I think it was after he lost his wife, obviously that's what it was.

It seems like most people say that. Tampa really went way downhill after his wife died. Do you remember her? Do you remember her dying? And do you remember going to the funeral?

I believe I went to the funeral because they had it at Cobbs Church. Yeah, Reverend Cobbs, I think that was where she was. Like I say, to me, he was a type of man looks like you would wait on him. He would wait and everything was brought to him. He wasn't the go-getter type, because I would pick him up and drop them off in the car. When we go to the gig, I would pick him up. Drop him off. I never knew him to drive. Pick up Johnny Jones, too. Johnny was in the backseat. It was dark back there. I had a car, a 1937 Chrysler—a seven-passenger car, my first car. And they're back there smoking. And that smoke was about to kill me. I didn't know what it was until he told me. I had to laugh, you know. [*Real high voice:*] "Don't do that back there . . ." The smoke was coming up there and was about to choke me. He had a thing—a weed or something, in a pot, or whatever it was. It was popular then. And he laughed about it—and I did too. "Man, don't be doing that in the car . . ." That was fun . . .

People would come around like Big Maceo. He came around, I never will forget because he did a tune I tried to do a called "Going Down Slow." At that time, he was sort of paralyzed in his left hand. And he was supposed to have taught Johnny Jones how to use that left hand. That's why Johnny can imitate him. He would stand up and he was a big fellow. I'd just look at him because I was in my twenties. And he would do that tune "I'm Going Down Slow." I never will forget. It's interesting. At that time, you're singing a tune and it didn't really occur to me what he was talking about. The sad thing here is even today, that's why some youngsters I guess feel that they don't like blues, because they're too young—they haven't lived yet. I think you have to live this in order to appreciate the value of it, because it tells a story. And the story he was telling, which is true. I'm at the age and condition now where I know what the man was talking about. "Going Down Slow." It has to do, I guess with the doing of things you shouldn't do, and then, eventually it catches up with you physically and causes bodily harm to you, bothers you in some cases, you know? And this makes you think and reflect—if I hadn't done this—if I hadn't done that I wouldn't be in this position. So, it's a feeling. But it's hard to explain the feeling. I think you have to live it. You have to live it. That's been a lot of the tunes that they do nowadays, they shout them but there's just no background to it.

When Specialty recorded Big Maceo, were you on that session?

Yeah. When Maceo did his thing, I was on that. Maceo would sing and Johnny was on piano.

How did you make the cowbell part of your identity?

I've always had a cowbell—always had a cowbell. See, the trick about the cowbell is you can be playing and you hit that bell one time and get a response from somebody in the audience. That's a quality bell now, you know some of them are duds [*laughs*]. Some don't ring with a resonant sound. All right then. But always I try to hit the bell when I'm on a session—so if I ever hear it, I know. A lot of us sound alike, see? But when I hear my bell, I can tell the difference—it's me. Well, it was an accident. I think I got a gig because of the cowbell one time. So, this gentleman sitting at the bar and on a break, he says you know I like the way you use that cowbell. He said, "Look, would you like to take a gig in Michigan for one night?" So, I did it. It was an outlying suburban area in Michigan somewhere just for one night, but it was nice, but the cowbell got me the gig, because he told me he says I like the way you use that cowbell.

Did you continue to play and record with Tampa after the death of his wife?

Well, I would say yes. I don't know what happened, but it seemed like things just fell apart afterward. Because something did happen there. I think the interest got lost with Tampa Red—and I went with Johnny Jones. We stayed together and he would hustle the gigs. That's right. And then we joined up with L.C. McKinley. It was just the three of us, you know, we could do well together. We were on Roosevelt Road and then we went to the Zanzibar. We were at Sacramento with Johnny Jones and L.C. McKinley. At that time, I was free and you could play with different people but mainly with Johnny Jones—but I played with Cool Breeze, too. He was located at the same spot—maybe on a different night. He was a bass player. He was very good and told a lot of jokes. He could figure his way through very well. We had a piano player named Johnny Williams. Very good piano player. He was with that group with Cool Breeze, and another fellow on saxophone, I can't recall his name, he plays drums now, but he played the nice saxophone too. So, it was the four of us. Between that, and Johnny Jones—I worked steady with Johnny the most. Definitely went to the Zanzibar with Johnny Jones and Big Bill Nelson, we stayed there the most.

I have yet to run into anybody who has anything nice to say about L.C. McKinley. Are you going to add your name to that list?

Who was the guy smoking a cigarette who said, "If you can't say something nice—don't say nothing at all"? Well, I know one thing—he was a sharp dresser. I think he was a presser but he was clean cut. He was a sharp dresser. T-Bone, that's who he imitated. That was his man. L.C. had a temper. He had a temper. Interesting, quite a temper. You could set him off in a minute. I experienced it. I sure did experience it. It was a scary situation. Johnny Jones had a brother who would always be around there—I think his name was Homer. Very nice fella. I don't mean to be technical, but L.C. would jump a lot of time—a lot of people don't know what that means. He would jump his meter and I would tell him he jumped his meter. He'd say, "What do you mean?" I said, "You jumped your meter but Johnny and I jumped with you to make you sound right. But you did jump." Then he said, "You know, you're the first one whoever told me I did that?" [*Laughs.*] He pulled out a knife. "If you tell me that again, I'll cut your motherfuckin' throat!" Well, Johnny Jones's brother was sitting out there and he jumped up on the stage. He said, "Now L.C., you know, you're wrong—you know you're wrong." So, he backed down and he apologized later. L.C. McKinley, he dressed clean all the time. He was a clean man. Clean man, I mean, a starched collar, that's what makes me remember him so much because he was clean. Very clean, sharp. Clean.

There were a few inbetweeners that I played with, like Buster Brown. Buster Brown is a harmonica player and a singer who didn't record you know. And then there was Little Henry Gray. And a fella that plays good time—I can't think of him but he was a tall boy, nice looking, and he sang his song, it was "Come Get It"—or something like that. I can't recall his name. But he passed but he, Henry Gray, and I played together for a little while.

How did the connection with Elmore James happen?

Well, we joined Elmo at the same time, Johnny Jones and I. We went to join Elmo. Elmo came from down in Mississippi, and he was looking for a group. He was hot then because he had just made "Dust My Broom" and came to the city. And then Johnny Jones and I joined him and played two and a half years. Here's a man who played with lots of feeling. And that's when we met Howlin' Wolf. We were doing a dance together—the Howlin' Wolf band and Elmore James's band—and I didn't know nothin' about no Howlin' Wolf, you know? But on a break, he came up to me and he spoke to me. He said, "How would you like to come work with me?" I said, "Well aren't you and Elmo good friends?" He says, "Yeah, we're good friends, but it's dog eat dog" [*laughs*]. "Oh—I couldn't do that." "Well, you decide you wanna work with me, you got a job." At that time, I was younger but I didn't think people did that, you know? Hey, good friend but he'd go behind your back and cut your throat at the same time. That's the way it seemed to me . . .

What was the band with Elmore? It was you, Johnny, Elmore, and who else?

That was when I met the harmonica player Mr. Rice Miller, Sonny Boy II—he joined the band too. I didn't know anything about him until he started working with us. Off and on. He was good. And then we had a saxophone player by the name of Boyd—I think his name was Boyd Atkins—very fine tenor man, who worked with Elmo a while. He didn't use a bass man when we worked in the tavern, but when he recorded, he used a bass man. Yeah.

But what about J.T.? Wasn't he part of the group?

J.T.? Ah, yes, yes, yes. He soon joined the outfit, too. That's right. J.T. Brown. Because he made a record. I was on it. He worked with Elmo quite a while, too. He was another clean, sharp man. Good-looking man, you know.

So, what was Elmore like as a person—as a bandleader? What was he like to deal with?

You have to be careful. You could set him off. People requested "Dust My Broom" most of the time. And after you do about two or three times, and somebody calls, "Do it again. I'll pay you!" Then "I'm sorry, Dear . . ." He would say, "Look . . ." it would be very insulting, I could almost hide under the bandstand the way he would insult people. "I don't want your money; I got enough money to burn!" But maybe when the man was talking so bad, it could have been because he drank some too. What he did, he did well. Ladies loved it; you know—but he had a temper. Like I say, he would let some words loose there, through the microphone, boy! I would just bang my head. Because he said it—he didn't bite his tongue. But to me it was sort of unbelievable. You wouldn't think that a man would do this, but just keep living—you find out a lot of things with different bandleaders.

I stayed with him two and a half years, and I only went out of town with him once to Indiana somewhere. But a lot of times we would play just a guitar and a drum, we would play out south, in the heights, where they have one big room there. You pay a quarter to get in. That was really nice—just a drum and guitar, the best experience you can get for a drummer. Of course, this dates back, that type of experience, when I played on Madison Street with a piano player. We stayed about three or four months—just drums and piano on the weekend. The best experience in the world for a drummer, because this fellow he was older, but he knew all the tunes and all the rhythms. And so, as a drummer, coming up, you get a chance to hear melody, rhythm, and you get a chance to apply yourself. It's a shame I can't recall the man's name. Because I didn't have a car, I would ride the streetcar. At that time, we had the red streetcar and I'll never forget, I had my drum case in one hand and my bass drum in the other and you get up on the streetcar, the streetcar fare was a dime. [*Laughs.*] And being young, I didn't mind it one bit. It was a pleasure. But that was such a good experience.

Then I had my share of Calumet City, too. I went out there a few times. You had drums, trumpet, piano player and a saxophone. But you play continually because you're playing behind striptease dancers. I never will forget that this girl had her bust insured for $250,000. That was a drawing card out there in Calumet City. "Come and see so and so and so and so—insured for $250,000 . . ." So, this was the place where we were playing. The band had to play behind a curtain. And when the announcer would announce the band, the band leader would stick his head out from behind the curtain—oh brother!

I stayed out there about three or four times that was enough of that. I didn't care about that because you're playing all the time but you weren't seen. But I could see the girls—because as the drummer, you have to see the girls so you can give them the bumps and grinds. The job was good experience, but I didn't stay out there too long—I got out of that. I was playing on Clark Street, I had a group—I'm going back a long way—and on Clark Street I had a fine bass man a fine tenor, man—you should know the gentleman because he had a name. But they both were strung out and I didn't know it. This is when I started learning about that word "drugs." And I was shocked because I was green, you know? Get through with a gig. Okay. "Would you take me to so and so and so and so?" "Sure." "Hurry up now." Huh? I thought the man had to go to the washroom. But no. We get to this certain address and he would run in you know? And he'd come back down and say, "Ah—everything's alright now." Then somebody would tell me "Did you know that he uses so and so?" No! I would get scared you know, 'cause the man got so that he wanted to tear the car up. Sometimes they'd go into rage because they couldn't get right. Lane Keys, a tenor man. He was a saxophone player. And the bass player was a dark-skinned fellow, but he played a good bass. But both these two were involved with drugs. And I didn't know it. Lane Keys would get on a tune and play almost twelve minutes—just one number. Then he'd just stand there and sweat. I didn't know what was going on. But hey, I was working with two cats in the group, and they were on the stuff. And I didn't know it. And it scared me because what could happen if the police had come in on something like that, you know? So that was a heck of an experience.

When did you and Elmore break up?

Let's see. After two years and a half with Elmo, I quit because he had a temper. We got into it a couple of times. Not really bad, but you know. And he was poor with people—very, very unmusician-like. You sit there and people being there to see you as entertainers. The man might insult the whole crowd. I would get too embarrassed—and I was always a black sheep in the band. I was a loner. You know, I didn't associate. After we take a break, I'd just go into a corner with my book or wherever it is that was, because I just didn't mix with the guys because they were smoking and drinking—and I wasn't. So, on a break. I'd just go somewhere, wait the time and come back, because that was it. See? I did that when I was with Little Walter. He told me "Odie, that music's gonna drive you crazy. But I can't say nothin'—because you're doing your job." At that time, Tucker, Robert Jr., Little Walter and myself, you know? Well, I was the black sheep, I just didn't do the things that they were getting involved with. That's all; I come alone; I leave alone. When it came to what I could do—who I could do, when it came to chasing-what does that mean? I didn't want to chase, or be involved in the drinking and smoking and stuff like that. Oh, well. I always consider myself a square. The conversations that musicians have among one another, can be very disturbing. You don't want to hear this type of stuff—musicians get together sometime and boast about how many women they have had. I didn't appreciate it the way they would talk about the opposite sex. I didn't want to hear it. So, therefore, I didn't mix with it. Because you come from a mother, you're married and so you don't want to hear all this type of garbage. Most of the time they weren't married. No. And so they had a lot of things to say when they talked about—and I didn't. So, I didn't want to hear that lifeline because I didn't have those type of experiences. So why should sit down and talk about something that you don't know nothing about because you haven't been involved in doing that. So rather than that, you just go get out the way somewhere. You know, go around the corner, get yourself a milkshake or something like that—just not to be around until it's time to go back because most of the talk was just garbage—off the wall talk. And you can talk sensible—a lot of loud cussing and swearing, and you didn't want to hear that. I didn't want to. So that's what will put me in that type of segment of being a loner or a square. If you did something—you keep it to yourself. I would, but a lot of guys would like to express this as making them seem big. And outstanding.

You probably weren't under the gun as much in Tampa's band because he was sort of a quiet family man himself, wasn't he?

Yes, he was very quiet. I would pick him up and drop him off. I hated it when a bandleader would get drunk on me because that would be so embarrassing. That's the part I didn't like. That's the part I didn't appreciate. I'd lose respect for that type of person because you got people who look up to leaders and you got youngsters who want to copy or be like so and so. People come up and figure they had to do this, or do that to be like you. Just to give an example; If a guy drank—J.T. Brown, that played saxophone, he drank, he smoked—and he sounded good. Well, to a youngster who would be watching and wanted to copy himself after this individual, figured he had to do the same thing to get the same feeling to do what J.T. did. Okay. Now, in my case, when a person wanted to give me a drink, they'd say, "What do you want?" I'd say, "Orange juice." "Orange juice?" They looked at me twice and a lot of times they would refuse to buy it, they would rather buy me something stronger. I'd say, "No—that's alright." Because the wonderment was, how could you do this and don't drink. And I'd explain it to them. I said, "In learning to do this I didn't have nothing to drink, it's a feeling—and I don't need anything to make me express my feeling—it's already there." A lot of times you drink or smoke, it can be a cushion, it's like a crutch you know? I'll give you an example; We worked at Zanzibar. Gin was Johnny Jones favorite drink and he'd do the first couple of numbers and say, "Wait a moment Odie—I got to get me a drink." Well, it was interesting. He showed me his hands and he said, "Look at my hands now." I'm looking. He said, "Now I'm ready." Well, his hands would be steady as a rock I guess before his hands would be shaking. But he was telling me something—and I was learning because I didn't understand. Because I think he was a couple of years older than me. But he said, "I got to get a drink." But I didn't understand why. I was just coming up in the ranks, you know? But that goes for a lot of them out there. I went on the road with Sunnyland Slim—my first trip on the road out of town. We played at a college—it was just three of us. But the band that we followed was a big band and then here came our three pieces. Okay, well you know Sunnyland is good for his strong voice, the way he shouts the blues, but he felt funny because he was just playing in front of college kids—and this is all we could do, play the blues. That's what he got hired to do. But after every set he would go into the back room and pull out that fifth and say, "Man, if I knew I was gonna come into this, I wouldn't have come. The lady shouldn't have sent me to anything like this." This was a suburban town; college kids and we were playing the blues but that's what he got hired to do. But I think what was getting him the most is because that's all we could do—the blues and it would get to him. He would hit that bottle, that was his crutch. It put you in another world, away from reality so you could perform. I understood that because I worked with people and they'd get halfway tanked on me. I started seeing the light but you have to be in it a while to find out. It was the same thing with Little Walter. We went down to Texas. We were in a nice big place where Walter was hot then. That was when he made Juke—I wasn't with him but then again, he was famous for making the harmonica really a standout at that time. He was a drawing card, you know? So, we would go up. At that time, we had Jimmy Lee Robinson was backup guitar player. The band was Jimmy Lee, [Luther]

Tucker, myself, and Little Walter. So, time to come on, Walter said, "Y'all go up, play about four numbers and then call me up. We went up an did about four numbers and then did some more and people in the audience were getting a little itchy. Well we found Little Walter about half an hour later but the man was tanked up. We had to leave the gig—but this was an example of how the stuff had taken over. I don't know whether it was nervousness or if the man got involved in drinking but we were doing all we can to perform but we weren't Little Walter. People wanted Little Walter—they wanted that harp. I stayed with him eleven months after we got back. We were playing at the Zanzibar. I never will forget. We were supposed to start at one o'clock and Walter hadn't shown up. The man said, "Where's Little Walter?" "Well, he told us to go ahead and start—he'll be here." Come an hour later, I got nervous. I got tired of this because they would always ask me, "Where's Little Walter?" I come alone—I go alone. I got tired. I quit—because this happened in a lot of cases. "Where's Little Walter?" Little Walter always said, "Y'all hit at nine o'clock." Well, you hit at nine o'clock, he won't be there. He might come in at nine thirty—or in time for the next set. This went on all the time. I would think that the guy just wanted to feel important. But here, your name is in lights. You're getting paid the big money—and I'm just a side dog. That went on for quite a while. So, I quit after eleven months.

It seemed like for all the artists that you worked with on record that you were basically the house drummer for the Cobra label. Did you work with the artists, say Buddy Guy, Magic Sam, or Otis Rush, outside of the studio before you went in with them? How did that happen? Otis Rush—did you work gigs with him?

Sure. I worked with him for almost a year on the west side, on Twelfth Street. I don't know how that happened—how we got together—how we meshed? You usually leave one group and somebody hears you playing out there, and they call you. I think it was really through Willie Dixon I got the meeting. We had a job in Oklahoma, once where I think Otis Rush was the star. He was hot then and we went there for a couple of days. I that's how I met Otis Rush. And then we worked on Twelfth Street for quite a while—almost a year.

Did you play with him before you recorded with him?

Yes, because he asked me if I knew how to play one particular tune. There's one particular tune that Dixon wrote that Otis did so well. I think it was "All My Love." It had sort of a haunting beat. Very haunting. He did it so well. Yeah. So, I stayed with him but I finally had to leave. The way he would pay people off, you know, he'd call you in a room one at a time. And you'd find out one guy is getting two dollars more than the other guy—and all that kind of stuff. At that time your basic scale pay was twelve dollars. They might give ten dollars to another guy, and someone else might wind up getting fifteen. We're going back a long way though. He was clean cut, a very good dresser, a good player but I finally had to leave.

Who was in that band?

Well, one time he had Earl Hooker in that band. Yeah, he had that double guitar that had the bass built in. He'd play the bass and then sometimes sneaking in a couple of licks on guitar while Otis was playing. Otis would turn around and look at him, you know, and Earl would be looking up in the air because he was a heck of a good guitar player but, he was basically uncontrollable. But, God, the man was good.

Who else played bass in that band?

Well, let's see. Lady Margot [Gibson], a lady bass player. She played with him quite a while—very nice. I think she had played with the Sweethearts of Rhythm at one time. She had a weak spot we found out. We were playing at the 708 Club one night. We were in the middle of a tune and she turned around and looked at me—and shot some words at me [*laughs*]. "Thank you, motherfucker." Once she got tanked up, she'd start talking about you. I had to take her home one time because she got so high. But she was good. She was a good performer. But that was the weakness, once she'd get high, she'd talk about you—and that's what she did. I haven't seen her in years. But it was funny. She could play that bass with Otis Rush.

Where were the Cobra sessions held?

I don't know. Wait, that was with Eli. Yeah, that was west on Twelfth Street somewhere. Yeah. Good old Eli. He was a cab driver—and a gambler. Interesting . . .

Dixon was actually the A&R man for Eli, wasn't he?

Well, the way Dixon would write, I think he was good for most of the musicians, because he was writing for most of them, I believe. That's why he knew them all and he was on most of the sessions because he was writing the material. I will put it that way. He was involved somehow, because we worked together out in Argo—Little Brother Montgomery, Dixon, and myself—and a guitar player—or a horn player. One thing, Dixon always let me drive. He said, I never will forget, "I feel so confident when you drive." We'd just be going to Argo, so I would go to his house, and we would take his station wagon going out there. At that time, they had the show out there with Little Brother Montgomery. He was very artistic on his piano, you know, but again, don't let him get high. Of course, I have to credit Dixon with quite a few of the sessions because Dixon was really a Chess man. And so, he got me on quite a few things. One of them was with Chuck Berry. I didn't know anything about Chuck Berry. I'm setting up my drums one day and Chuck walks in, draped with two ladies on each arm. He looked at me—I looked at him. And that was it. [*Laughs.*] Because I didn't know who he was. He didn't say hello. We got started and that was it. I remember people asking me about that relationship. I tell them, "I know you better than I did him." All I know, I was setting up the drums. He walked into the studio—that was it. And when the section started, he told me what to do and that was it. Hello, shake hands? No.

You're on one of my favorite Chuck Berry's—"Nadine."

I like "School Days" myself. That's the one I remember. He made a session after that because at that time, there was some trouble. And they had myself and another drummer come in. They were going to record a double session with him. He was on his way up the river.

You played behind the Buddy Guy on Artistic?

Yeah, Buddy Guy. I think I was on his first. That's when I met him on the first record. And we're going back a long way . . .

"This Is the End" and "Broken-Hearted Blues."

I don't know the name. But I know I was on a session with that young man—probably his first session. Yeah.

How about Harold Burrage?

Yes. Yeah, I recorded with him for Cobra. Yeah.

Was that just work in the studio—or on the bandstand as well?

No—we were on the bandstand as well. We played and we would play practically every weekend in Gary, Indiana, and we had Harold Burrage on that show. Harold Burrage—he worked very hard. His main tune was "Hi-Yo Silver." That's one he would really work on. That was one of his strong numbers, "Hi-Yo Silver."

Magic Sam, how did that happen?

I think Dixon might have something to do with that because I think Dixon is the one that named him. I think Dixon is the one that gave him that name. Magic Sam.

You actually played with him on the bandstand?

Yeah. For a little while. Sam, Shaky Jake, and myself. And on bass was one of the Johnson brothers [Mac Thompson], play nice bass.

Mac Thompson?

Yeah, Mac Johnson at the time. It was a very, very nice group. I like the way Magic Sam played. He had a good sense of rhythm. You know. He was a nice-looking boy too. And Shaky Jake, he was a smart cat you know, he's very smart. And that's about it for that group. I don't know how we dissolved—I really don't know how we dissolved. It was interesting. When I left the boy, I happened to be looking up and then I saw that he had passed. But I'm going back a few years.

After Magic Sam, what happened? Where did you go? Who did you play with?

Well, now you can throw Louis, Louis Myers and the Aces in there. I stayed with them for almost five years. Musically, you couldn't beat them on playing the blues, you couldn't beat them. Tight.

Who is your favorite bass man to work with?

Well, Ransom was steadying as a rock at the time—because he could read you know, he's a reader. And now, here again, when it comes to the bass playing, as far as steadiness, you got to throw Dave Myers in there. Or you got to fill margin now. You got to throw him in there because he's as steady as a rock, you know. And now you talk about the electric bass. Now, you got your standard base and Willie [Dixon] is one of the leading ones but he was a Bluesman. Then novelty wise, he could slap that base.

Did you ever run across Judge Riley?

Judge Riley? [Judge started as a drummer and later switched to bass.] Yeah, I think I met him one or two times. That's true, with Blind John Davis. I played with Blind John quite a while. We were at The Lemon Twist when I met him. Because I used to pick him up—really nice.

Did he drive?

No, no. I'd drive with him. I enjoyed working with him. We played down Tony's Cellar for a while. Blind John—I liked his touch on a piano.

I've got a list here of people that I think you recorded with and maybe you can even tell me if there's any others here. Tampa, we know about Elmore, Chuck Berry, Otis Rush, Buddy Guy, Magic Sam. I see you have a session with Jimmy Rogers. Do you remember that?

Yeah, I guess so. Yeah. It's very, very vague. They don't stand out too much.

Well, no big hits came from it.

Well, probably, but don't take my word for it.

Okay, how about Memphis Slim? Did you record with him?

Yes, but Memphis Slim, then you've got to go way back. Yeah. Way back.

But you recorded a Chess session with him I think during the '50s.

I could have.

Who are some of the others you've recorded with that I haven't mentioned?

Gina Gibson made a session at the studio over there on Wabash. And then I was on Eddie Chamblee on "Lonesome Road." And then I worked with the cat that made "See You Later, Alligator," Bobby Charles! I wasn't on that record, but we did a later session for Chess. Then, you've got Arbee Stidham's "Mr. Commissioner." I was also on one set with Muddy Waters—"Don't Go No Further." Yeah, well, I worked with him when his drummer got sick. Now, that's as close as I worked with Muddy. His drummer got sick. I worked one weekend. It was Elgie Edmonds. Yeah, because he was a nice little drummer—a nice fella. Nice fella.

Willie "Big Eyes" Smith

Willie "Big Eyes" Smith was a good drummer and a great guy. He was best known for his work as the drummer in Muddy Waters's band. It was one of the few bands, along with Frank Frost, who played "old-time" time—which meant playing way back in the pocket as the veteran Blues players all used to. When Muddy's band left Muddy *en mass*, they stuck together and became The Legendary Blues Band with Guitar Junior playing lead guitar. When that band reached the end of the trail, Willie became a frontman and a bandleader on his own. He won a reputation as the blues equivalent of Art Blakey—a bandleader and mentor to a generation of up-and-coming blues players. He gave them jobs in his band and took them out on the road. As he got older, he switched back to his original instrument—the harmonica. In his new role as bandleader, he was in and around Chicago and I got to know him. I invited him to come down to the station and tell his story.

■ ■ ■

I was born January 19, 1936, Helena, Arkansas. Well, I suppose I was always involved in music. They tell me even when I was really small, even before I could remember, that I used to be walking around beating on tin cans and trying to sing. We had gramophones at that time, you wind up you know. And when they put that thing on, I would just feel good. You know, I'd like a lot of the tunes that my grandmother had and I wanted to play them. So, I would get me a top and pretend I was a Seeburg [popular brand of jukebox]. I'd put a straw in my mouth and put a record on top of it and spin it around and listen to it. [*Laughs.*] I stayed with both of my grandmothers really, on my daddy's side and my mother's side, but my grandmother on my mother's side, she was all the way religious, you know. So, I wouldn't dare to sing those "reels" as she called them, around her, but when I would come to live with my other grandmother, she had the gramophone, and the music, and that's what I would like—I liked to listen to it. In her day, it was Victoria Spivey, Bessie Smith, Blind Lemon Jefferson, and Blind Boy Fuller—just all the way back, Leroy Carr, and Roosevelt Sykes.

Did anybody in your family play any kind of instruments?

Well, I had a cousin that could play a little guitar, but he never did try to play professionally. Nobody, as far as I know, in my family ever, ever played professionally besides myself, but I guess it was always there. But nobody ever used it. Besides, we were farming at the time. They didn't have time . . .

How about any live musicians you might have seen in the area? Anybody of note that we would know today?

Well, during that time—no, because they didn't ever really come to that area. They'd get up to Memphis and West Memphis and Little Rock, you know, all around. I was just in what you call a little one-horse town. It was just a small town. So, there was nothing there but a lot of country people—and they'd only go out on a Saturday night and have a ball. And musicians didn't ever come down until later years—like in the mid-1950s. When I think of the early years, if you remember Rosco Gordon, he used to come but this was in the early '50s. Howlin' Wolf used to come around, that was in the '50s. But going back during the years of the 1940s, I was really small and probably wouldn't got to see anybody anyway. But they never came there. All people did was listen to the Seeburg. When I really got interested was when I was coming to visit my mother here in Chicago for two weeks. I was seventeen. And during the two weeks that I was here, she took me over to see Muddy Waters at the Zanzibar. And from that point on, I really knew I wanted to play because I just enjoyed it so much. And it was something that I really wanted to do, so I had a talk with Henry Strong, the harmonica player Muddy had at the time. And I talked to Muddy, also. I talked to Henry about how I wanted to blow that harmonica, how good he sounded—he did sound good. This was on a Saturday night. The next week I told my mother I wanted some harmonicas and an amplifier. So, she went and bought me an amplifier and I got a whole keyboard of harps. I got started tootin'—that's all I was doing tootin'—sucking and pushing, pushing and sucking, along with the record player that we had. And after about two or three weeks, I could kind of hear a little tune coming out, and from that point on, I just started blowing harmonica. This was like 1954. So I just started blowing and blowing and I got pretty good with the darn thing. After two weeks was up, I wrote my grandmother and told her I would be back because we were gonna start picking cotton. I really didn't like to do that but I figured we had started a crop; I would go back and help them finish it—and then I was gonna leave again. I'd gotten big enough that I could be on my own if I wanted to anyway, but I told them to let me know when they get ready to start picking cotton—I would be back. That was about another two weeks. So, after those two weeks was up, I got me a job. I was making something like $50 a week in a factory job, you know, that's pretty good money at that time. And she wrote and told me they were starting to pick cotton. Okay, I told her I had to make this next paycheck, I'd be back the next. So, what I did, I bought myself a car. I was gonna drive it back, you know. But then every week, I was starting to play a little bit every weekend with Clifton James, Bo Diddley, Billy the Kid Emerson—we all got to know each other at this particular time. And when we weren't gigging in some place, we'd all be on the back porch, just playing music and drinking beer all night, and that got good. There was a lot of writing, writing, and writing. I said, "I ain't coming back, you'll have to forgive me for this one. But I won't be back." I stayed right here.

What was your harmonica style based on? Who were you trying to blow like?

Who else—like Little Walter—that's it! [*Laughs.*] As you go along, you know—most people create their own little style. But as far as Walter's sound goes, or some of the licks that he would do, you hear him in most harmonica players today—you still hear that. Even though they got their own style, you still hear that little click, those notes that he was hitting. They always do that. Just like a guitar player, when he learns the stuff that T-Bone Walker played—I don't care what he plays—you will always hear a lick or two of T-Bone in there—even though he's got his own style. You can't get away from it. Well, I don't care, even if you try to play like Walter note for note even if you tried to do it—No. No, you can't think like that man. You don't know what he was thinking. You might be able to feel some of what he was feeling, but you're not thinking what he was thinking at that particular time. As you keep playing, you just automatically create your own style, because that's you. When we were playing together, what we were trying to play, because we didn't have any other ambition at the time, because we were real, you know, young boys, eighteen years old—we didn't have any other choice but try to play it note for note. Most of the little taverns that we played in, if you couldn't play Little Walter, Howlin' Wolf, or Muddy Waters, wasn't no use of you even going in there.

Walter was on his own at that point, right?

He was on his own at that time.

Who was in his band when you saw him?

I had seen him with Dave and Louis, and Below. I had seen them all together. But when I really got to where I could go around him and talk with him, he had Robert Jr. and Luther Tucker and Below was there. I remember Walter was playing at this place at 38th and State. And I lived at 43rd and State. So, I used to walk down there, you know, that was walking distance for me. And Tucker and I were basically the same age, and Robert Jr. and Below. So, I used to talk to Walter and Walter used to call me up to play every set, up to blow every set because I was almost like Willie Anderson. And you know how Willie Anderson got to be Walter the second? Well, I was really headed that way, but I guess I wasn't around him as much as Willie Anderson. And we laughed and talked, just like we did you know, because we did some. We did some gigs together and as a matter of fact, he played with the band when Muddy had to go to the hospital for his hemorrhoids. And I think he was gone about three weeks or a month and Walter was in the band during that time He was always nice to me, you know, from the first time that I met him he was nice to me.

How about Henry Strong? How much of Henry Strong did you actually see?

Not too much. Not too much. Because, matter of fact, I think Henry Strong must've got killed, must have been 1954. I believe it was in 1954, the same year that I came to Chicago, I came to Chicago in July and this was somewhere during that fall, somewhere along when he got killed, yeah.

Do you remember any of the things that he said to you?

Not really, because, you know, I was just asking him how he blew the harp in the lead. He said, "It takes a lot of practice." And I wasn't playing at this particular time. I wanted to play but I wasn't playin' nothin', you know.

How would you compare the two harmonica players, Henry Strong and Walter? We hear a lot of nice things about Henry Strong. Would you say he was on par with Walter or how would you assess him?

Me personally? Yeah, I would say so. And if he had lived, he and Walter probably would have had a lot of competition because the man could blow. The man could blow you know, though I'm not sure whether Muddy ever recorded with him. I don't know whether he ever got a chance. I think at that time Walter was hot, and they were using Walter to do the blowing for Muddy. But shoot—when you'd go to hear them, I mean, until you walked up there and looked, you couldn't tell the difference.

How'd you catch up with Clifton?

I had seen Below playing somewhere. They were playing I believe it was 38th and Indiana, but I couldn't get in there. I could just see through the window, but I could hear and I saw Below playing drums so I decided I wanted to play, I thought I could do that, too. And I had my drums set up in my little bedroom and I just started playing. I had the drums and harmonica all at the same time, but this particular day, I was sitting up starting to play on drums—on a set just like that one right there. Well, this building we were staying in, I was living 4345 South State. Clifton was living at 26 East 44th Street. Clifton's brother was a plumber. So, the guy that owned our building, got him to come do some plumbing work on the floor where we were. He was back there doing his plumbing. He went out and got Clifton and brought Clifton back. Clifton was trying to learn how to play drums but he didn't have no drums. For some reason he didn't have any drums, but he was learning how to play. So, he got Clifton and brought him back around to this house. Clifton came in and when he saw the drums, he just went crazy. He really wanted to play them. So, Clifton started playing the drums and I guess I went and got the harmonica and we started to playing. At that particular time Clifton wasn't really into blues. He was into the Swing stuff but he wasn't into the blues. So, I put on a Little Walter record and I'm sitting here blowing and he was sitting here trying to learn how to beat it, you know and I'm still trying to learn how to blow it, too. We got good together and then we met this boy, his name was Bobby Lynn and we formed him a trio. As a matter of fact, when Clifton left to go with Bo Diddley, I should have been going too but I didn't want to go because I had just gotten married at that time so, definitely, I wasn't going out on the road then. [*Laughs.*] When Bo cut his first record "Bo Diddley/I'm A Man," Billy Boy Arnold was on it—that Bo Diddley thing that he did. And Billy Boy came back and went to Vee-Jay and cut a record. And Bo Diddley said that was the record that he was going to do when he came back here for Chess. So, Billy Boy and Bo fell out, because at that point it was dog-eat-dog. Billy Boy started doing his own records, and Bo was getting pretty big, because his first record was a hit. I wasn't playing with Bo, but he wanted me to play with him. Yeah, when he made that first record, he was getting ready to go on the road. And after I couldn't go, he got Lester Davenport to go with him.

In the discography it lists Billy Boy on the first session, the second session was Lester, and you were on the third session.

I remember that "Diddy Wah Diddy." I don't remember exactly what session it was.

Did Bo keep a harmonica all the time or just for the session?

Well, no, he kept the harmonica all the time until recent years. Then he didn't use a harmonica anymore. I guess nobody could blow that style for him anymore, you know, but he had a harmonica a long time. Clifton went with Bo and I stayed home. During that time, I formed my own band for a while. Then I played with Big Boy Spires for a while. I had a play-brother, his name was L.T. [This is the artist that recorded as Kid Thomas—real name Tommy Louis.] He introduced me to Big Boy Spires, because he was trying to play drums at the time and he was trying to blow harmonica, too. But he was playing drums at the time. L.T. went somewhere and Spires needed a harmonica player. And he called me—that's how I got to meet him. Matter of fact, we were playing at 258 West Roosevelt at the time.

Where did that famous picture come from with you and Big Boy Spires? You're blowing harp . . .

Well, that was at 258 West Roosevelt Road. Do you see that drummer sitting in back there? That was Kid Thomas on drums. With Arthur [Big Boy] Spires on guitar and Johnny Williams on guitar—Uncle Johnny . . .

I saw you listed with Big Boy Spires for Chess. Is that true?

Yeah, we did. We did but they never did release it. Yeah, this was during the fifties also, but he never did release it. "Murmur Low" and I forgot what the other one was ["One of These Days"], whatever it was, I know, I've never heard it.

Do you recall who was on that session?

Let me think now. I'm not sure, was Kid Thomas on that session? I believe Uncle Johnny was on it—either Uncle Johnny or Johnny Shines. It was either one of the two was on that session. I remember.

There's a handful of recordings with you and Big Boy Spires. When did those take place?

Those took place somewhere in Al Smith's basement. [*Laughs.*] That's where they took place. And I remember doing it—it took place in Al Smith's basement out south. I remember doing it but I can't remember exactly when. It was in the fifties though, I know.

Was it supposed to be a rehearsal? Was it supposed to be a session?

Actually, it was supposed to be a session, really. It was supposed to have been a rehearsal, too. But I didn't hear of it until way later.

Those were never issued on record, though. Right?

I guess not. The tapes just sort of laid around in the vault. Yeah.

What were you playing on that session?

You mean what instrument was I playing? Harmonica.

Who was the drummer? Was there a drummer on that session?

It either was Ted Porter—or Kid Thomas.

Ted Porter—that's a new name to me.

Well, he goes way back. He was old. He was an old drummer. He was a blues drummer, but he kind of played on the style like Big Boy Cruddup, with some of those type of drums on it. Something like that. After that point, that's when

I got my own band for a while. That's when Freddy King made his first record for King, which was on the Federal label. And the kid that I'm telling you about now, that used to be my play-brother, L.T., they called him Thomas, he made a record for Federal.

Kid Thomas, is that right? The harmonica player?

Harmonica player, drummer and he also was trying to learn how to play guitar. They made records for Federal. Willie Dixon, somehow, he left Chess and went to the Cobra label, with a gentleman named Eli [Toscano]. Cobra was the label that recorded Magic Sam and Otis Rush. So, he talked to me about cutting but at the time, I was a little bit too smart for my own pants because I asked him what kind of money is he talking? He said, "Well, I tell you there ain't no money in it, but you'd be making a name for yourself." I just flat-footed said, "Man, let me tell you something. I already got a name. Shit. I need some money. I mean, I can't see myself coming in here, and ain't gonna get nothing out of it but maybe a hot dog." I couldn't see that you know? And when I said, "What kind of royalties do you get?" He's told me something like, one percent or two percent. I said, "Listen man, you got to be crazy." That's just the way I said it. Yeah. And I never did try, because they were full of baloney. I didn't realize that you had to give up something to get some, I didn't know. But I was looking at it from my point of view about what should be happening, but it didn't work that way. So, I never did get to record. During that time, I was hustling—trying to hustle gigs for myself. Now, I was still hustling as a harmonica player. I didn't go to the drums till I started playing with the Red Devil trio [w. Little Hudson]. And that's when I went to the drums. I played harp and this was our last weekend at this place where I was playing harp. Kid Thomas came and got me. Little Hudson, I didn't know him at the time—Kid knew him, Kid said Hudson needed a drummer, and ask if I would play. I said, "Yeah, I'll play." So, I went down and set in and he liked the way I played. He had a steady job. And I just started playing drums at that point. He was working at a place called Vi's Lounge, at 52nd and Wentworth. At the time, he didn't have nothin' but a trio. He was playing guitar. And I was on the drums and he had a piano player, Lee Eggleston. That lasted from about 1956 to 1958, that quick, I didn't have to hustle no more on harp. I mean, matter of fact, I would only blow harp then occasionally. Maybe on a Saturday night if somebody came in and played the drums for me, I might blow harmonica, but other than that, I had a full-time job playing drums. But then rock and roll came in, you know. And then harmonica players were starting to starve to death. There was no money to be made unless you have somebody like Wolf or Walter—they still had it, but everybody else was really starving to death. Besides, if you were a drummer, and you were playing good, you could work five or six nights a week. Well, I had a day job too, but I was doing both. The money that I made playing music, that was my get-away money. [*Laughs.*] Just that quick I started playing and Muddy was giving a matinee every Sunday, at Smitty's Corner, at 35th and Indiana. And we used to go down there every Sunday, because there really wasn't anything else to do but go down and jam—so we all went down and jammed. And Muddy liked the way I played. So, he got ready to do a tribute album to Big Bill Broonzy. And he asked me to do the album with him. That was my first recording with Muddy. I wasn't really in the band at that point.

Well, I tell you about one thing about Muddy, when you first joined the band, he was gonna give you hell anyway. He was gonna give you hell. I didn't care what you did, he was gonna give you hell. It wasn't right to him—even if it was right. He would always put everybody through some kind of a test. Even though he knew that I knew what I was doing. We talked about it later. He knew I knew what I was doing, but no matter what I did, it was always gonna be one beat off here or there's gonna be something wrong out here. And he'd look right at Spann. "Yeah, you know, you was wrong, yeah." So, I'd go home. I know I didn't do that. But I would go home and I put this record on and I would listen to it. And I would sit there and you know, just kind of strum along with it and I would be right there. Now we go back. He was just that type of person. He told me in later years, "It made a better man out of you." That's what he said. "You don't get too confident in what you're doing." That's what he said. And he's always looking at me and say, "Motherfucker—I made you a good drummer!" [*Laughs.*]

Were there any of his tunes in particular that gave you any trouble?

Yeah. One. It would give me some problems. And that was "Louisiana Blues." [*Sings.*] "Get me a mojo hand . . ." that gave me some problems. But I learned to work it good. You know, he was like a father figure to me because, well, actually, when I started, I was no more than twenty-one or twenty-two. And I was wild. He talked to me a lot about different things. And I learned a lot from him. It's just like a husband and wife, really, I mean, we broke bread together. And we'd have our differences, you know. He cussed me out, I cussed him out and we go around, and then go to work, you know? He got drunk, I got drunk. [*Laughs.*] He was just a fun guy. He was. He was just a fun guy. I mean, he was just like everybody else. Yeah. He would have his ups and downs. There was a time when the music didn't sound right. And you got to blame somebody, you ain't gonna blame yourself. So, he'd blame somebody and we just sit down argue and, that's it. Keep on having fun, man.

Was he an easygoing guy?

Yeah. Yeah, he was an easygoing guy.

He wasn't a stern taskmaster?

No. Oh, no, no. He liked his champagne. He was a champagne man. Dom Perignon High Priced at that time, it was like it was like $25 a bottle, then you know, and he was drinking a couple of them a day, man. Because he was making the money then you know, so he could afford it. As we went along, we kind of persuaded him to let us go up and do two or three numbers before he came up. But he used to always want to come up with the band if we had a short show to do, he would come up with the band—but when we'd be working in one of those clubs, where you're doing three shows a night—three one-hour sets, it was different. So, we would go up and work like maybe fifteen or twenty minutes before he come up on each set. Then he would come up and sing four or five and then the last tune maybe one of the guys would take out the last tune.

What actually happened when you guys split?

Nothing between him and I or the band personally. It was the management. That's all it was, just the management was beginning to get screwed up, you know.

Who was the manager at that point?

Scott Cameron was the manager at that time. Honestly speaking, Muddy was sick, even before we left. I knew he was sick. But I didn't know—I didn't even dream he was that sick. Actually, we left about May of 1980 and he didn't really do too much more work after that. I think he went to Europe and he came back and he did a couple more things after that. But you know he stayed in the hospital a heck of a long time.

Did you see much of Wolf?

Yeah. Well, I didn't ever play with him as far as working with him. I sat in with him a lot. But, that was about it. And he was nice to me, you know, matter of fact, after I quit in 1964, he wanted to hire me then. But I had heard that Wolf would always want to whup his guys, you know, which I found out later it wasn't so. I didn't tell him but I said no, I'm ain't gonna work for him because I know I ain't gonna take no whuppin'. Nobody, you know, I'm grown. So, I found out in later years, we were at the Depot there, Muddy was there at the 47th and Drexel. It was before they closed, you know, a few years before they shut it down. And I was talking to him and I told him why. Wolf said, "Man, you been playing with Muddy Waters. I tried to get you to play with me." And then that's when it all come out. I told him you know what I had heard about him. "Man, I don't know why people want to go around and lie on me like that." I just told him that's why I never did work with you. He said, "No, no man. You treat me like a man, I treat you like a man." I could relate to that. I quit music period in 1964. I quit period for a quick moment in 1969. That was a time when Muddy really wasn't making no money, man. I mean rock and roll took over everything so we really weren't making any money. And what really made me quit—this was like coming up in 1964, we just had come from Europe, Muddy, me, and Spann. And what really made me quit, they had booked Muddy somewhere for like, three months. But even while I was playing with Muddy, I started driving a cab all the time. I was playing with him, because we were only playing just the weekend. We were playing at Pepper's on 43rd and Vincennes, and shit, we weren't making any money. So, I got a job driving a cab. Finally, the agent got Muddy a job about three months out of town. And I told him I wasn't going because I was making more money one day driving a cab than I was making a whole week playing at festivals. So, I told him I wasn't going. At this particular time, he had, let's see, Jimmy Lee Morris was on bass, Peewee Madison was on guitar, Mojo Buford was on harp. And Otis Spann was on piano.

How much of the decline of Little Walter did you see?

Well, if you said decline, he must have started declining somewhere in the 1950s. I remember when we had this disc jockey called Sam Evans. I heard him say, I had missed Walter for a while, but I heard Sam Evans say Walter had got shot in the leg. He was in the hospital and you know, from that point on, I think he never was the same. I never did see a decline in his health. No, I didn't see a decline in his health. He had been off for a while. He really hadn't been active. You know, if you don't stay active, you begin to lose some of it. But he knew what he was supposed to do. So, he was starting to push, besides, he was getting older and you don't have all of that wind you had when you were twenty-one years old. During the time when Walter got killed, I had heard that Muddy was thinking about putting him back in the band with him.

Was Cotton in the band at that point?

No, I think Cotton might have been doing his own thing about then.

Is that right? That was like Walter got killed in 1968, right?

Yeah, Cotton must have been doing his own thing about then because I started back with Muddy in the last of 1968.

And who was holding down the harp position at that point?

Paul Oscher—but in the meanwhile, we had formed our own little thing. By that time, we got it together. Originally, it was Pinetop, Jerry Portnoy, myself, Louis Myers, and Calvin Jones—The Legendary Blues Band.

You've changed personnel considerably over the years . . .

Yeah, we changed considerably because the management there was bad, too—and if you ain't working you can't keep a band together. But Pinetop had notions all the time that he wanted to do his own thing—so, when it got a little bit slow, he just moved out. We talked about it, he and I did. I said, "Hey man, more power to you!" So, he took off and then we started to change and change and change. So, it got down to where there were only two of us left—Calvin and myself—and he retired. When he got old enough to collect his money, he said, "To hell with it." And he quit. That leaves nobody now but me, so that's why I'm going through a lot of changes. As a matter of fact, I'm changing everything around. Instead of just the Legendary Blues Band, from now on it'll be Willie "Big Eyes" Smith and the Legendary Blues Band. So, it won't be all LEGEND now. You know, they called me a legend. I don't consider myself a legend, but everybody else does. So, it'll be Willie Big-Eyes Smith and his legendary blues band from now on.

Who's in the band right now as we speak?

Big Nick Moss, he's on the bass. And I have Willie Philips on guitar, and myself of course is on the drums. And right now, I'm using Dave Waldman because my work is kind of spaced out around here. My main harmonica player lives in Louisville. His name is Mark Hoekstra.

Casey Jones

In addition to the front-line, first-call, Postwar Blues drummers (Fred, Odie, Earl, S.P.), there was a generation of younger Black drummers playing blues during the early 1970s. They seemed to have drifted from soul and funk into blues—guys like Dino Alverez, Merle Perkins, Roosevelt Snake Shaw, and Tyrone Century. Another of the younger generation that I saw on a regular basis was Casey Jones. Casey was first-call among that younger group and was good enough that he was hired to play behind even some of the Postwar elders, like Howlin' Wolf. I can't recall Casey displaying a double-shuffle, but he had such a solid backbeat that he was in demand everywhere. I never had the opportunity to talk with Casey on the band scene and didn't know him personally, but word went around that he was battling cancer, so I called him and we got together for the following interview.

■ ■ ■

Really, the first time I saw the little town that I was born in was about two and a half years ago. I went down to my mother's funeral in Greenville, Mississippi, and I was going down to one of my sister's house. And I'd happened to see the signs that said Nitta Yuma not too far from Cameda(?), Mississippi. I said, "Oh, that's where I was born." And I had to stop. There's nothing there but about 15 or 20 people, something like that. I don't even remember being there. Well, I got into music because I liked the sound of those drums and trumpets and clarinets and stuff in the marching band. That's where I came from, a marching band. I was in a band and in Greenville, Mississippi was called the Coleman High Tigers—that was the name of the football team. But every Friday they were playing so we had to do the march thing down on the street every Friday night, then we go to the park and perform there. I couldn't wait until Friday came, man! I was in love with that [*laughs*]. I was just playing the snare drums. That was in 1953. I started in the marching band. And I didn't start really playing the drums, you know, the whole set, until I came to Chicago. I came to Chicago in 1956. When I came to

Chicago, I was seventeen. I came with my family—my mother, my younger sister and my niece. Matter of fact, the one that brought us up here was my brother-in-law and my sister. She's still living in Greenville, Mississippi, Adaline Luke. They're the ones that bought me my first set of drums, and put me in the union. And I remember my first job. The first job I had, I was with my brother-in-law's brother, Otis Luke. We were called Otis Luke and the Rhythm Bombers. Our first job was on 55th, which is Garfield and State Street—Spruces Liquor, no bandstand. We went there and played that night, and each made five bucks, big dough to me. And I said, "Don't give me no dollar bills. I want all change. I want nickels, quarters, and half dollars and dimes. I want everybody to know I had a lot of money, you know, there it was a rattling in my pocket. I didn't want to no dollar bills, I wanted to show off. [*Laughs.*]

Well, we were playing stuff like B.B. King or Bobby Blue Bland. Percy Mayfield. When I started singing, which I really didn't want to do in the beginning, I just wanted to be a drummer.

I played up until 1959 just doing the drums and in 1959, that's when I started singing. We had a guy in the band named Herman Owens, he passed away. He was the only one in the band that knew how to sing, he played the piano and sang—and he was good, too. And one night, we were playing in a club called the 1959 Club on Damen and Roosevelt. Later on, they named it The Blue Lagoon. Herman got pulled over for a traffic violation. And when the cop pulled him over, he had a gun in the car. So, he didn't make that gig that night. They took him to jail [*laughs*]. So, guys in the band said, "Casey, you got to do something, man—you can sing a little bit."—because when he used to sing, I used to sing behind him—to myself, you know. I only knew three songs. I would sing one song per set, and the rest would be instrumentals. And the next set I did another vocal. You know, I found out I could scream and holler like Little Richard. It was all over. I was ready to start singing then. [*Laughs.*]

Let's go back and talk some more about your drumming. Did you own a set of drums? On your first gig, where did that set of drums come from?

My sister Adeline Luke and my brother-in-law Prentiss Luke bought me my first set of drums in 1956 and put me in the union. I didn't have nothing but bass drum, snare drum, and a mounted tom-tom. They bought it from Frank's Drum Shop, down on Wabash, up under the el. They were Leedy & Ludwigs.

What color were they?

You name it! [*Laughs.*] They were all different colors. They weren't at all matching. I just was glad I had a snare drum, bass drum, and a mounted tom, because they just made up a set for me. I liked them, too. Man, I kept those drums for a long time. And I used the ride cymbal was also the crash cymbal for me, too. Because I didn't know you're supposed to go for the ride cymbal—I thought you were just supposed to hit it. But I always was pretty smart about what I was supposed to do with the drums behind people that would sing or play instruments, you know.

Did you see any of the other big-name drummers here in town when you were young, like Below, Odie, or Earl Philips, any of those guys?

I used to see Earl Phillips. He used to play at a place with Left-Hand Frank. Left-Hand Frank and Willie Black, they used to play on Lake Street, Lake and Homan. I used to go by and see them all the time because they were good friends of mine. Left-Hand Frank and my brother used to work together. I'd just go by and watch you know, but I really wasn't really influenced by anybody. That's just something I wanted to do. Same thing with my vocals. Just after I start singing, I just wanted to do it. But after I got into it, I started doing different styles, you know? Fats Domino, Johnny Taylor, people like Little Richard, Wilson Pickett, Otis Redding. You know, anybody that came to see my show, they never saw me do strictly rhythm and blues or strictly blues stuff like that. I always believed if you got the talent, show it.

When you played with that first band, was that just a one-time thing?

It was a regular gig because it was a family thing. It was a weekly thing over there, Friday and Saturday, every week.

Was that all you were doing at that time, just playing those two nights? Or were you doing a day job as well?

No, I never had a day job before. My first day job came in 2000, because the music got a little funny, so, you know, you got to do what you got to do. But I never had a job in my life.

So, did you try to find a whole lot of other gigs playing like every night of the week kind of thing?

Oh, I was busy, I was. Once somebody saw me play, the word got around. I had no problem getting a gig because everybody wanted to use Casey Jones.

Can you remember various guys you played with—and when?

I played with Eddy Clearwater back in 1957/1958. I played with Eddy; his uncle had a hall up there on Ogden—upstairs on Ogden Avenue. We used to play up there all the time.

Who was in a band with you and Eddy at that time?

Let's see, I can't remember that bass player. Abb Locke hadn't gotten with them yet, he was still playing with Freddy King. I can't remember the bass player's name.

Were you on any of Eddy's records?

Yes. Well, I did a couple of things on his label, Cleartone—"Two x Nine" and "Nashville Road." I did a couple more with him. We stayed together. And then things got a little slow. After I stopped playing with him. Then I started playing with people like Morris Pejoe, I know you remember him. We were playing at the Happy Home. And I used to play with Freddie King on a Friday night, because the drummer he had, T.J. McNulty, he had a day job. So, what happened, on Friday, Freddy would always need a drummer. And Mojo Elem told Freddy, "Why don't you use Casey Jones?" And I showed up at the Happy Home one night and that was when I started playing him, every Friday, every other Friday, you know, whenever he needed somebody.

Where was the Happy Home?

Happy Home was one of the main clubs back then. It was on Madison, right off Oakley. Oh, man. It was a jumping spot. I was at the Happy Home, too. That was after Morris Pejoe.

Who was in Morris Pejoe's band?

I wouldn't know. Every now and then he would use Mighty Joe Young on the second guitar.

Was Henry Gray on piano?

Henry Gray. No, he wasn't there. I know Henry Gray. He's the one who's played with Wolf. But when I played with Magic Sam, Johnny Jones was on the piano. It was me. Mac Thomas. You know, Mac Thomas? Jimmy Johnson's brother? We were together with Magic Sam. Sometime he would use a piano player, but most of the time it would just be us three. Just like when I was with Freddie King, most of the time it was a three-piece thing. Oh, Fred was known for that. I use a three-piece a lot of time now, but when you use a three-piece, hey, you got to be on top of everything. You gotta keep the gaps filled . . .

We've got Eddy Clearwater. Then you went with Freddie King for a while—and Magic Sam. Who else did you work with?

Jimmy Johnson. Jimmy Johnson had his brother, Mac on bass, too. It was Jimmy, Mac and me—it was three pieces.

What kind of stuff were you guys doing at the time? Was it blues?

Jimmy is the type of guy who likes to mix it up, you know? He will do B.B. King or Bobby Bland people like that. Then sing Little Johnny Taylor's "Part-Time Love."

How did you join up with Jimmy Johnson?

Well, I had been playing around you know, and guys would say, "Give me your number. I can use you sometime." And when I was playing with those guys, I passed out quite a few cards that I had printed up, and when a gig came along and they needed somebody, my name just spread. They would call me. Everybody would say, "Man, that guy you got really can play. Casey Jones, he's like a little kid!" because I was real young. I always was—until now. [*Laughs.*] So, the word got around that I was the one you should have.

And when you hired on with the various frontmen, did you get any opportunity to sing, too?

Every now and then I would do stuff like "Lucille" or "Stagger Lee." Back then I wasn't particularly really into singing like I am now. I just wanted to hit the drums and learn what I supposed to do behind somebody. That's why I get mad about people who play behind me now—especially the drummer—because I expect them to be the same as me, you know, really careful and try to make everything go like the person I'm playing behind wants it to go. It's kind of hard to find a guy that does me that same way. I know a lot of people say, "Why did he jump off the drums anyway? He's the real thing, he's the deal." But, that's me, that's what I want to do.

How did the thing with Magic Sam happen?

He just called and said, "I got a gig open tonight if you want to play it. We start at so and so time . . . " That was at a place called the Tay-May, over on Loomis and Roosevelt. It might have been called the Alex Club at that time, because it just kept changing names. So, I was over there playing with him but before Sam, I used to work with Otis Rush for three years.

How did you hook up with Otis and who was in the band?

Oh, we had one of the best bands in Chicago. We had Otis on the guitar. I was on the drums. James Green on the bass. Mighty Joe Young on second guitar. And we also had Abb Locke on saxophone—that's all he had one horn, and he was singing through the amplifier. No PA system. We were knocking fire though. Oh man, we were strong. Well, we played with purpose. We played at Peppers—the original Peppers on 43rd Street—we also played the Castle Rock; I think it was around Kilpatrick and Roosevelt. Oh, it was a jumping club, too. It was like the Happy Home—everybody played there and it was packed all the time. Also, we went on the road with Otis, a few times, not that much at that particular time. I never did play Theresa's with him either. But we had private things that we would do, little dances and stuff like that. Another place, well-known, called the Twin Lounge, located where three corners come together—Cermak, Ogden and Pulaski. We used to play there all the time, too.

You recorded with Otis, didn't you?

Well, the sides were done in a studio over on Delaware. Willie Dixon was the one who called me for the session. I was in Otis Rush's band at the time, but Willie Dixon was the one called me. Otis told him, "Hey, I want Casey on the drums." I want to use my own band, you know, we went in and did a couple of songs. It came out on the Duke label.

I guess what I was trying to figure out was if the sides issued on Duke and Peacock were done down in Houston . . .

Oh, no, no, we didn't do that. We did that in a studio over on Walton. I'm trying to think of the studio name [Universal], but no, that wasn't down there, that was here.

So, you never got a chance to meet Don Robey?

No. Produced by Willie Dixon.

And what songs came out of that?

Well, one side was called "Homework," [*sings*] "I can't do my homework anymore!" It was a good song, too. That's the only one I've ever seen was "Homework"—I think that may be the only one we did. There was a white group in Europe that did that song—and they did a good job, too.

Did the changing trend in music have much effect on your work and the bands you played with? They went from downhome blues to R&B, then to soul and funk. How did that affect you and your work?

Oh, I loved it. I still do. Yeah, because that way you're not caught in any one band. See, that's good for your mind, believe it or not. Because anything they throw out at you, you're on top of it. It didn't bother me at all. The best way to put it, I like some of all, but not all of any. I don't care what it is as long as it sounds good, it's good music.

After I worked with Otis Rush, I started putting together some guys for my own band—putting together about maybe four or five different bands. And after that, I started working with Wolf.

Well, what happened, I was in bed one night and Wolf was playing at the Burning Spear. Okay, S.P. Leary was playing the drums with him. So S.P. was bringing the drums in and he never made it into the club. He was so drunk he fell out flat on his back. [*Laughs.*] Eddie Shaw got on the phone. You know, he's from Greenville, Mississippi, too. And he called me and said, "Casey, what are you doing man?" I said, "I'm in bed sleeping." It was about 10:30. "Well, I may have a gig for you. Wolf needs a drummer because S.P. just fell out in the middle of the street and we can't wake him up." I said, "Man, I haven't played the kind of music Wolf plays in a long time." "Man, you can do this—just get up and come over. It ain't nothing but a piece of cake." I said, "Okay, let me go downstairs and get my drums and I'll be right there." I went over and we played the first show and after that Wolf fell in love with me. Wolf says, "Oh man. You play really good. Play like you playin', you're alright with me." [*Laughs.*] He's called me Long Hair, because I had a long process thing hanging down to my shoulders, you know? Yeah.

What did you find Wolf to be like, the time you spent with him?

Oh, man. He was alright with me. I'm telling you. A lot of people, you know, they will disagree because I think a lot of times the guys would say he was really mean and stuff. He had his ways, I got my ways, sure—you got your ways. Probably, the reason was, he would tell somebody to play something or want you to play it like it is on the record. Then they want to do it their own way. See, I don't have no problem with it. You have somebody tell me to do something, even if it's wrong. That's okay. And you might say, well, that's not gonna work. You see, I don't think that's going to be good for this. Well, just play it and see what happens. Then I don't go no further with it. If they're satisfied, I'm satisfied with it, because I don't care what they tell me to play, I can do it. I might have a better idea, but hey . . .

I think everything I heard, you just played straight backbeats behind Wolf.

Yeah, right. Because I remember one night, I was playing with Wolf—I think we might have been up in Canada. I think we were playing "Forty-Four"—"I wore my forty-four so long . . . " It was grooving, and I was getting into it because I really liked that song. And I put something in there that wasn't supposed to be in there—like a riff. He didn't like that. We came down, he said, "Well, you play good Long Hair, but that spot there—you put that little beat in there. You keep that out of there . . . " Okay. You'll never hear it again, you know, I'm working for him. You know. If I say, "Well, man, that sounded good to me." Well, you know, there's gonna be an argument. Why am I gonna argue with the man? It's his show. But that's the only time he said something about me playing. I knew what to do then—lay back, straight backbeats and play as close to the recording as possible.

Did you work with him on a regular basis or for very long?

No, I worked with him about maybe it was a year or close to a year because he was on the machine [dialysis] at the time I was working with him. Yes, it was close to the end. You're right.

I remember there used to be a really beautiful Black waitress—a great big afro—that worked at Peppers and he would sing "Shake For Me"—and she would come up there and dance in front of him. Was that a regular thing, or did I just happen to stumble in on the right night?

You just got lucky! [*Laughs.*]

Have you got any stories you can tell about Otis Rush that listeners would find interesting?

Otis and I were really cool. Like I said, most everybody I played with, I got along with them, because I was very disciplined—whatever they told me to do, I tried to do it, just like I do to this very day. If somebody calls me and I accept the job to play drums, I play just as well as when I'm playing for myself. With Otis—he was back in those days, just like he is today—real quiet. When I was working with him, he was really quiet. He didn't do too much talking to anybody—nobody, except maybe for me—he might say a few words. That's about it. He doesn't sit or stand around on intermission. He'd be off, you know, by himself. Then, when it was time to go back, he'd go up there and knock fire. He was playing and singing too, partner.

What do you think happened with him? It seemed like emotionally he had difficulty later on.

It might have been that he had been messed around quite a bit, you know, with certain business deals. Not everybody can take it. Some people will get aggravated when you get into a bad deal, or you get tired of management and you can't do anything about it. You know you should be free and making more profit just get to it.

How about other guys we could talk about that you worked with?

Oh, man. I worked with Johnny Winter, just for like a couple nights—though I've been on a lot of his recordings. He was a good guy to work for. He trusted me in the studio. He used to tell me all the time, when we'd do a recording, he'd say, "Casey, watch me. If I get away, just hold me. Yeah, because I get to feeling happy and start to get away, you do what you're doing because you're good for me here."

Is it true that you did a recording session with Muddy Waters?

I never did work with Muddy—but I did a session with him down at the Chess studios. I had been playing on records with different people around town. Willie Dixon was in charge of the session and he saw me play behind Magic Sam—and Shakey Jake—and he thought I would be good to do the Muddy session. I got a call and we went down and did it. Ernie Johnson was on that session too. He's an in-law of mine. When he first came to Chicago, he used to run [tune] his guitar down, just like Mojo Elam used to run his guitar down. But Ernie was one of the first in Chicago to start playing bass.

What can you tell me about Earl Hooker?

Oh, man. A great player. One of the best slide guitar players you ever want to see. He was the type of guy you kinda had to watch him—because he could play really good but you'd rehearse a tune three or four times in the studio. He did something you'd hear and I'd want to put a little something on drums at that spot to go with it, but come time to record, you might not hear that again because a lot of times he wouldn't play the same thing over [*laughs*].

Did you work gigs with him?

Yeah, I worked gigs with him—locally, but not out on the road. I was so busy—I got so many phone calls from everybody, I just didn't have time to say, "Okay, I gonna settle down with you guys."

Did you work with Ricky Allen?

Yeah. He had good records, man. I played on, I think, four of them. I never did work gigs with him. He would come by where we were playing and sit in on the show. I knew him really well though. The band would be A.C. Reed on saxophone, Ivory Park on guitar, I was on drums, and Ernest Johnson on bass. We used to call him Peter Rankum. [*Laughs.*] That was just one of them old Mississippi names! [*Laughs.*] He got hung. When I did that with them, I was playing at the Twin Lounge. Otis would play there on a Thursday, and on Friday and Saturday we were off, but they would call me and I would play Friday and Saturday over there with them.

Didn't you and A.C. have an association for a while? You were friends and working partners for a long time . . .

Long time. Well actually it started when we worked over there at that Twin Lounge. We started talking and he liked the way I played, and I liked the way he played and we kept playing on certain gigs together and something just clicked. We became friends and kept in touch. This was around 1962 or '63—something like that.

Were you on his Age records?

No. When we first started really talking, we were in the studio with Ricky Allen. He said [*imitates A.C.'s voice:*], "Man, you sound good man. You sure can play. Give me your number man. I could use you on some of my stuff man." So that's how it really started—we started being really close. So, the next time he went into the studio, he wanted me to play behind him.

Here's another one—didn't you record with Margie Hendrix?

It was on the Mercury label. I never did hear the recording. I don't remember how that happened, but what I do remember—what happened on that particular track they had another guy play the drums—I won't call any names—but he had messed up the time, the tempo. He got loaded or something—and they wanted me to come in and straighten it out. They pulled him off and overdubbed my drums on there.

Well how the hell can you do that? Isn't the time already set?

Oh man—don't ask me! [*Laughs.*] It happened twice! [*Laughs.*] I hope it never happens again. Man, that's a hard job. I did it with Margie Hendrix and I also did it with Guitar Red. That's a hard job—but I got it done. I believe that was down at Universal, too. Universal was located over on Walton. Margie was covering something that Ray Charles did. It might have been "Night Time Is the Right Time," because I remember her doing that chorus singing "Baby!"

When we talked on the phone you mentioned that you had recorded with Major Lance?

Right. I did "Hey Little Girl." I can still remember the line that Ernest Johnson was playing and Robert Borden—he's an in-law of mine too. I remember the line, because Curtis Mayfield said, "Hey you guys play this—blah-blah-blah." I never will forget it—[*sings the melody:*] dah-dah-dah-da-dah-da-dah . . . It stuck in my mind all this time. It's called "Hey Little Girl." It came out on Mercury.

Did you ever strike gold with any of the records you were on—were any of them big hits?

No. The biggest person I recorded behind was Lou Rawls. I don't know if it was a hit or not. That was on Philadelphia International. This was after all his stuff on Capital. He wanted to do a record with a blues sound and with Chicago musicians from Bruce Iglauer and Alligator Records. Bruce is the one who put us all together—like me, Lonnie Brooks, Allen Batts. He put all of us together and we flew to New York to do that session. Lou Rawls was crazy about it. Hank Crawford was on it—and David Fathead Newman. Hawk Crawford was crazy about it. He said, "You guys can play partner."

Did you work gigs with Fenton Robinson?

Yes. We used to be in a band together. When I first met him, Fenton used to come by a place called the Trocadero. That was down in the basement—all the bad guys used to hang around down there. I mean, you want to get stepped on by not being able to play, go down to the Trocadero. There were all kinds of musicians hanging out down there—if you didn't know what you were doing you didn't have any business down there. Fenton used to come by there. On Mondays they used to open up about eight or nine in the morning and go all night. Guys out in the audience would come up and sing—just like a jam session. Fenton used to come by quite a bit, and I used to hang around there. I liked to hear him sing and play and we just got started talking, you know.

How about Reggie Boyd?

[*Laughs.*] Oh yeah—Reggie's cool! He was alright. I haven't seen him in a long time—I wish I could see him and talk to him right now. Reggie didn't lead any bands—he was mostly a session man. The guy that he taught was a session man and used to play with Singing Sam—Matt Murphy. Singing Sam was a bass player and he and Matt Murphy played behind Memphis Slim. They had a sax player named John Calvin, Sam Chatman was on bass—I think Al Duncan on drums—and Matt Murphy on guitar. They used to call him M.T. Murphy back then but it was Matt Murphy. Reggie taught Matt and Phil Upchurch. Singing Sam and the Sparks—man. They were rough, too. They'd do stuff like the Coasters, whatever was popular or on the radio—and they'd mix in the Blues, too. They say Reggie Boyd's wife used to play too. She was a bass player. I never met her but people used to talk about her—she was really good. I used to work with McKinley Mitchell too [*laughs*]. I used to call him pretty boy. He had a strong voice. I never worked gigs with him but he wanted me to. Luther Allison too. He was always after me. "C'mon man and work with me . . . " But I wasn't interested. I'd rather just stay around Chicago. I really didn't want to travel. I still don't like traveling but I have to do it now.

In talking to the veteran drummers, I heard many of them say when things got slow, they'd go play in Calumet City . . .

Well, I worked in Calumet City, too. I worked with Cozy Eggleston. I never will forget. I was seventeen years old when I did that. The union got me that job, with Cozy Eggleston, at a place called the Paradise Club. I was so glad to get that job but when I worked there, I pretty much kept to myself. We got up there and did the show—and then break time, I was underage. I couldn't move around visiting from table to table—I couldn't move around talking because I was only seventeen years old and they had to watch out for me. Cozy was my guardian. I'd just find myself a booth or back to the little break room and nod until time for the next show. The same thing when I first started working with Magic Sam. We were working the Black clubs with Shakey Jake. Shakey Jake was Sam's uncle. It was time to go back up and Sam would say, "Where's Casey? He's not here." and Shakey Jake would say, "D-d-d-don't worry about Casey! That boy quiet—He'll be here! I'll bet he'll be here! You go on up—I'll bet he'll be there!" Shakey Jake knew, I didn't want to talk to nobody. I'd just study what I had to do when I went back up on that bandstand for the next show. When Magic Sam got up on that bandstand—Magic Sam or anybody else I worked with—if you get up there, I'm up there! I kept my eye on things. I didn't roam the streets. I was just a quiet guy—Hard to believe huh? [*Laughs.*]

How did your work with Albert Collins happen?

Well. Bruce Iglauer put the two of us together. I had been hearing about Albert Collins because when I was working with Otis Rush, he used to play

"Frosty" all the time—and he'd play it note-for-note. Bruce decided to record Albert Collins. I first got to record for Bruce and the Alligator label with Lonnie Brooks on *Bayou Lightning*. My drum captain down in Greeneville, Mississippi was playing with Lonnie Brooks at the time. Lonnie had a pair of tunes he wanted to record—"Two-Headed Man" and "Watchdog." Lonnie called me at home and asked me if I could come over and rehearse with them, because my partner couldn't handle it. So, we had one rehearsal and then I killed it. And that's when Bruce said, "Hey, I better start using this guy . . . " Bruce decided to record Albert Collins, brought him up here and we met up at the Wise Fools. That was the beginning of it . . .

I understand you were friends with former boxer Ernie Terrell. Tell me about that.

Ernie is an old Mississippi boy, too. He used to live on the Westside, over there on Drake. I used to live on 16th and Millard. He used to come by to see us all the time when I was with Otis Rush. He used to hang around places where we worked, like Peppers, Twin Lounge, and the Castle Rock. Ernie always used to come in because he always wanted to sing and play guitar, too. Otis would let him come up and play sometime. I found out where Ernie lived—and he found out where I lived, we were almost next door so we just started hanging around each other. He'd come by my house and I'd go by his house when they were over there rehearsing—he and his sister and a couple of brothers. He asked me, "Would you mind working with us for a little while, until you get something else going?" So, we got together and formed the band with me in it. We started traveling—we traveled quite a bit. It was a fun group and this was while he was still boxing, too. He was boxing heavyweight. He's real heavy now, as heavy as this building. [*Laughs.*] He fought Muhammad Ali back in 1967 back in Texas. He fought Cleveland Williams, Oscar Bonavena—he fought all of them. We used to talk all the time; we were like family. We made one record together. We went to New York to do it with the guy who was producer for Brook Benton, Clyde Otis. We recorded one called "A Hammer and a Nail." It was a nice song but it didn't take off—a whole lot of songs don't take off—you know how that is.

Also, tell me about Saxy Russell.

He played alto sax but sounded like a tenor. That's when I was with Otis Luke and The Rhythm Bombers—at 2525 Madison Street in Chicago. We were rehearsing and he was riding by in his car. He heard the music and parked his car. He came in, "Y'all rehearsing? I play sax too. I don't have my horn with me." "Well, go get your horn, man. We just started." "I'll be right back!" He was living on Avers, there—just around the corner, 1814 Avers. He went and got his horn. He said he'd be back in fifteen minutes—I think he was back in five!

[*Laughs.*] That guy was blowing, too, guy. So, we were rehearsing and that's when we started doing gigs around town. We did just little gigs—also, around Gary. We used to play a place called the F&J in Gary. He could sing a song or two but he had a limited repertoire singing—but he could blow. "Honky Tonk" and "Rambunctious." We're still close—we're real tight. We always keep in touch.

I used to travel with Albert Collins. We use to have a lot of fun—laughing and joking and talking. But we could always tell when Albert was getting ready to start an argument. He usually drank Jack Daniels—he liked Jack Daniels, but just let Albert drink I.W. Harper and then the mess would start. A.C. Reed would look at him and go, "Aw, shit! I imagine we're gonna start some shit now. We're gonna rock out and he's gonna bullshit when we get off of work!" And he wasn't wrong! [*Laughs.*] He'd get that I.W. Harper in him, that was it—that's when the argument commenced—and it wasn't about nothin', you know—and the next day it's like it never happened [*laughs*].

Phillip Paul—One Last Story

Phillip Paul was based in Cincinnati and was the house drummer for the Cincinnati-based King Label. He's reputed to be on over 400 recorded sides. He was still around—and playing(!)—in his mid-nineties. I made arrangements to do a phone interview, but time was catching up with him, and overall, the interview was not a success but what follows is a fun story he shared during our call.

■ ■ ■

A buddy and I would go out every weekend and play wherever people would let us play. People were willing and ready to let us play and learn what we could—all from good professional musicians. Every weekend this buddy and I would go out and try to get to sit-in, because we thought if we got to sit-in and we sounded good enough, they might hire us. And that's what we did. My buddy, he believed in just trying everything—and try as hard as he could, and it would happen for him. And he did that with me. He pushed me to go up on stage. On Monday nights, Dizzy Gillespie and all the guys were there—and they would invite you on the bandstand to play if you felt halfway certain that you could do it. So that's what my buddy did—he entered my name. They said, "Anybody who feels like he can come up and play with Miles Davis and Charlie Parker are welcome." Miles Davis had the same old habits—he wouldn't speak to anyone and he'd turn his back to the audience—oh man! They got us up with the guys that were big on letting you play. They said, "Just take it easy. We're going to find the right key and tempo and everything." So, we heard a little tapping like this: "Tap—tap—tap—tap-tap-tap-tap-tap-tap-tap-tap-tap . . ." [*Speed of light tempo.*] We wondered what that was—and that was the guys kicking off "Cherokee"—"Cherokee"!!! Can you imagine that? That's what he did with us, he stomped off—that's what they called it. To tell you the truth, I couldn't do two choruses at that tempo—it was so fast. I'm just a young drummer—I don't know that's coming. They played an introduction and Miles Davis stood with his back to the audience—and God, I was a nervous wreck. I said to them, "I gotta give it up—I can't play this!" They said, "That's alright—we invite you to come back anytime you feel like you can do this again." It took me about two years before I even had the nerve to ask to play. But it turned out to be a good thing because I got an opportunity to play with Charlie Parker. In fact, they complimented me for having the guts to do it. They said, "Hey, your old buddy Miles Davis, he does this all the time to us!" I felt great! I went home early that night, my buddy and I got some gin and went home and played the records!

Part Two **The Guitarists**

Roy Gaines

Roy Gaines came to my attention through a pair of instrumentals, "Gainesville" and "Nightbeat"—but neither of these sides indicated to me that he was one of the leading T-Bone Walker disciples. I was surprised to learn that Roy was still alive—and had recently resumed playing Blues after ventures in other music genres. He was booked to perform at the 2003 Chicago Blues Fest. I made arrangements through the Blue Fest selection committee to interview Roy when he came to Chicago. I recall this interview specifically because the interview was scheduled to take place after his fest performance. He and his wife were staying in a hotel in the River North area. I remember walking from the Petrillo Band Shell to his hotel, toting a duffle bag with a full-size, studio deck DAT recorder, microphone stands plus cables and mixer—quite a load. The hotel room was quite compact so, both Roy and his wife sat on the bed and while I sat in the only chair. They had a very early start that day, leaving their California home around 3 a.m., so his wife soon nodded out, but Roy talked for nearly ninety minutes. When fatigue finally caught up with Roy, we agreed that he would discuss the later chapters of his career at our next get-together . . .

■ ■ ■

Can you tell me when and where you were born?

Yes, I was born in Waskom, Texas, August 12, 1937.

Did you come from a musical family?

Yes. My brother Grady Gaines is a great saxophone player. He's what you'd call a Texas honker. He played with Little Richard, Sam Cooke—a lot of great musicians. And he still is very popular as a musician in the Houston area. And he can really get the house excited, like in the days of Big Jay McNeely, they take them one note [*Daa Daa . . .*] and they can really get a house worked up. He's a great, great musician and a great entertainer.

What was your first exposure to music?

Well, my father was a blues man. And he never worked with a band or anything like that. He worked in train yards and lumber yards. He played the harmonica and you could hear him coming home from work, walking on a railroad track, singing the blues and playing this harmonica. That was his musical career. But before him, his father played the banjo, back in that time—that was just after slavery. And they were still going back to the plantations to play plantation parties. He played mandolin, he played violin and banjo. He was a string-man. So maybe that sort of wiggled down to me. That's the most I know about any music in our family. My mother played some piano—and the way I found that out, when I wanted to play music, I wanted to play piano. I didn't know anything about a guitar. I wanted to play piano. So, she bought a piano. And the first day the piano came. She sat down and played a song called "Blues Jumped The Rabbit"—and run him for a solid mile. Well, I said, "That's kind of interesting, I didn't know you played the piano." And I started taking piano lessons from the time I was six until I was thirteen. I thought I'd be a piano player. I played with my brother's band for a while until one Sunday we were playing just outside of Houston, at a little old place and my brother—like I said, he's a showman with a saxophone. His band was playing this wild song and he went all out in the audience. And when he came back to the stage, he had all these girls following him, you know. I said, "Well, I think I better get me an instrument that I can take off the stage." [*Laughs.*] I laid awake at night wondering what I could do. I didn't want to play saxophone because I got hit by a train when I was quite young, six years old. We're going crawfishing and the crawfish hole was across the other side of the railroad tracks. I was crossing the tracks and two trains were coming. All the noise sounded like one train. So, I walked into the one that was backing up the caboose steps hit me and cracked my skull and my mother said that they thought I shouldn't play any instrument that would cause a lot of pressure from blowing. While I was thinking about getting off the stage and coming back and have the girls come after me, you know, I got this idea. I saw Guitar Slim, I saw T-Bone Walker and they have these long guitar cords. And T-Bone would make turns and circles. And he would do "whips" and "cracks" with the guitar—Big Band "pops" and "cracks"—Big Band sounds and then he'd come in and play a line—And then he would do the splits and he would put the guitar behind his head. Guitar Slim had maybe 100 feet long cord. He'd go out the door if he could, and he come back in and the people were just screaming and hollering. So, I said, "That's got to be the way to go, you know?" [*Laughs.*] So I had the idea that I would get a guitar and learn to play as fast as I could, so I get in on some of the action. This was in Houston, Texas, I passed a jewelry store called Crowns Jewelry. Crowns had guitars there—and they had little amplifiers—and it was a nice-looking little guitar. And I can remember what it was—it was a Kay. The guitar cost $85. And the amplifier was a smaller pretty brown amplifier with white triangles painted on the front of it. And that little amp cost I think $35. So, it was all totaled $120.

We were paying my mother $5 for room and board. I started throwing [*news*] papers from watching my brother at the age of six. By the time I was eight or nine, I was a station captain. So, I told my mother that I wanted some of the money that she had been taking for rent room and board. And I told her I thought that the guys down the street, and everybody I know, all the boys that threw newspapers, they didn't have to pay rent. And that if I was paying rent, she could surely let me have some of that rent money, or come sign for me—or just make a way for me to get this guitar. This conversation went up against a brick wall. She wasn't going hear any of that. So, my mother told me, for a week or two, there was no way I was going to get a guitar. So, I come down on her again, I said, "Well, I don't think it's fair, that I pay in rent and you don't have any of that money." And I thought she was saving the money. I said, "Nobody else is paying rent—nobody! I gotta get a guitar. I'm not paying any more rent until I get the guitar. And then I can resume paying rent." I come like that. And she said, "You want that money? I got every penny of it. And it's in that trunk over there. You go in that trunk, and you look down in the bottom, and you get all the fruit jars. Every penny—just how you gave it to me—is in those fruit jars. But, if you go get this money that I've saved for you, you will be broke all the rest of your life. Because you will never want to save nothing. Just like you don't want to leave that money over there and have some later on. You're not going to save money. You will not learn this lesson that I'm trying to teach you." [*Laughs.*] And that scared me so that I didn't want to get the money. I thought I'd be able to get the money—but I'm going to get just enough for the guitar, if there's enough over there. There should be, because I'd been throwing newspapers quite a while. And so, I went in and got me $145 but I got just enough I thought for the guitar and the tax. And I come out and I consider the rest of that money taboo. I don't ever know, whatever happened to that. [*Laughs.*]

And then I wanted to figure out how I could finance learning to play it. I'd been taking piano lessons so I could read music. I knew enough about music to move along very swiftly, but I needed a teacher to get me started properly on the new instrument. So, I found a man who had stopped in Houston, Texas. He had an ad in the paper. He had been teaching. He was a white man. His name was Steve Hester. And Steve had been playing with big bands. He had an ad in the paper as a music teacher. Well Houston was kind of an exciting town to be in for musicians. Jobs were plentiful—musicians could get work. Some of the great musicians like Al Grey, that played with Count Basie, musicians would come here and stay. And these musicians were the reason well-known artists like Gatemouth Brown, Johnny Ace, and Bobby Blue Bland were able to have great musical sounds behind their singing on Peacock Records, which was the big record company down there. These guys could come in, they could write music from being in a big band, they knew how to arrange music and make it sound really good and swinging. That enhanced the music and provided the swing for Texas swing music. Steve was a big band guitar player, he played in the big band style and he knew how to read music. And he could teach guitar. So, I went to him. I learned in three months. How to play like Gatemouth Brown, T-Bone Walker, and Lightning Hopkins. I figured out how to go once he taught me the skills and then I added the different things that I already knew about from the piano. It all made a nice wonderful transition for me very fast. So, in three months, I was ready to go play my first job.

Was it unusual for a white guy to take on a Black student at that time?

Not him, because he was an international traveler, you know, with the big band. And I don't remember where he came from, but he was different in that sense, because he was a big band guitar player, and he was around music. I used to go into his neighborhood which was the white neighborhood to take my lessons.

I was playing with a man named V.S. Freeman. V.S. Freeman was basically my age then—maybe a year or two older. V.S. Freeman, you would know if you followed B.B. King. He became B.B. King's drummer and bandleader. When I was fourteen and had been playing three months, V.S. Freeman offered me a job. I went off to his house and rehearsed. And when the time came for the job, I'd catch the bus all the way into his area and then I was to meet him on a corner at six o'clock in the evening. He would pick me up and take me to this job—that was the plan. Well, the bus got there late and it was a deal that turned out very bad for me. V.S. already left. He was gone. I sat there and I sat there and waited with my guitar, my new guitar, my Kay, and my new amp. And I'm thinking man any minute somebody could come along here and rob me. And it started getting dark, and now I'm getting really scared. Because I'm only fourteen so tears started coming out my eyes, I was trying to figure how I'm going to get out of this. In those days they didn't have cell phones—and you couldn't call Mama—you had to make a decision. So, a man came by in a Cadillac, a brand-new Cadillac. He let the window down—he mashed a button and the window came down! That was spooky right there. [*Laughs.*] He said, "Kid—what are you doing with that guitar? Can you play it?" "Oh, yes sir." "What're you crying about?" I said, "Well, I was supposed to go play a job with V.S. Freeman." He said, "I know V.S.! He lives right down the road from my house." So, I said, "Yeah, I was supposed to play a job for him, but he left me—and I ain't got no way home—and I don't know what to do." He said, "You get in the car with me, and you come go to my house. I'm going to change my clothes. I'm a mechanic and I fix cars. I know a place where I can take you and you can play all you want. We're gonna see if you can play that thing. If you can play that thing—you got a job!"

I was kind of leery of him but he looked like a nice man. He had a very pleasant face. I got in the car with him. He went to his house and he was married. And he took this good long time taking a shower because he had his head dirty from working on cars. And he had cars in the front yard—all over, all you'd see were cars and car parts—and dogs barking, guarding his cars at night but it was nice house in a nice little neighborhood. And he took his shower. He come out of there *sharp* man. His name was Hot Papa. Hot Papa became a very, very interesting part of my family. He started fixing all our cars, my mother's cars, my uncles and my brother's cars. He just became a great part of our life, because he fixed them at a good deal. He was just a good mechanic and he didn't charge a lot. So, he takes me off to this club called the Whispering Pines. And there was a man there with a corsage in his coat lapel. And he had like a gold/beige looking suit—double breasted. And he had his hair slicked back and he was a good-looking man. He stood tall and his shoes were shined—and his club looked something like Roberts Show Lounge here in Chicago. The dance floor was lit up. In the center of the floor was just straight out and all the chairs and tables sat around the dance floor and the bandstand. The bandstand was at the end of the dance floor and elevated, maybe two feet up—because you walk up steps to get on the bandstand. It had rails around that. So, I used to walk out when I was going on that first night. I knew three songs. I knew "Boogie Rambler" by Gatemouth Brown, and I knew "Cold, Cold Feeling" by T-Bone Walker, and I knew another song "Going to the Station—Catch the Fastest Train" that was by T-Bone as well.

I was ready for them—I had my show. I told them what I wanted them to play behind me. And I kicked the song off and, man, the house went wild! Wow, they saw this little young kid playing that guitar with a baby face and playing it behind his head—all the same stuff I do today. I'm sixty-five, I've been doing this job for fifty-one years.

And that night I just kept increasing the pace. When I finished the first song, I didn't wait for them to applaud—I kicked off the next one and I was gone. You know, and it was because the people were throwing so much money at me and I got excited—Wow! I never had as much money before. If I had worked with V.S. that night, I would have made $3.50—and then got left on the corner. Well, the audience threw over $100 out there, at least—maybe $200 just by the time I finished the first song. Once they started throwing that money, I just keep playing that same song. And then the man that brought me out there, always carried, I found out later, he always carried $1,000 in his pocket. It was in $100 bills. And he would wave these $100 bills up around my guitar then stick it up in the neck, that's where the pegs are. Right up there and I'd be going around to the next table. And boy people started throwing fifties! And twenties at me on the floor. It must have been $500 easy out there on that floor after I finished those three songs I knew. And the man told everybody, he said, "Would y'all like to have him back here on a weekly basis every Friday and Saturday?" They screamed throughout the hall—and they hired me right there in front of all the people—and he was paying me. I was getting $14 a night. So, I went from $3.50 to $14 just like that—and tips. And Mr. Oakman, he had a cleaner in town, and he kept all his clothes so clean, nice. He was just a sharp man. He must have been in his early forties or late thirties. But he ran a great club. And I worked there and made my name from there. T-Bone heard about me from that club and everybody that came to Houston would hear about me from that club. Because I was so young. And I was entertaining.

I was only doing shows. I never had to play with another band. I didn't even play with my brother's band anymore. I never played guitar with my brother's band because of that. I didn't play guitar with any other band, because I was featured all over town. I got so popular. They called me "The fourteen-year-old sensation." I got so popular until I would play at the Eldorado in the mid part of the night, I would play at a place called the Gypsy Gardens, on Lawrence Avenue, where all the main little clubs were—where you could hear, if anybody got a hit record, you could hear this going down Lawrence Avenue. You could go from one club to another to another. When B.B. King had a hit record, "Please Love Me," you could hear the intro in one club and then when you're in the next one he's singing, "Well please love me baby . . ." and hear the record finish in the next club. And it was just that way all the way down. That was exciting with all of these beer joints. They didn't sell whiskey in those clubs—they were beer joints. They hired me to play. There, I would start the night out at Whispering Pines—that would be my first show. I'd do my three songs there—I still didn't know but three songs—and then I'd come over and do my songs way out in the Third Ward—and then I'd come back to the one on Fifth Ward, on Lyons Avenue. So, by this time I'm going to play my last show at the Whispering Pines. See, the Whispering Pines gets two shows, but the rest of them only get one. Yeah, because we had to be out of those clubs at 12 o'clock. Their time was from eight to twelve—that was the way the law works—Saturday night they could go to one o'clock. That's the way it was in my early childhood.

T-Bone Walker heard about me and he wanted to know where this kid was from. They said that this kid plays just like T-Bone. He mentioned that he would like to see him. So, when T-Bone came to town, I didn't give him a chance to look for me—I took my mother, and she carried me to where he was playing. He was at the city auditorium, which was a big venue. And T-Bone, at that time, was bigger than life. Well, T-Bone was a very generous man—and he was that way until he died. Maybe people have changed over time, but back then he'd let somebody that he knew played guitar and were popular in a town or were trying to make a start, or start a career, he would call someone up on the bandstand and have him play a song in front of the entire audience—maybe 1000 or 2000 people in a big auditorium. So, when I went to see him, I was trying to figure out how to get back where he was at—and I just went to the side of stage. The band was playing. And I spoke to the guard. He told me I couldn't come back there. I said, "Well, this is my mama. I'm Roy Gaines—I'm the one that T-Bone wants to hear play. I play like him. And I heard he wants to meet me." So, the guard said, "Stay right here!" and he went behind the curtain and he came back in no time—when he came back, he said, "C'mon!" So, I walked to the back of the stage, the band was there—and who's standing there surrounded by people? It's T-Bone! And T-Bone broke up the circle of people that were surrounding him and he said, "Come here! Are you the little boy I've been hearing about?" "Yes sir." And he said, "You stay right here. I'm going on. And I'm going to call you up and you're going to play some after I do three songs." Oh-oh what did he say that for? I wasn't expecting anything like that. And you can just imagine someone that's walking up to their idol—and I'm a young guy. I mean, I'm just still fourteen, and I had made a little noise before, but not on stage with T-Bone, you know. And I started thinking about it and I didn't have time to discuss it with him—he's already on stage, he's playing and people screaming and hollering in the audience—and I'm getting more scared by the second. I felt like I was on a Ferris wheel. I was tightening up. I wanted him to call me up—but at the same time I didn't want him to call me up because I didn't think I could handle it. But he called me up, just as he said, after that third number. And when I came out people started screaming and T-Bone said, "There's a kid here that they say plays just like me. I've never heard him and I want to hear him myself." He called me up—and he took his guitar and started putting it on me. He took the guitar strap and made it shorter for me. And then just as he made me afraid by calling me up, he made me relax—and this is all he said. He said, "I'm going to sing and you're going to play." He said, "We're going to do 'Cold, Cold Feeling,'" and that just relaxed me, because that was one of the three songs that I knew—I was home free. He told me to kick it off because it was a guitar intro. I played that little arpeggio and he came in singing "It's a cold, cold feeling . . ." and when I hit those licks behind him, and played them just like he did, those people went crazy! And T-Bone and I were friends until he died.

How did you make contact with the Groove Label?

I had a Black manager in New York. He was a very unique man; his name was Joel Tonarrow. He wore a process like all the guys did back then. I had one and just about everybody had one. He was a very intelligent man in the music business. He was educated, he was a good writer. When I say writer, he could write songs—and write articles about things. So, he took me on as a client. And we discussed the way I looked at the time and the possibility of directing my career.

When you say "the way you looked," because if you were young and handsome, you would have star quality?

They thought it would be easy to make that move—I'd make a lot of money as a young teenage idol, you know, and they could make a lot of money as managers and record companies. It didn't quite turn out that way but there were several records made. I don't know if you have "This Ain't Love," "Skippy Is a Sissy," "Dee Dat Dee Dum Dum," "Right Now Baby" and those songs. Well, all this music we're talking about came because I was young and good looking. Everybody's been young and cute at one time—and I was just like Chuck Berry, and Elvis Presley and Jerry Lee Lewis and the Big Bopper and different people that came along at that time. And records that I made reflect my crossover attempt—to be what Elvis Presley was, "Skippy Is A Sissy" was a crossover attempt to be where Little Richard and Chuck Berry were.

When you use the word crossover. You're basically trying to find a white audience?

Yeah, yeah—Rock and Roll. Yeah, they were making the kind of money that I just dreamed about. I was fortunate enough to be recorded on same label as Elvis Presley. "Skippy Is A Sissy" was on RCA Victor, Groove is a subsidiary of RCA Victor, when we started doing more stuff. At that time, King Curtis, the great saxophone player, he was a session musician. He's playing solos on my records. And George Rose the conductor went on to become Sammy Davis's main conductor. George was my arranger on "Dee Dat Dum Dum," and "Right Now Baby," and a lot of those things I did on Groove. "Night Beat" sort of snuck in there as an offbeat instrumental that we would play just before I'd bring Chuck Willis on stage. It was a song that people liked every time we played it. And I said to myself, "The next time I record I'm going to record that." And I did—it's on the Deluxe label. Do you have any of the Deluxe recordings? "Gainesville," that was on Deluxe. Do you know why they have such distinct sounds? There was a man named Andy Gibson, who was an arranger for King Records in New York. These are the King Record guys in New York, and he wrote those horns arrangements on "Gainesville." And those guys were veterans of the big band era.

Clarence Hollomon was the inspiration for me wanting a guitar because I used to see him before I knew I was going to play guitar. He had a brother named Sweets Holloman, and Sweets Holloman was a pianist who played exactly like Charles Brown. Sweets copied the actions and the whole flamboyant way to present a blues—and, he knew how to encourage Clarence to play in the style of Johnny Moore and Oscar Moore—players who played with Charles Brown—and they played together as a quartet. They had drummer, bass, and Sweets on piano. Sweets was the leader—and he was a costume maker, he made clothes. He made uniforms for different people. So, their group was always sharp. They were always looking sharp. They were playing in a place called Tip Top Inn. And Clarence—I just admire him so much. Clarence was this little thin guy and he was little all his life. They called him Gristle. His nickname was Gristle. He was a little guy. And he was one of my best friends. He taught me the first chord on guitar. Before I went to Steve Hester, I called Clarence up and asked if I could come to his house and play. And so, he said, "Come on over boy." So, I went over and he showed me a B flat chord or two-finger B flat chord, which is three strings. And he said, "Let's go outside and play." I said, "I won't be able to concentrate." And he said, "No, c'mon, let's go out and play. You don't want to learn too much at once." So, he's out there throwing the ball and a big Doberman Pinscher came running around the corner and he's got this dog—and this dog's as big as both of us. And he said, "I'm going to give you another lesson." I said, "What's that?" He said, "When you see a dog that scares you out of your wits—don't move! Just don't move. And watch—he'll come up here, and he'll go away—but don't move." Oh man, that was a hard decision for me to make. [*Laughs.*] So I figured Clarence called me over to his house to play and then told me to go outside and play—and had his dog come up to me and make me stand at attention—and wet in my pants! That's almost what I did! I said, "Oh God, this big dog, I hope he goes away soon . . ." and he went away. Clarence said, "See?" But that lesson did come into play.

Once, when I was in Houston, I was waiting to hear a tape Clarence played on. He had played with Don Wilkerson. Don Wilkerson was a very important musician in Houston, Texas. And he and Clarence played together because Clarence could play jazz with him. They both could play jazz together. And this guy who played bass with Bobby Blue Bland had this particular tape of Clarence playing with Don Wilkerson. I saw him on the street and he said, "I got a tape of them together." So, I went over to his house to hear it. When we pulled up in his yard, he got out and opened the gate. We pulled in and he went back and closed the gate. Then he tapped on the window where this big dog was hitting at the window. Then he opened the garage without talking to me—without telling me, you know, he's going to open this garage. And I started to say, "Hey man . . ." But then I thought about what Clarence said and so I decide not to move. You know. So, he opened the garage door and his big Doberman Pinscher came out. Man! He hit that dog on the face with a paper. He said, "He thinks he's bad—but he's not bad." So, we went on in his house. We went into a little room and he let me hear the music. Yes, he put the tape on. As he put the tape on, the dog jumped up onto his recliner chair right across from me. But after he put the tape on, he left the room. He walked right between the dog and I, and went out the room. Me and the dog are there together but the guy's gone. I wanted to say, "Hey, man, don't go—don't leave the room," but the dog would have picked up on it. And I sat on this little couch here—the dog's here and I'm just sitting right here. Well—I tried to stay normal at this point, because I remember what Clarence said about—don't move! So, I didn't move—and I wouldn't give the dog any eye contact. And I wouldn't move. And I was listening to Clarence's tape. So, the guy left the room and he's gone too long. The dog wanted me to look, you know, he wanted me to look at him. I won't look at him—and I won't move. And I didn't move. But about two or three minutes went by, maybe more, I don't know. It seemed like an eternity for me. So, the guy came back. And I said, "Hey, you know what?" I spoke very calmly. I said, "I've really got to go. I started some things back at my house that I've got to finish. It just won't wait." So, I got out of there, man, and he was taking me home, dropping me off. And I gave him a piece of my mind. I told him how uncomfortable he had made me. I didn't care—I didn't ever want to see him again—and I never have seen him. So that's how Clarence taught me a second lesson that day. And if I hadn't gone outside and played with him and listened to him, I wouldn't have known that dog lesson.

Guitar Shorty

David Kearney, known to Blues fans around the world as Guitar Shorty, came to my attention through a series of recordings he made for the LA-based Pull record label. The Alligator label was handling Shorty at that time, issuing his CDs and booking him into Buddy Guy's Legends in Chicago, on a regular basis. I got in touch with the folks at Alligator and they were kind enough to arrange the following interview on Shorty's next trip to Chicago.

■ ■ ■

My name is David Kearney. I was born in Houston, Texas; raised up in Florida. And I've been trying to play a guitar ever since I was six years old. And my mother, before she passed, was telling me all the things I used to do when I was a little baby boy. She said I used to crawl around on the floor, get up—this was before I knew anything about a guitar—get up on the piano. Of course, she had an upright piano in the house and she said that her and my daddy noticed that I would take and pick up notes on the piano, on the piano playing the boogie-woogie style. They said [*in a deep bass voice*]: "Dum, dum, dum, dum." She noticed I was doing that so she said to my father, she said, "The boy's got talent." And he looked at me and laughed. He said, "Oh, he's just playing around. He can't do that anymore." And she said a few days later and she noticed that I was doing the same thing again. And, any time I heard music, I'd be dancing to the music. It was as though anything that came up, I was just all over the place trying to dance. And my grandmother had a little harmonica. She said I would pick the harmonica up but don't know how I found it. I'd be blowing on the harmonica. Couldn't play but I was just making all kind of noise on it. So anyway, they had considered that I had talent. And my grandmother—she was the one that raised me.

So, my uncle, which was her son—his name was Willie Quarterman—he had a guitar. And he used to take the guitar and he'd be walking down through the streets at night after he had got off work. Going out through the neighborhood. He would take the guitar—he would take anything, anything that you said, he would make a song out of it. He was that kind of a guy. I always wanted to be like my Uncle Willie. I would take his guitar, when he'd go to work. I would take it—pull it out from under the bed [*chuckles*], take it out of the case, lean it up against the wall and I'd fram on it. At this point, I was six years old. And I would fram on the guitar and try to do things. Try to bend the strings like I saw him do. And because I couldn't bend the strings, I would have a tantrum. A baby tantrum. Fall down on the floor and be just screaming and hollering because I couldn't do it. My grandmother, she would run in the room where I was. She'd say, "What's the matter with you, boy?" And I'd say, "Grandma, this thing just don't do what I want it to do. I hate it! I hate it! I hate it!" You know, just mad. She got tired of running into the room after me. I just thought this over—so, one morning, my uncle was on his way to work. She called him, she said, "Willie." He said, "Yes, Momma." "Would you do me a favor?" And he said to her, "Yes, Momma, if I can." She said, "I want you to teach this boy how to play that guitar before I kill him." [*Chuckles.*] And that's how it started with me learning how to play guitar. Whenever he'd come in from work, after we had our dinner, he'd get the guitar and go out on the porch. And he'd sit up there and fool around with the guitar. Then he would take me and set me on his lap and put my hand on the neck of the guitar and put my fingers against the strings. Because my hand couldn't go around the neck at that time because I was too small. And he'd press my hand, my fingers up against the strings. And he'd say, "Now, son, this is what you've got to do to get the sound that I'm getting." And he said, "I'm going to teach you every evening when I come in from work. I'm going to show you as much as I can. But you're going to have work with what I'm showing you." I was tickled pink! I was so glad my uncle was helping me. And every day, he would go to work. When I'd come in from school, I'd go under the bed and get that guitar. Do the same thing over and over and over.

But, by the time I reached seven, for him showing me all this stuff, my grandmother decided she was going to get me a tutor—from school. His name was Mr. Washington. He would help out with music at school. And she got him over and they got together on a price that she would pay him. Because my grandmother was very poor. They couldn't afford to get me an outright teacher. So, they made an agreement for me to take lessons from him. And Mr. Washington was about—I'd say he was about that tall. He was as tall as a midget. He was a dwarf. And he was left-handed but he played guitar right-handed. If you heard him playing guitar, saw him playing right-handed, you'd swear up and down he was right-handed. Anyway, he would come in and he had a Nick Manoloff Guitar Book. That's what I started out with when he started teaching me how to read notes and chord changes and stuff. And what he did was he took the book and started me from scratch. Showing me how to stroke the strings with a pick. He showed me how to hold a pick and everything. And after he showed me that, he showed me how to tune my guitar. This is out of the Nick Manoloff Book. And after he got me squared away on that, he took me right on down from point A to point B, right on. And I was so hung up on learning out of the book, when he gave me a lesson to learn, when he came in—like in the middle of the week, I'd gone two or three pages ahead. I was advancing that fast. Finally, he told my grandmother—he said, "Look, Ms. Quarterman. Why don't we do this? This boy's learning so fast on this guitar," he said, "Why don't we just—I'm going to give him a lesson to get out. And after he's gone in that book as far as he can go, when you see him starting to have problems, you call me. Then I will take the lessons that I taught and if he's got that straight, then I'll go over the other pages that he went through to make sure that he's got it correct." And that's the way I really started moving on my guitar.

I started playing all kind of stuff on guitar. The first thing I learned how to play on guitar was "The Huckle Buck," "The Boogie-Woogie." And I would listen to B.B. King at that time, "Three O'Clock in the Morning." Those are the three songs I learned how to play first on my own. The next thing I know, Mr. Johnson, Walter Johnson, which was Miss Pearl Johnson's son, he taught music at school where I was going at. And he had a wife named Judy and he had a little old small orchestra that he had put together for the weekend. They would go all the way down to Tampa, Florida. They went down to Tampa, Florida, and they had a little old place down there they were playing at, Club Rouse. And he told my grandmother, he said, "I want to take him with me." He said, "This boy's got a lot of talent." Saying, "I want to be responsible for him. There won't be no alcohol on the table where he's sitting." And he promised that he would not let me out of his sight. When I was with him, I was like his own son. So, when he took me down to Kissimmee, Florida, he said, "This is what I want you do to, son. I want you to take your guitar and amp, put the amp behind you." He got a little stool about this tall for me to sit on. He had a little small . . . you've seen these metal music stands? He said, "Now I'm going to put this music in front of you. And I want you to look at this music." He said, "Each time that I call a tune off," he said, "I want you to make sure you move the page and be looking at the same stuff that we're playing. And I want you to keep the guitar turned down, and the amplifier. I don't want any noise. Go through the motion, and stroke like you're playing the rhythm." He said, "One of these nights, we're going to turn that guitar up and you're going to be playing the chords." And that's what I did. I did that about . . . maybe I'd say about two months. That's what I did. I called myself being sneaky. I went up on the bandstand, I went and turned my amp up a little bit, turned the guitar just a little bit so I could kinda hear it. And I started playing chord changes along with the stuff that they were playing. And I could see him kind of looking back at me, smiling. He could hear me. So, when I finished that night, he put his arm around me and he say, "David, you sound good. Keep it up but don't turn it any louder. Let it stay where it's at." [*Chuckles.*] Because I was making mistakes but I was thumbing through it.

Can you tell me what kind of a rig you were playing at that point?

I was using a Silvertone. I had a Silvertone amp and I had a Silvertone guitar. You don't see them anymore. I don't know what the pick-up was then. The pick-ups, they had, they called them lift-tick pick-ups. They were round and had chrome. And I understand those guitars nowadays, if you find one, it's worth a lot of money. So that's the kind of guitar I had.

But anyway, I gradually was getting better and better as time passed. So, I was with Mr. Johnson all the way up until I was nine years old. I was playing then. Bending the strings like a grown person. And so, by the time I reached the age of thirteen, Mr. Dewey Richardson, out of Tampa, Florida, that booked Mr. Johnson in this club—because he was like a booking agent. He came in and made an announcement to the crowd, he said, "Ladies and Gentlemen, next week I'm gonna bring to you this guitar player. His name is Guitar Shorty." And he said, "I'm going to make all of you surprised to see this young man. This young man has got a lot of talent." He said, "Are you ready for a show next week?" They said, "Yeah, it's about time you brought somebody down here." You know how people are when they're drinking. And he said, "Well, next week, Guitar Shorty will be here." So, he walked off the stage. When he walked off the stage, right away, I grabbed Mr. Johnson. I said, "Mr. Johnson, this guy Guitar Shorty," I said, "is he really as good as Mr. Richardson say he is?" He said, "Oh yes. He's a great guitarist." I didn't believe him then when he said he was a great guitarist. I was worried. So, I went to the horn players and asked them. Everybody was taking a break. They were all giggling at me and said, "Oh yeah, Dave. You've got to see this man. This man here is blistering!" Then I got nervous. And I thought I was going to lose my job. On Monday, I went to school. When I came in that evening from school, and I put my books and everything down, and I went straight to the kitchen. I cleaned up all the dishes and everything. Took out the garbage. Went in the room, my grandmother's room, and cleaned it up. I mean, I had that house spotless when she got home. And so, then I went in the room and picked my guitar up. I was working hard on my guitar then. So, when she came in, I heard her say, "Oh my, what's this?" She went in her room and she said, "Oh my God!" I'm fooling around with the guitar like I didn't hear her, you know. So, she came in the room and she said, "What happened?" I said, "What are you talking about Grandma?" She said, "What's the occasion?" I said, "Nothing." She said, "Well you cleaned all this stuff up and I didn't have to even ask you!" I said, "Well, I'm supposed to, right? I thought the best thing for me to do is clean up. You know, you're always taking care of us." She said, "Oh, son, I really appreciate it. Thank you." She said, "Are you sure you're okay?" [*Chuckles.*] I said, "Yes, ma'am." "Everything's all right, son?" I said, "Yes, ma'am." "Okay." So, she went on back in to her bedroom and turned the radio on. She didn't care too much about TV. And I kept on fooling around with my guitar. She came in later on, she said, "Are you sure everything's okay?" I said, "Yes, ma'am, Grandma. Everything's all right." And every day, I'd come home I do the same thing. All the way till time for us to go back to Tampa. We went there every weekend. So, when Mr. Johnson came to pick me up, he said, "Are you okay?" I said, "Yes, I'm alright." My grandma said to him, "I don't know. He's been awful spunky lately—Cleaning the house up, and I don't have to ask him." He started laughing. So anyway, we got down to Tampa. We did one set. And the second set was supposed to have been Showtime. But the whole time I'm up there on that stool, I'm looking back behind me at the door. The green room for the musicians was behind the stage. And the door was cracked, about like this, you know. Where people stand around and look. People were peeping—they'd look at you. I kept looking at that door and it never moved. I kept looking at it and it was still cracked. And anyway, when we took the break, you know, to go off the first time, I asked the guys again, I said, "Where's this guy Guitar Shorty?" "David, don't worry about its Guitar Shorty. He'll be here." [*Chuckles.*] I said, "But I want to see him." He said, "Well, you'll see him in time." I asked Mr. Johnson, "Mr. Johnson," I said, "when is Guitar Shorty coming?" He said, "He'll be here . . . he'll be at the Showtime, son." And so, I'm sitting at the table. I was so nervous I didn't know what to do with myself. So, time to go back on the stage. We went up. The band did a show tune. And when they got through doing the show tune, Mr. Richardson walked up on the stage, said, "Ladies and Gentlemen, it's now show time. Are you ready for a show?" And everybody said, "Yeah!" So, you know, I made you a promise I was going to bring this guy up here named Guitar Shorty. And I'm telling you he's a helluva guitarist." They said, "Yeah, bring the young fella out. We want to see him!" And while he was talking about all these things, he's going to be doing the weeks ahead, I'm sitting on the stool, looking behind me at that door. It has never moved. Still cracked. So, he said, "Ladies and Gentlemen, I guess I've said enough. Why don't we get down to business?" And he said, "Well, I'd like to bring out front to you right now, at this moment, the one and only—Gentlemen, he's come a long way. . . . He's a great entertainer and a guitarist. He's a young fella by the name of Guitar Shorty." And when he said Guitar Shorty, I'm still looking behind me. My heart went boom, boom, boom. [*Laughs.*] And, anyway, the band had kicked off a tune that I always played, and I'm looking. Didn't see no Guitar Shorty. When I looked around, he was standing with the mic in his hand pointing back to me. And when he did that, I froze! I just couldn't move. [*Laughs.*] I couldn't do anything—nothing. The horn players put their instruments down, came out and picked me up and carried me out to the mic. Put me in front of the mic. And I had to do all three of those songs that I learned on my own. If they'd asked me to do something else, I'd be in trouble. "And so, ladies and gentlemen, what do you think of this young guy?" Everybody starts whistling and screaming. Throwing a little bit of money out there for me. And Mr. Johnson made a crack. He said, "I should be Guitar Shorty. You're making more money than me!" [*Chuckles.*]

And so, Mr. Richardson said to me, he said, "Son, I want you to keep this name. You keep this name; it's going to bring you luck. As long as you stick with Guitar Shorty, it's going to be many people in show business, record business or movies that are going to ask you why don't you just use your own name? Say, David Guitar, or Guitar David." He said, "I want you to keep that name." And just like he told me, there's been a many people that ask me why don't I just stick to my birth name and just say Guitar David or David Guitar. And I tell them, I say, "Look. I'm sticking with this name as long as I'm living. And when I'm gone, there's nothing I can do about it."

What kind of stuff were you, were you playing with that band?

They were playing a lot of standards. Like they were doing stuff like "Body and Soul," "I'll Remember April," "When Sunny Gets Blue," "April in Paris." All that kind of big band stuff. And right today, I can still play that stuff. I've been with many bands; they can't play it. And when they put horns behind me, I'm home! That's what I grew up on, playing to the horns. And if you listen to where I solo, I don't play guitar solos like the average guitar player do. I try to make my instrument sound like a tenor sax! That's the way I play my lead. And I was telling a good guitar player about that along not too long ago. He says, "I notice that your style is unique and it's altogether different from any guitar player I've ever heard." I said, "That's where it's coming from horn players." I said, "I don't listen to guitar players any more like I used to because I'm trying to be creative. It's good to listen to other people, but you don't have to listen to the same instrument that you play. You can listen to something else, like a guy playing a Hammond organ or somebody playing keyboards." And that's what I do.

I was down in Tampa, still fooling around with Walter and them. And this guy had a pawn shop there. Its name was Pawn Shop Louie's. B.B. King loved the ground he walked on. And so, Mr. Louie was called . . . kind of managing me, trying to help me. So, he said to me, he said, "Son, say I've got something for you." I said, "What's that?" He says, "Me and Willie Dixon, we're going to take you to Chicago." I said, "What?!" "They want to record you. Cobra Records want to record you." I said, "You're going to take me to Chicago to record me?!" He said, "Yeah." I was seventeen years old. And so, he said, "Yeah, Willie Dixon really likes you." He said, "This is a good stepping-stone for you, son." He said, "Now to make this official with you, when you go," he said, "I got a little present for you." He took me back to the pawn shop. Got a little Fender Deluxe amp and gave me my first strat I've had in my life. Stratocaster guitar. And he said, "This is for your birthday, son. Happy Birthday!"

I didn't know what to do with the guitar because I'd never had nothing like that play so easy. So anyway, about two weeks after that, that's when they flew me into Chicago to record. And the first song that I ever recorded was called "You Don't Treat Me Right" and "I Got a Girl Named Irma Lee." [*Sings:*] "I got a girl named Irma Lee. And she's just like honey to me." I used to sing that one. "I want to stay with her, to sleep with her, stay with her all my life."

Where did you record when you got here?

I don't know where the studio was but it was for Cobra. I think it was right down from Chess, Chess Records.

It was a bona fide studio? Because I know a lot of their stuff took place in a converted garage that they had rigged to be a studio.

Yes, it was, it was a studio because I do remember, at that time, Otis Rush was playing rhythm guitar for me. Yeah, I remember that.

The rest of the band were all Chicago guys?

Yeah.

You don't have any recollection of who they were at that time?

No, I don't. I do remember Otis. I remember him, very well.

Dixon was producing. Did you know any of the rest of the guys from Cobra at all?

I remember the guy that owned the company, but I don't remember his name. Those were the first two songs that I'd written. I tried to sing them at the time and couldn't. And Willie shut the whole thing down. He said, "Oh, son, I tell you what I'm going to do. You going to come with me and I'm going to teach you how to sing this stuff we have. You can't sing them this way. We'll never get a recording."

He took me away from the studio for two days and we got that stuff worked out. He took me back in the studio and I ran it down like clockwork. Then after that, the next thing I know I was hearing my stuff on the air. Didn't even know how to follow up. I didn't know anything about it. All I knew was I had two songs out there. It was a 45.

My first break out of Florida was with Ray Charles. Ray took me on my first tour of my life, of my career. I was a young kid. And when we went down through Florida and down through Georgia and Alabama, round through Louisiana, we got far as New Orleans, Louisiana. Then I got scared and wanted to go back. Yeah, I told the manager that my grandmother was sick. [*Laughs.*] I told a fib to go back. He said, "Okay, Shorty." He said, "I hate to see you go but since your grandma's sick, you've got to go home." So, he says, "You got our itinerary and all you have to do is when your grandmother gets better, call me. I'll make sure you got a flight, have everything taken care of for you." I said, "Okay, I'll do that." But when I got back, I just decided to stay back there. The next thing I know, Guitar Slim came through. When I got with Slim, I left there with him to Tampa. And we toured all over the same places I did with Ray. We went all through Mississippi, Georgia, Alabama, all around through California and around through Seattle. We went to New York. And by the time we finished the tour, we ended up back in Louisiana. Then I was staying at a place called Thibodaux, Louisiana. That's where Slim was staying at, with his manager, Hosea Hill. And so, we're staying there, working in and out. I stayed with them for about a little better than three years. Then I decided it was time for me to leave. Slim had a good band. In fact, I was with him when he had Lloyd Lambert on bass.

Was there room in the band for two guitars?

Well, I was opening the show for him. So, I opened the show. He had me. Also, he had Carol Fran and he had a guy named Thunderbird. His name was James Davis but he took the name Thunderbird because he loved Thunderbird wine. [*Laughs.*] And you'd say, "What's the word?" "Thunderbird!" "What's the price?" "Thirty twice!" [*Laughs.*] And him and Slim? Oh man, they used to get wiped out on wine. Guitar Slim had recorded a song called "Love Is Just Like Quicksand. You can't stop when you're sinking down." And when Slim would get ready to do his show, he would start doing that song. When he'd start "Love's like quicksand; you can't stop when you're sinking down," I know he's gettin' ready to act crazy. So, I started watching him as he'd do his show because his valet was very tall. He was like about 6'2", 6'3". He would back up to the stage and Slim would climb up on his shoulders. And put his legs across his shoulders and this valet would wrap his arms around his legs, like to hold him. He'd walk down through the crowd with the guitar behind his head, playing the guitar, walking around through the crowd, as far as he can go. When he reached the length of the cord, then he would stop and turn around and come back the same way he went. Get back to the stage. Slim would get off his shoulders. And then when he got off this valet's shoulders, he would hit the floor and run all the way back out as far as he can go with that cord. Then he would turn around and run back, fall down on the floor with the guitar and roll over on his back. Don't care what kind of suit he had on. He didn't care. Put the guitar across his chest and he'd just begin to playing it. Then he would take the guitar off his chest and he would roll over, put the guitar behind his head, with his side leaning on the floor, play that guitar. And when he'd get up, he'd be so dirty it looked like somebody had drug him all over the place! [*Chuckles.*] But that's the kind of show he'd put on for the people and they ate it up! And that's where my show came from. It's a take-off of Guitar Slim's show.

When he kept doing that, I said, "If he can do that, I can turn flips." So anyway, we had some time off. I would go back sometimes to Florida to see my grandma. So, this particular time, I went back and I decided to call Barney Louis. Barney Louis used to work with BB. His real name was Hubert Louis. We called him Barney Google Louis. And Barney called me up one day and wanted to know what I was doing. I said, "Just lying in bed, man, waiting for something to happen." But I said, "If anything come up as far as work, I got a surprise for you!" "You do?!" And I said, "Yes, I do." He said, "Well, why don't we do this." He said, "I've got something happening in Daytona Beach. Do you think you can go to Daytona Beach?" I said, "When?" He said, "Can you be up there Friday?" I said, "Yeah." "Okay, meet me at the el." And he gave me the address. So that night we were playing up there and we got through playing the first set, he said, "Okay, Shorty. What's that surprise you're going to show me?" "Okay, I'll show it to you on the next break, man. Come up and do a show and I'll show it to you." So, anyway, when we went back up, they did a show tune. Then he said, "Now, ladies and gentlemen, it's show time now. How'd you like to see Guitar Shorty do his stuff out in front?" And everybody started calling for me. I sang about three songs. Then when I got back, I walked back up to the stage—because I had to do my show out in front of the band stand, out on the dance floor, I said, "Okay." I said, "Give me a little thing in the key of G." So okay, I kicked it off. I gave them the tempo I wanted, and I walked out, and I started singing. "They call me Guitar Shorty. I came here to play in your town. If you don't like the way I sing the blues, I will not hang around." I'm doing all this and I kind of clown with the guitar and dancing out on the floor with the guitar. And I walked back up to the stage whilst I'm doing this. He said, "Is that your surprise?!" I said, "Just wait a minute. I got it. Let me show it to you." And, man, I started running with that guitar. Jumped up in the air. Tried to flip and landed right on my head! I'm trying to walk the hurt off, I'm wobbly in the knees. I hit that concrete floor. And so, I kinda of look around at Bonnie. Bonnie's playing the sax. His jaw's all puffed up. He's trying to keep from laughing. [*Chuckles.*] So, anyway, I walked to the stage, still playing guitar and clowning a little bit. People thought it was in the act! They didn't know I was hurt. I said to him, I said, "I'm gonna' get it taken care of for you, man." He said, "Is that your surprise, man?" I said, "Just hold on. I'm gonna do it, man. This time." Like that. I said, "Just bear with me." By the time I made up my mind, I said, "Lord, please, let me do this. Don't let me get hurt again." I got that guitar, man, I and started bending the strings and clowning with it. And started running at the time and jumped up in the air and hit that floor again, right on top of my head. This time I hit it so hard I could see blood stars. You know, how when you joke? I got up. I was dizzy that time. But I managed to hold on when I'm trying to walk that hurt off. By the time I had a big knot on my head! [*Laughs.*] By the time I got back to Bonnie, Bonnie said, "Shorty, is that your surprise?" I said, "Just hold on, man. I'm gonna do this if it kills me!" He said, "Shorty, I'm not gonna stay up here and play for you until you kill yourself." And I looked back. All the horns walked off the stage. The rhythm section was still playing. And they didn't know what was going on. They thought that it was in the act. They kept right on playing. So, by them playing, it gave me another chance. I started praying and talking to the Lord. I said, "Lord, this time please don't let me get hurt." I got up and I started running—and I guess this time I got enough speed going on. What you call that force and everything. And I jumped up in the air and give myself a good boost and I landed on my feet. I closed my eyes because I thought I was going to fall again! And when I landed on my feet, the people jumped up and started throwing money and everything on the floor. And the janitor had one of these long push brooms and started pushing the money up to the band stand. And by that time, the horns went back up and took the song out for me. They had joined me again to finish it up. And so, after that, there was a guy that was watching me. He was an old guy. His name was Billy Preston. And every time I tell people Billy Preston, they would think I was talking about THE Billy Preston. "No," I said, "this was a white guy." And he handed me his card and he said, "Son, I see what you're trying to do." He said, "Give me a call. I can help you." I was hurting then. I said, "Okay. Yeah, okay." [*Chuckles.*]

When I went home, I told my grandmother what happened. She saw that knot on my head, she said, "What'd you do?" So, I told her. She said, "What are you going do? Commit suicide?!" [*Laughs.*] I said, "No, Grandma. I've just got some idea and I've got to work on it and I'm gonna develop it." She said, "Be careful. I don't want you to kill yourself." Anyway, I told her about this guy. She said, "Why don't you give him a call?" So, I called him up and he told me he was waiting on me to call him. He said, "Come on over here, son. We can have a little talk and I can help you." I went up there and he had a gym. He took me through and it had everything you could think of in there. Guys go in there to learn how to box, martial arts, and . . .

Wait—he's not going to book you—he's going to teach you how to tumble?

Yeah, he did. [*Laughs.*] He taught me how to do it. And next thing I know, I got involved in it so much. I loved it so much because I had this body control. And I did the flips all the way up until '84. I got hurt in '84. I got run over by a car. This leg here, I can't hardly use it sometimes. Sometimes this leg hurts so bad I can't walk. But anyway, it worked for me all the way until '84. And then he worked for me from the '80s all the way up into the '90s. Thirty-six. . . . I can't think of the play I was but it was in Indiana. And the club had a bandstand about six foot above the floor or better. BIG gigantic stage. And I was doing my show there and when I was doing my finale, that's my last tune. When I was singing "They Call Me Guitar Shorty," I ran across the stage. I went to the left, flipped. And then I turned this way . . . because when I turn a flip and land, I would actually turn and go back the other way. And I did a flip that way and when I turned to go back this way . . . I was gonna turn a flip then I was gonna roll back and flip up, stand on my head and my shoulder. That didn't happen. I went this way and I turned around to go that way, the guy had a spotlight right in my face. I couldn't see my footing because he was following me with that light. And I felt something hit my feet—because I was going, trying to do the flip—and I knew then that was it. I knew I was going to get hurt. I had to do some fast thinking. Hit the floor on stage or fall off on the dance floor and kill myself. So, I hit the floor on the stage, dislocated my right shoulder. And I ended up right here, in Chicago, afterward. I went to the hospital here. The company I was with—some of their staff was here and didn't know I got hurt. It was in the papers and everything. They came here, when I got to Chicago. They said, "You ain't going on tonight. We're going to take you to the hospital." And when I got hit, they even told me at the club, "Shorty, you don't have to turn no flips here. We know you're hurt. You play enough guitar; you don't need to be turning no flips." So anyway, they took me here and the doctor x-rayed my shoulder, my right shoulder. Said, "We don't see where it's dislocated now." And I told them about the noise that I heard after I left—because I was driving, with this hand. My drummer was sitting on the passenger side and my shoulder had raised up and it was swollen really bad. And when he heard the noise, he said, "What was that?" I said, "I don't know but I heard it too." So, I kept on driving and all of a sudden, I started feeling better driving. And later on, down the road, he asked me, "How do you feel?" I said, "I feel fine." "How's your shoulder?" I said, "It's a little sore but not as sore as it was." I didn't know that it went back in place. So, when I told the doctor that he took x-rays, and he said, "Your shoulder went back in place, Mr. Kearney. You're a lucky man that we didn't have to put it back." Because he saw a hairline crack where it had been, where it had moved out. He said, "It was dislocated but by it going back in, it saved you a lot of pain. You THINK you was in pain," he said, "if we'd had to put that arm back in place to your shoulder, you woulda had some pain!" Before I left the hospital, they gave me a sling to put this arm in. I still have it. They said, "When you're not using it, keep it in the sling." They wanted me to do it for at least six months. And I did what they asked me to do, but it sure was hard. Keep putting my arm in the sling. Anyway, that's where my show came from. It's a take-off of the Guitar Slim Show.

We're down in Ft. Lauderdale. Yeah, 250-foot guitar cord. He would go all the way out in the street with the guitar, as far as he can go. And do that. Do anything to draw attention. He did that. When I saw him doing all that there, I said, "Well, I might as well join him." I ran across the stage a couple of times with the guitar, doing a flip and did my little thing. There were some tables right up close to the bandstand. I backed up and got a running start, jumped over the tables and hit the floor when I flipped. And when I got through with my little show and everything, I came back up on stage and took it out. So, when Slim got through doing his song, he was gonna try something different. Up, over the bandstand, there was some racking like frame, that you could grab. Slim had been drinking. If he hadn't been drinking, it wouldn't have happened. Slim got around to playing that guitar and he ran and jumped up and grabbed the thing. He grabbed the rack and didn't quite make it, and his hand slipped. There were tables and everything down there. [*Laughs.*] He went down on top of the tables. There were drinks that were flying. [*Laughs.*] People nowadays would probably get mad at you. But back then, people would come out to have a good time. That's what they did. And he got up off the floor, and this lady had a brand-new gown. She'd just got married. She had come out for a good time. And she didn't get mad. She was screaming and hollering, just laughing—And her husband—he was in tears. So Slim, when he got back on the stage, he said, "Ladies and Gentlemen, I'm so sorry." He says, "Sir, all of you up front here.

Don't worry, so the management will take care of you." When he said that, everybody started laughing again. [*Laughs.*] I'll never forget that. I've thought about it. I wish I'd had a camera and got a picture. T-bone had a long cord too, you know. He used to walk out in the crowd with his guitar. There was Johnny Guitar Watson—he did the same thing. Albert Collins did the same up until his last day. But actually, me and Guitar Slim was the first ones started that.

I told you about James Davis. Okay, now, his nickname was Thunderbird. What happened was they was going to Houston, Texas twice a week with James Davis. And I found out from other people that they were recording James Davis.

Recording for Don Robey (Peacock Records Houston)?

Yeah. No, I was interested in going with Don Robey but at that time, all I wanted to do was get away from Hosea Hill. I figured I'd get a break if I got away from him. And, I said to myself, this is not right. I'm the one that's holding the shows up for Slim. They should be recording me. And when I talked to Hosea Hill about it, Hosea said to me, "Don't worry Shorty, we're gonna record you." I said, "But you should be recording me now, don't you think?" I said, "I'm out here fronting Slim. Holding his thing together when I should have stuff of my own. You know, that's something I can fall back on." "Just be patient, Shorty." So, I kept seeing this happening over and over. So, I just got tired and I said to myself, I said, "Boy, I've got to do something with my life because I'm not gettin' any younger."

Had you made a record to this point?

No. And so, I went to him and told him that I was going to leave. He said, "Well, Shorty, you don't have to do that." I said, "No, I think I better. I've got to find a way to get outta here. I've got to do something for myself." So, what that was—we had some gigs coming up. We had about a month worth of work. And we end up in New Orleans at a place called The Eagle. It was a club called The Eagle. And when we played there, Frank Pania was down there. The guy that owned the Dew Drop Inn. Frank said to me, he said, "Shorty, I heard through the grapevine that you were thinking about leaving Slim." I said, "Boy, news sure travels fast!" [*Chuckles.*] And he said, "Well, if you decide to leave and you want a job," he said, "I got a place for you." He said, "I can't pay you no money right now," he said, "but I can give you a place to stay, make sure you got plenty of food, take care of your clothes for you." So, when we finished up with Slim, went back to Thibodaux, Louisiana, that's when I told him I was gonna leave. We didn't fall out. He said, "Well, Shorty, let me tell you, if you gotta do that, I'll do everything I can to help you. If you need us . . . need anything from me, don't be afraid to call me."

So, with me working there, for Frank Pania, I got a chance to see many groups come to that little old place—the Dew Drop Inn. I saw Little Richard come through there. T-Bone Walker. Earl King, Gatemouth Brown, Big Joe Turner. I saw many of them go right through that place. But Sam [Cooke]—I never seen Sam come in there. Sam played the Longshoremen's Hall in New Orleans. It's a big place. And what happened was I had just gotten through doing a show that night at the Dew Drop Inn. That morning by, say about four o'clock, somebody knocked on my door. And I said, "Who is it?" He says, "It's me. Bob Tate! Open the door!" And I'm sitting up there trying to think of Bob Tate. I don't know a Bob Tate. [*Chuckles.*] And he said, "You gonna let me stand out here, man? It's cold out here!" It was cold. So, I opened the door and let him in. And I said, "Have a seat." I said, "Whatchu doing here? Why you come here?" He said, "Somebody told me that you are a helluva guitarist." I said, "I don't know about being a helluva guitarist." I say, "I work hard and I try to do the best that I can and give the people a good show." He said, "Well, Sam Cooke is interested in you." I said, "You with Sam Cooke?" He said, "Yeah. I'm Sam Cooke's band director." He said, "My orchestra is the one playing behind Sam." That's when Sam Cooke had Lou Rawls and George McKern with him and Cliff White—plays rhythm guitar—for the Ink Spots. He was playing for Sam at that time. So, I said, "Okay." I said, "What's the money? What's in it?" So, the price they gave me—I said, "When do you want me to come?" [*Chuckles.*] He said, "Tomorrow. We got to rehearse tomorrow. We want to hear you. We want you to audition for him." So, I went the next day and played one song, and went to go into another one. And he gave Bob the okay sign. So, I said, "What's up?" He said, "You don't have to play no more. You're hired!" So, I said, "When are we leaving?" He said, "We're leaving in the morning at nine o'clock. Can you go?" I said, "Well, my clothes are packed. Man, I'm ready!" So, of course, I had to talk to Frank and let him know that I had a break to get away from there. He hated to see me go. But any way, I got on the road with him and we toured all over the place.

Me and Sam Cooke were doing a show in Orlando. We were doing a show there. I'd just walk out there on stage at night, jewelry on, all my chains and all that stuff. Decked out, shirt opened. Sam did the same thing. And I'm playing guitar along with him. We were doing a finale. We made a mistake and got too close to the edge of the stage. The crowd, women, everybody just grabbed us and snatched us off the stage before we could get away! [*Laughs.*] The stage hands were trying to get them away from us and by the time they got to him, the crowd took all Sam's jewelry, and got mine. [*Laughs.*] I'll never forget that! They didn't try to hurt us. They were just over-joyed. And when we got down on the floor, whoever was involved took advantage of it. But now, if you see me on stage, you'll see . . . I still stand back!

Pull Records—that was Charlie Reynolds. His main label was Flash. Pull was like a little branch off of Flash Records. I recorded "This Is a Hard Life" and "Ways of a Man." I can't think of all the stuff I did for him; it's been so long now. But I recorded enough stuff for Charlie Reynolds to do at least a couple of albums. It was a small company; didn't have a whole lot of money. I got to Pull through Bob Tate. Bob Tate lead the band with Sam Cooke. When we got to LA, the group broke up. We were supposed to have been going back on the road but it never happened. So, with me lying around in the streets, night life with Bob. He finally ran up on Mr. Reynolds, talked him into recording me. So that's how I got with Flash Records, which is Pull.

Didn't you run across Ray Charles?

Yeah—In fact, I found out at that time that he was playing with Guitar Slim. He did Guitar Slim's "Things I Used To Do." That's when he was with Guitar Slim. I didn't even know that. I just found that out say a few years after I knew him. And if you listen to the keyboard play on there, you'll see that's Ray Charles.

What was it like playing the Silvertone guitar?

The Silvertone, it was playing like a solid body but it wasn't. It was like a semi-hollowed body type thing. But that Fender sounded so much better—to me, at that time. The feel was a little softer on the Strat than it was on the Silvertone. I tell you what it was—the Silvertone didn't have a maple neck. It had what's called rosewood. That's the kind of board it had on it. And Fender had a maple neck, which is so easy to bend the strings. I guess that's why it was so easy for me to play it. And I had that guitar all the way up until I think that was '75. I had some work done on it and all the parts and everything replaced, brand-new neck. Got the body work done on it. It looked like a brand-new guitar. And I was playing at a place called The Wild Goose in La Puente, California. Down in Orange County. I had a little small band called Narcissus. That was the name of the old band I had then. Went out there, set up to go to work on a Friday. I brought my guitar back with me. And I had some songs. I had a book about that thick of songs I had wrote. And just coming back in my car, all of a sudden, the car heated up on me. I had a 1960 Lincoln. So, I pulled over to the side and it wouldn't start. And I got out of it. Turned the hazard lights on. I was going to try to call a cab, hitchhike a ride, or whatever to get to the place where I was staying. This guy pulls around the corner and I waved at him. He kept going. He stopped and he backed up. He said, "Can I help you?" So, I explained to him what happened to my car and everything. I told him I didn't live too far away. I was about maybe three or four miles away. I said, "If you give me a ride home, I'll pay you." And he said, "Where you say you live?" I told him again. He had on coveralls. Could see he'd been working. "I better not do that, son. I gotta go." [*Chuckles.*] He said, "I've been gone too long. My old lady's mad at me now. I'm in bad trouble with my old lady." So, I said, "Okay. Thanks a lot. No problem." So, he pulled off. Drove about the same distance he did before and stopped, backed up again. He said, "Where do you live?" I told him again. "Okay. Come on. I'll take you there."

I went and got my stuff out of the car, put it in the back of his car. He had a 1967 Cougar. Blue. I'll never forget it. Every time I see one today, I go back to that. And so, got all my stuff and put it in his car. I had the doors open. Police pulls up. "What are you doing?" And I explained what was going on. And he said to me, he said, "You can't leave that car there." I said, "Sir, I only live up the road a piece. I'm gonna go up here and get my other car. My old lady's gonna come back with me and we're gonna jump this one and move it right away. It's not going to be here no more than. . . . It won't be an hour." "You have to move it there, Sir. You can't leave it there. I don't care about your hazard lights or whatever." He said, "Some old drunk will come in there and fly into it!" So, I said, "Okay, Sir. I'll move it." The guy was sitting there in the car, all my stuff laying in his car. My guitar and all are in it. I opened the door and . . . I was pretty stocky. I could put my shoulder up the car and push it by myself, so I pushed that car. I was at Palmer and Beach Boulevard, right there in Anaheim. Right across the street was Knott's Berry Farm and on the other side was a big old flower shop. And that flower shop is still there. And Knott's Berry Farm is still there.

So anyway, I'm pushing this car, having a hard time getting . . . because it wasn't a big but with that being a Lincoln, it was heavy. So, I'm pushing like a dog, trying to get that thing up in the parking lot. And I heard a motor revving up [*makes three revving sounds*]. Like somebody getting to race, getting ready to race. And I look around. Wasn't nobody and the police done gone. Left me. And the guy sitting in my car—in his car, with all my stuff in it. I knew what he was getting' ready to do. So, I said, "Hey, hold it! Hold it!" [*Popping sound.*] Took off so fast. The fool closed the doors and I mean, he just went on down the road. Right away, I was so hurt. I said, "All my stuff. That was my life that just went down the drain." I found the phone book right away and called 'em, told 'em what happened. I explained everything to whoever was on the phone, told him what went down. "Don't worry, Mr. Kearney. Somebody will be right there!" Within I'd say two or three minutes, those guys came right back where I was. Same guys. They wanted to know what happened. And I told them, "You know something. That's really cold. I lost everything I had. Doing what you guys asked me to do. And you didn't even stay here to make sure I got in the car with this guy. You just took off and left him sitting there. I was just like a sitting duck." "Don't worry. We're going to get this stuff back." I said, "No, you won't. You'll never get it back." And he said he was sorry. I said, "Don't tell me you're sorry." I mean, I just read 'em everything I could think of. And I never got that guitar back. That was the one that Mr. Louis gave me when I was a kid. Then, I had to go to work. I got lucky. I got a job at a service station, a Shell station, working out in Anaheim. And Mr. Richard Kellogg, he liked me because he saw I was good at automobiles. He sent me to Scrat [?] Institute. That's how I really got to know about cars, working on cars, working at night until I got enough money to get me some more instruments. He did that for me. I worked for him for about, I'd say, four years. He gave me permission I could work there as long as I didn't get a bay closed up or leave the cars tore down. I could work right there for him. And that's what I did. That's how he helped me get on my feet.

I was booked at a place called The California Club there in Los Angeles. On the show with Johnny Guitar Watson and Big Jim Wynn and Jackie Kelso Quintet. So, we worked at that place for two months, The California Club. People's coming every week to see us! In that area, all the people still never got to see us because it wasn't a big place; it was small. So, when we finished there, Jim decided he was going to go to Canada. And I was packing my stuff up the last night, after we had closed down. And I heard him talking. He says . . . the owner saying, "Yeah, we're going to Vancouver, B.C. and we'll be up there about two and a half months. And what we'll do, is we'll probably come back here. That's what we're thinking we're going to do. I don't know what we're gonna do when we get back." Like that. So, when I heard him say that, I said to him when I was going out with my guitar and stuff, . . . I said, "Hey," I said, "You say you're going to Canada. You didn't even ask me if I could go." He said, "Of course, Shorty. You're going if you want to go. Do you want to go?" I said, "Yeah, I want to go!" Of course, see at that time, I had been in LA for a long time. You know, fooling around at the night clubs and things. And there was a little girl was chasing me, wanting to get married! I didn't want to get married. So, I said, "When are we leaving?" He said, "We're leaving out of here Monday, say around twelve o'clock. You think you can be ready by then?' I said, "No problem. I'll be ready." [*Chuckles.*] So when we took off, before we got to Canada, and he was talking about all these things that happens on the road, and he mentioned T-Bone Walker. I said, "You mean to tell me we're going to be working with T-Bone Walker?" He said, "Yeah," he said, "I'm his band leader." I said, "You're T-Bone Walker's band leader?" He said, "Yeah." He said, "I've been with T-Bone for years, Shorty." Why didn't you tell me when we were doing shows?" He said, "Well, I didn't see no reason to say anything about it. I thought you knew." [*Chuckles.*] I said, "No, I didn't." So that's how I ended up working with T-Bone Walker. We got to Vancouver, BC, worked at a place called The New Delhi. And when we finished there, getting ready to leave to come back, and when he told Mr. Leo Baggery [sp?] that he was . . . he was going back and T-Bone was going to New York because he had to record. That's when he was with Atlantic Records. And so, when I heard him say that, I said, "I'm not going back." "What you mean you're not going back?" I said, "I'm not going back to California!" He said, "Well, Shorty, this is not for you asking. You can't stay here." I said," I'm not going to go back." I said, "When you all go back, I'm not going back there." So, Mr. Leo said to him, he said, "Well, if he wants to stay, I'll be his sponsor." He said, "You telling me you'll be Shorty's sponsor?" He said, "Yeah, I'll be glad to keep him here." "Okay, Shorty. You got it!" He said, "You got nothing to worry about now." So, I stayed there with Mr. Baggery for almost six years. Working off and on. Because I would work there, worked down at Easy Walter's Place, working there at the Cave [a supper club]. I worked at a place down there called the Smiling Buddha [also a supper club]. I worked the PNE Amphitheater. I mean, I've been all over that place. Worked with Danny Vecellio there. Then I started gettin' kind of tired of the scene and I wanted to find something else to do. And so, I asked Mr. Baggery was it okay for me to go to Seattle. I wanted to go check things out. "Sure, you can go. You've got a job here as long as you want it." I went to Seattle and start hanging around different places. I met Dave Lewis. Dave Lewis and I got to be really tight. Then I started going in doing guest spots. When I come out of Canada, do a little guest spot, doing a little show thing for them. Then I ended up working for Dave Lewis. Dave Lewis has some hit records called "Dave's Moves," "Little Green Thing." [*Sings the tune.*] He had a lot of stuff out there. And the guy that was managing him—his name was Dave Leavy! And Dave Leavy was Dave Lewis's manager. And he loved Dave so much, like he was his own son. Leavy tried to get him to leave the place. He wanted to take him out, tour the US. Couldn't get Dave to leave. He wouldn't leave there. But anyway, that's what I was doing—working with him in and out of the places.

So, I got to hang around there, doing a little thing like—I was working in a little place called The Black and Tan. I worked in that place up until they shut it down. They opened back up again under The Blue Room instead of Black and Tan. And, I found out later from working those places, everybody who owned that club was dead. They got killed some kind of way. And Earl—his name was Earl, the guy that had it this time when I was working there for The Blue Room. He ended up in a bad accident, killed himself. The next guy had it, his name was B.J. Darrett—Benjamin Darrett. He got shot down at the bottom of the stairs in the same place. At that time, it was The Blue Room, still. And what happened was this little kid came down. He wanted to see—I think it was Jack McDuff. . . or Jim McGriff. . . . it was one of them that was working there. He went to the window to get a ticket and B.J. looked at him, and he said, "Can I help you, son?" He said, "Yeah, I want a ticket." He said, "Well, it's gonna cost you ten dollars to get in." He said, "But I only have five dollars." He said, "Well, that's not gonna get you in, son." He was only teasing him. Because he saw he was so young, he knew he was just barely age to get in. B.J. turned to get a ticket to hand to the kid; the guy shot him in the back. Shot him in the back. I think it was just a . . . I think it was a nine-millimeter. I think he shot him about nine times in the back. Then he turned around and said, "Son, I was going to get a ticket for you. Why'd you have to shoot me?" By that time, everybody had grabbed him. They got the kid. They almost killed him right there. Tore him apart. Got B.D. to the hospital and they moved him off of the critical list and put him in the ICU? Yeah. Put him there. And he was doing fine. The next thing you know, pneumonia moved in on him and that's what killed him. Now everybody that owned that place, at the time I was staying in it, they had some kind of tragic death.

Tell me about your contact with Jimi Hendrix.

Well, during the time that I was coming back and forth, that was when I met Jimi's stepsister, Marcia. And when I leave to go to Canada, some kind of way when they find out that I was going to be at this club—it's called the Continental Showcase. I was telling you earlier, that Dave Leavy was very crazy about Dave Lewis. What happened on that was Dave Lewis ended up owning the club. So, when I come in off, coming from Canada, and when I come in there to play, I had a spot. That's when the Beatles was very popular, and they had "Hey Jude" and I was supposed to go to her table. Well, I went to the table and met her. I was young and, you know, shy. And she says, "Well, I like the way you sang "Hey Jude." When you go back will you sing that for me?" I said, "Sure, I'll be glad to." When I went back, I sang "Hey Jude"—two times in one night. [*Chuckles.*]

So, it got to be a regular thing. The next thing I know, her and I were going out together. And going out to breakfast and stuff. The next thing you know, the time passed, she ended up being pregnant. And so, we ended up having a beautiful baby daughter, named Tammy. She's still in Seattle today. And then things got really bad between her and I. Just before Jimi died, Marcia and I split up. We had split up like two weeks before his death. And so, with me going back and forth to Seattle, to Canada, and back and forward, when they finally brought Jimi after his death, I was there. Helped put Jimi away. And I decided it was time for me to leave. So, I left Seattle and came back to California.

I knew Jimi from the time he was working with Little Richard. And I'd seen he was working with other groups as well. Jimi knew me, and when I found out all this stuff here about him going AWOL to watch me play—I got that from him. He said he went many times to see me and hear me. And he said to me, he said, "Shorty," he said, "you are the most amazing guitar player I ever seen in my life!" He said, "I don't think you'd mind the few little things I borrowed from you." I said, "Hey, man. It's in the family now." I said, "I'm in the family, right?" He said, "Yeah, you're family now." So, he showed me a lot of things that he had picked up from me. He said, "But one thing I did try," he said, "you can have it." That was the flip. He turned the flip and got hurt. He tried to do a flip and got injured. And so, he started setting his guitar on fire. And if you listen to "Hey Jude," "Just a Voodoo Child," or any of those stuff, I used to do all that kind of stuff on stage when I was setting up, fooling around with my guitar. Just playing around with it. And he took it and did something with it! So, I can't say he took it! I mean, I'm just doing it. I mean, those are ideas. I mean, guitar players today—they're still watching me and picking up ideas from me. When I find out they're doing it, I'm flattered. I'm happy they're doing it.

Did you spend any time, or been around Percy Mayfield?

Percy Mayfield wrote me two songs before he died. And if you get with Tina Mayfield [Percy's widow] today, she'll tell you the same thing. But, anyway, he wrote two songs for me. He called me up one day. He said, "Shorty, you asked me to write some songs for you, didn't you, son?" I said, "I sure did." He said, "I got them." He said, "But you gotta come over here." He said, "I got 'em. I've already written them out for you." And what he did, he played 'em and sang 'em over the phone to me. And I really liked them. But he'd taken ill. I had gone on the road. He'd taken ill whilst I was gone. And when I got back, he was so bad, I couldn't go see him at that time. And he didn't come out of the hospital. He got really bad and we lost him. So, I told Tina about it and she said, "I remember the songs. He did write 'em for you." she said, "But I'm gonna try to find . . . I'm going to try to find them for you." And when I talked to her about it again, about maybe I'd say three months after he was gone, she said, "Shorty, I've torn this place up. I can't find them songs." She said, "But I know for a fact that he wrote those songs, two songs for you."

Floyd Murphy

Floyd Murphy is renowned for his guitar work on the classic Jr. Parker recordings done for the Sun Label in Memphis during the early 1950s. In November of 2000 Floyd was living and working in Rockford, Illinois, the second largest city in Illinois. Floyd was working with a group, Geneva Red. Geneva got in touch and asked if I would be interested in interviewing Floyd—and so we got together for this interview. You'll notice by the number of questions I ask, that nobody would mistake Floyd for loquacious but compared to his famous, notoriously mute, guitar-playing brother, Matt "Guitar" Murphy, Floyd was a chatterbox . . .

When and where were you born?

I was born in 1935, in Memphis, Tennessee, at John Gaston Hospital.

How many people in your family altogether?

Oh man, I can't count them—there's a bunch of us [*laughs*]. Man, it's a bunch. I got four brothers and two sisters. After my mother died, we all went down in Mississippi and lived with my Auntie. And so, she raised us on up till we got big enough to go to school. Well, some of them went down south—what I'm saying down in Mississippi, you know, and, but then when I come over, I used to go to school back in Memphis when we started living with our father again.

How old were you when your mother died?

One year old. I stayed down there until I got to be old enough to go to school, I was about seven. I stayed down there from one to seven. So about six years, I stayed and my Auntie took care of all of us during that time. While we were in Mississippi my brother—Matt "Guitar" Murphy—would listen to old records and stuff by old blues players and stuff like that. Well, we had a Victrola that winds up you know, and that's how he learned how to play—how *we* learned to play because then he taught me.

How old is he compared to how old you are? And where do you all fall in the order of the brothers and sisters?

There was another brother in between me and him. See, I'm the youngest brother and then you got Melvin and you got Matt—and then you got Dan. And then all my sisters come after that—they go on up the ladder being old this year. Matt is the one that taught me how to play. Yeah.

Have any idea who he was listening to back in those days?

We listen to Blind Lemon and, and the old Sonny Boy Williamson. All the Spiritual singers, all the stuff like that. We listened to all that stuff.

Was your Aunt a music fan?

Yeah, she loved music. Yes, all of us were music lovers. Yeah. They all like music.

And what was the situation when you moved back to Memphis with your father?

When we come back, then we start going to school. We all started at the Manassas high school—I think that was in north Memphis.

Were the schools integrated at that point or was it strictly black and white?

No, they were all segregated.

Had your father remarried?

No, he wasn't married at that time. But he took care of us all, you know? So, we got big enough to do a little work, and help him out. We went into the cotton field, picked a little cotton and helped him out. We did whatever work we could find around to do you know . . .

Was that what your father was doing—farm work?

No, I think he was working at a hotel—and he took care of us, you know?

Do you happen to recall any of the addresses where you lived in Memphis?

Lion Court—we live in Lion Court. And then we moved from there and we went over to a place over there on the south side. 852 D LaMoyne Garden. That's where we lived.

You were exposed to music through your brother through the records. He was the first one to take it up. How did that happen? How did he get his hands on his first instrument? What did he start playing?

We ordered a Prep [guitar brand]—you know, a Prep we ordered from Sears & Roebuck. They made Silvertone and Prep. We ordered Prep from Sears & Roebuck. And that's what we had and how we learned to play.

Did you have more formal instruction? Or would you learn from people that you were acquainted with who would teach you how to play?

Well, I would always watch anybody that played—and if they played something I liked, well, then I'd take that on home. [*Laughs.*]

Did your brother precede you in earning a living in music—And you followed him?

Yeah, actually, I didn't want to play but he got me interested in it. And after getting involved in it, then I found out that it wasn't too bad, you know. Hey, you can make some money at it. And that's one of the things that I can use—to make some money . . .

Who was Matt working with?

He started out playing around Memphis there with different guys and then eventually he got with Howlin' Wolf. And then he and Junior Parker formed a group call the Blue Flames. He played with that group for a while, and then he got with Memphis Slim. He went to Chicago—playing around Chicago. And then after playing around Chicago for a while he met up with John Belushi and the Blues Brothers. So, then he got into that. So that's how he got here today. You know,

When you came on the scene would you play in bands with your brother? Would you work together—or avoid working together?

Well, sometimes, I would go with him on some of his gigs and sit in and play sometime. That's how I got used to playing—I'd sit in and play. Yeah.

And would you say that your style closely resembled what your brother was playing?

Yeah, it's related—closely related. Yeah. My style and his style, but he does it so much better. [*Laughs.*]

Would you say that there's any one person in particular that Matt took his cues from musically, a guy where he got his guitar style?

Well, he started out playing like T-Bone Walker. That was the one guy that really enthused him. Yeah T-Bone. But he had his own style and had his own ideas about what he wanted to do so, but that was one of the guys that got him from one place to the next. By listening, he was able to go to the next level.

What time are we talking about when your brother first broke in on the scene in Memphis?

When I was around that had to have been like, 1945/1946. I was around twelve somewhere around there . . .

How old would that have made him?

About seventeen I'd guess—he'd be about seventeen. He was four years older than I was.

I could see how a guy who was seventeen could get out there and get in the bars. Did you go to bars? You were a young boy at that time—how would you catch up? Would you go in taverns, bars, clubs, where they played?

When he first got out there and got started, even he was too young but at that time you could get in a place back then—things were different back then, you know. If you could get there, you could get in. But once he got going, a few years later made him on up to around about twenty. So, then it was some years later than I started going with him—I was still too young but I was with my brother, you know?

Can you recall any of the people around Memphis that he used to play with that folks might know today?

He's played with this band Tuff Green around Memphis there. Play with him. Played with that group for a while. He actually played with some of everybody, you know, different groups. Yeah.

How many of these guys you think went on to record?

Most of them did, you know—he played with Howlin' Wolf—and Junior Parker. He played with Sonny Boy. He played with all the guys. Well, I don't know if he played with Little Walter. I never heard him say that he played with Little Walter. But he played with a lot of people—a lot of them I don't know. But he played with Willie Johnson and those guys. He made a recording with Bobby Bland. When Bobby was first starting out, he was in Memphis.

How about Rosco Gordon?

Yeah—he played with him. I remember when Rosco was around there. He was writing and doing his thing.

It's obvious that your brother had ambitions to have a career in music. Did you have those same ambitions?

No, not at first. My thoughts were not on music. So, I was just open until something came along. Music—I wasn't even thinking that way—but that's what it turned out to be. I guess he looked at me and he saw that he really could help me out, that this music thing would do me some good, later on. So, he figured he would do something to help in case I wanted to play music. It would give me some else to do—another trade.

So, were you just in school and playing?

Actually, my brother left and he went back out in the country again, and I went back out there too, and that's when I learned to play. He was farming—we were all farming and he taught me how to play, and then he left again. And then he started playing with other groups. It's kind of fuzzy the way it all happened. Because we were down in the country two different times.

If you were going to describe what vicinity in the country—where the area was when you went both times?

We lived around Ashland area there, Michigan City Junction [Tennessee]. And then you had Holly Springs [Mississippi], around in that area.

When you were learning to play guitar, did women come into it at all? Didn't that help you with girls—or were you too young to be interested in girls at that point?

Yeah—it helped—girls love to hear you play. But I was more interested in how to play than messing with girls. I was more interested in learning how to play after I got started . . .

I guess that shows how young you were.

Yeah. [*Laughs.*]

When did you decide that's how you wanted to make your living?

Well, it didn't dawn on me at the time. But I kept playing and kept practicing and learning stuff, you know. And then Willie Nix came down and played in that area. And I went down to see him. And he knew me, he knew my brother and he knew that I could play so he asked me to play with him. So that's what I did. I just went home, got my clothes and left. And I've been playing ever since.

Did you ever make any records with Willie Nix?

No—I attempted to make one, but it didn't go through. He wanted me to play with him, but then he decided not to—he wanted to keep it like it was. But I played with him for a while—a long while.

The impression that some folks have gotten about Willie is that he was just about crazy. Was he just crazy later? Was he just crazy for white folks? Or was he always crazy?

No, no, he wasn't crazy. He just didn't want to take no stuff. You don't really try to meet up with trouble but if that's just the way you are—it's just a matter of time until you're gonna run into some. So that's the way he was. He'd treat you nice, you know, but then he just wouldn't take no stuff. That's the way he was . . .

It's nice to hear somebody who has something nice to say about him. I think he was a fine artist. What exactly did he play?

He played drums and sang.

What kind of stuff were you guys doing at that point?

Well, we do all old blues, you know, mostly the real blues. That's what we do—the real real blues, low down blues.

When he put a band together or he had a gig, how many pieces would you have? And what would the lineups be at that point? Who was in the band?

At that time, we had drums and two guitars, maybe a harmonica player.

Were you playing amplified?

Yeah.

Were you amplified right from the beginning?

Yeah.

So that's how you learned to play, basically was to play amplified?

Yeah, I'd been playing on amplifier all the time. Not back when I learned I didn't, you know, like when my brother was teaching me—we just had a regular guitar, you know, just open face.

And when did you change over?

Ah, well, the change to amplified came when I started playing with groups, then I knew I had to get me an amp. I bought me a brand-new guitar and a brand-new amp. Yeah.

What were the amps like at that point?

Well, at that time, they was all tubes—transistors weren't out at that time. All tube amps. The first amp I got was a Fender. And then I had a Gibson guitar.

It seems as if, when we talk about it today, back in the late '40s and in the early '50s, there was a Memphis style. Would you agree that there was a Memphis style in particular, as opposed to anywhere else?

Well, I will say, a southern style, not just Memphis. It's a southern style. See the people in the South play different?

I was thinking, particularly when you got to amplify blues, how they cranked the amps up, and have it be distorted.

Distorted, yeah . . .

Who led the way on that—do have any idea?

Well that came about, because the amps weren't strong enough to sustain a clear sound. So, by turning it up too loud, that was done—not intentionally, you know, and it developed a good sound. And pretty soon the people would hear that, and they were enjoying it. But, you see, we didn't know. What we were trying to do was just play loud enough. Those amps weren't built to take the load you were putting on it. So, it developed a distorted sound. See? And that's what happened. It wasn't intentional. That distortion came about by accident when we turned up too loud. When you turn up too loud you get feedback, actually, that's all it is—feedback. Yeah. So that wasn't done intentionally—we were just trying to get that volume up, you know, and you get that feedback. And it sounds good. So then people come along and developed that you know, they turned that into a thing. That Jimi Hendrix thing—that Marshall amp—that's where the idea of a Marshall amp came from—from distortion. They build distortion into it [*laughs*]. And every note you hit would be distorted [*laughs*].

Who were the guys that were playing guitar on the scene there in Memphis—and around that vicinity? Who were the major guitar slingers?

Well, during that time, B.B. [King]—and my brother [Matt "Guitar" Murphy]. And you had Willie Johnson and Hubert [Sumlin]—and he had this other guy called [Joe] Willie Wilkins. Joe Willie Wilkins and this other guy he played with, Robert Jr. Lockwood. Yeah. Yeah. Those were some of the promising, top guitar players.

So, there's nobody that played around Memphis, that's been totally forgotten today? And, basically, everybody that was there playing made a name for themselves?

Yeah, they did. Yeah.

Do you remember when Wolf went to Chicago?

We formed the Blue Flames with 'Struction [Destruction]. And me and 'Struction and Dickey, and all the guys, you know, the drummer and the bass player. We formed the Blue Flames. But Wolf and them left a little before that time, you know. We formed the Blue Flame—so, I had to be seventeen . . .

What kind of regard was Chicago held in at that point? Did it seem inevitable that everybody was going to come to Chicago—and, would you keep track of somebody that you knew if he went to Chicago?

Well, most everybody left and went to Chicago, because everything was happening in Chicago. But we stayed there, and we still made some recordings. So, we still could make our recordings and still get something going—but everybody else went to Chicago. We stayed there. We formed this group. We made some recordings—and got a couple of hits.

How did you decide to form the band?

Okay. So, Junior Parker was still there. And then the 'Struction.

What did 'Struction play?

He was a piano player. And he was the one that was teaching everybody. He would teach everybody. You want to know something, he could show you how—so, he got us all started on the right foot. He helped us with the music and everything. But it was my ideas that got everything going, but with his ability to write words and stuff, that helped. We all just got together, but me and him mostly. Me and 'Struction were the guys that constructed the band and the songs. Yeah. So, we get together—we had 'Struction on piano, me on guitar, we had Kenny Banks on bass, Dicky on drums. And I don't know if we had a saxophone player. I don't think so. Um—maybe we did put Wheeler on saxophone. But I don't know if we had a saxophone. But anyway, that's how we formed the group. And so, we got together and went over there to Sun [label] and made those recordings and then they made the hit.

How did you get to audition for Sun? How did that work?

Well, he was always open, you know, you could just come in and tell him what do you want to do? And he will listen to you. He would give you a chance, you know, he was open. His door was open. You could always go there. If you had something, he'd listened to it. And if he thought it had a chance, he'd put you wax, you know?

How old was 'Struction—and what was his real name? Did you ever know his real name?

I did, I think, at one time but I just got so used to saying 'Struction that there just didn't seem to be any other name that'd fit him. [*Laughs.*]

Was he an older man—or your age?

No—he was old. He was old. Much older. That's why he could tell us because he had experience. He could write, he could read—and everything.

Just for those unfamiliar with your work—what were the records you guys made?

Well, we made "Feeling Good," "Love My Baby," "Mystery Train," and "Mother-in-Law Blues" . . .

These are all classics by Junior Parker.

Yeah. The Blue Flames, we'd all broadcast over in West Memphis, KWEM. We'd play live. We all had a certain time to go on. After one group play and then go off, then another one come on. And we would just stand up and look at the rest play, and then we go on, do our thing.

Would you have a sponsor in particular for your program?

No. I don't think so. I don't know how they did it. All I know, we went over there. I don't know what it was. They had a sponsor, you know, for us, but it could have been. We had an hour worked out—what we're gonna do first. We probably do like two or three songs, you know? But we'd have it all worked out what we're gonna do.

What time during the day would you do that?

Well, our shows were usually later in the day. They could go on for a while, you know, because a lot of groups came in and you'd hear Joe Hill Louis and other groups that had to go in and do their thing. We would wait for our turn, and then go on in.

. . . and did the band stay together and work with him after that?

Yeah, we stayed together. Eventually, we joined up with Johnny Ace. And Willie Mae (Big Mama) Thornton. I was a guitar player for all those groups, you know, at that time, so I had to learn all their stuff.

When you worked with Johnny Ace, Johnny is a piano player. Did you have 'Struction on piano with Johnny Ace? Did Johnny just sing?

Well, Johnny would play during the time that I worked with him. He would handle the piano because he had his own style of playing, you know. And he felt more comfortable performing, sitting down at the piano.

Did you record with him?

No—I didn't do any recording with Johnny Ace.

Was there anybody other than Junior Parker that you recorded with for Philips?

Yeah, I recorded with the Tiger Man—Rufus Thomas. I did some stuff with Rufus.

How did that happen?

I don't know how it happened. But I know I made that recording with him.

Were you a part of his band?

No, no, no, this is just studio work. I just come in and play this part with him. You know, we'd sit down and we had this thing. Come up with some ideas on the spur the moment thing, you know . . .

Are there any well-known titles that we'd recognize that you did?

I think the one I did with him was "Tiger Man."

When you made the records with the Blue Flames what label did those come out on?

On Sun. Yeah, Sam actually put those out himself.

What kind of places would you play when you went on the road with the Blue Flames? Would you play big auditoriums—or fish shacks? Did you go to big arenas?

Clubs—big clubs. Yeah. Big clubs. Nice clubs. Play all down in Florida, Texas, Alabama, Arkansas. Oh, man. We went to some nice clubs.

How did you travel?

We had two station wagons—and then we had a car.

Did you have uniforms?

Yeah. Yeah.

What did the uniforms look like?

Well, we had gray uniforms with vest and pants and—matching shirts, stuff like that.

And how many pieces did you have all together?

We had the same group—basically the same group, the Blue Flames. Drums, bass, guitar, piano. We traveled light. I think upright bass was still being played at that time.

How long did the Blue Flames last?

Well, it lasted a pretty long time. I think I played with them on the road at least three years.

How did you and Junior Parker fall out?

I was tired of the road—you know what I mean? One time we came back to Memphis. I got tired of traveling and they were heading out to California. So, I told them, "Y'all go ahead without me." So, they got another guitar player. After that I left. You go to sleep riding and you wake up riding—and eat riding and I just had enough of that riding. Every time you look up, you're getting in the car and taking off, going to the next place. It keeps you on edge all the time, you know, you're trusting somebody else with your life. They're driving and you think about all that when you're riding. I just got tired of it, you know, so just get somebody else.

At some point didn't Junior go with Don Robey?

Yeah, we all went up there. We all left after that. See, after we started playing and we got on the road, we spent a lot of time in Houston, Texas. While we were there, we got connected with Don Robey and we went on the Peacock Label.

Did Robey have just Peacock or did he have more than one label?

I think he had one called Duke, too. Did we record on Duke—or Peacock? I don't know. We could have had recorded on both labels. I don't know.

And were you guys free to record with other people? I mean, you weren't under contract?

No—no contract. We just made a recording, you know, we weren't on a contract. Back at that time, you could just go in and record—if you want to record—and if they figured your stuff was suitable. They put the money out. They wouldn't sign a contract that you couldn't record for nobody else. You know.

I've read that Robey was a crook and a thug. Guys say he was a tough guy. What was your impression of Don Robey from what you saw?

He was nice to me. He was nice to me—yeah. He was the one who took me downtown and bought me a brand-new guitar and amp. Yeah, so you know, I never had any problem. But I guess if you're dealin', taking care of business then you never get to see that part of him. But because I didn't get to take care of any business with him—he was nice to me. So, to be honest with you, all I can say as far as I'm concerned, he treated me nice.

Where was the material coming from that you were recording for Robey?

I don't know who was writing material. Somebody else was writing it—"Next Time You See Me" and "Mother-in-Law Blues" and stuff like that. I just lay stuff down the blues stuff down for him on "Mother-in-Law Blues."

And those were tunes that you guys didn't have on the bandstand or had been working with? You actually worked those out in the studio?

Yeah, we worked those out at the studio—but other tunes like "Feeling Good," "Love My Baby," "Mystery Train," stuff like that—we had been playing that on bandstand for a long time.

Any idea where "Feeling Good" came from?

"Feeling Good" came from that song from a guy in Mississippi, Landon Bogay.

And where would you see him? Did he ever record—or is that just somebody you saw in person?

He was a friend of mine down south. And he used to play that song out in the country all the time.

And at that point, were you still making your living just strictly through music?

Yeah. That's all I was doing. Whatever the situation called for—if I'm making enough money playing—then I would just play—but then if money got tight—then I'd go and do some work.

How long were you actually able to stay out in the field, just making your living through music? How many years did you actually do that?

Well, it was mixed up all away, you know. At the time when I was on the road with Johnny Ace, and making good money—I did it straight for maybe three, four years, you know?

Talk about Johnny Ace and his death. Were you anywhere in the vicinity when that happened?

We had played the last gig in Dallas with him. He asked me if I wanted to be his guitar player. I told him no. I told him I've been playing with the guys here and I can't do that, you know? As a matter of fact, I didn't know him that well. So, I was gonna go with the guys I knew and could trust. So, we played the last gig in Dallas with him, and shortly after that is when he got killed. [Johnny Ace killed himself playing Russian Roulette backstage on a Christmas Night gig, 1954.]

Are we talking about a couple of days later, a couple of weeks later, a month later?

I don't know how long it was. But I know it wasn't too long of a time after that. It could have been the next month or next. But it wasn't that long. It was shortly after that.

Were you shocked to hear that?

Yeah. Because I mean, he wouldn't be the kind of a guy to do something like that. He was a jolly guy, you know, and he was sharp—he was smart. I just can't picture him doing something like that.

How long were you off the road before you decided to pick up with Eddie Snow again?

I was there for a while. I don't know how long, but there was this tenor player. He was playing up there in Cairo, Billy Duncan. You remember Billy? Billy Duncan. He's the one that made "Three O'Clock in the Morning" with B.B. King. He was the horn player on that, yeah. But he was living up in Cairo. So, then he had come up—and so when he came up, he asked me if I wanted to play in Cairo. So, I told him, "Yeah, I'll go." So, I just got my girlfriend, me and my girlfriend got all our stuff together and we took off and went down there. That's when I started playing with Eddie Snow. That was nice because it was a nice town, I could go fishing and stuff like that. And they had everything round there. You could pick cotton and do other things to make money. So that was pretty nice.

How far away from Memphis is that?

About 160 miles . . .

Do you ever have anything to do with the St. Louis scene? I think that's where Ike Turner and all those guys were at—running back and forth between St. Louis and Clarksdale.

I met Ike in Cairo. He was learning how to play guitar, at that time. So, he went on to play and play good. After that I left Cairo and I went back on the road with Junior Parker and Bobby Bland in 1955 and then went back on the road with them and played with them for a while. When I left, I went to Chicago. And right after that, I had to go into the army in 1958. I spent two years in the army and got out in 1960, and then I came here [Rockford, IL] to stay.

Where were you stationed during your service?

Fort Hood, Texas.

So, you never got out of the states at all?

No, I went to Germany. I went to Gelnhausen around Frankfurt.

Did you play at all while you were in the army?

No—I didn't play. I wanted to but I couldn't get it. I was a foot soldier. In the armored infantry.

There actually was a thriving little blues scene here in Rockford for many years. I've heard the guys in Chicago, people like Sunnyland Slim, and Floyd Jones, and everybody talk about the fact that they would come out here to play. Can you shed some light on what was going on out here? You seem to be the last remnant of it. Maybe you could tell me a little bit about it.

Yeah, well, when I come here in 1961, I had a thing going on with Birdlegs and Pauline. We had a group and we made a record and it hit. When I first came here it was nice. Yeah. It was good. This was blues country then.

That surprises me. Was there a large Black population in Rockford?

Yeah, I mean, there was enough—we didn't actually have too many groups. Maybe that's why it was so good—because there weren't too many groups here. But, yes, there were a lot of Black people here that were working in Rockford.

Where were Black folks working in Rockford?

Most of them were working for John Atkins[?]. That's a place where they make quills and moldings and stuff like that for heavy industry. Yeah. So, the people work there—they worked at Roper. There was a lot of work here. A lot of good jobs. Yeah.

Did/do any other blues players stay out here besides you?

During that time, they would come here occasionally. They never stayed here because in this town, there aren't many music connections. You know, first try to make a record and then move on because this side of the city is sort of closed off. Actually, when you come here, you trapped as a musician . . .

Well, what were the clubs that the guys would play when they'd come here?

Well, you had the Regatta, the Town Lounge, one of them was Rock Tavern. You had the American Legion, and the Elks Club. Where you have places up in Freeport where you can play, too.

Tell me about Birdlegs and Pauline. How did that happen for you?

My brothers hooked that up because they knew my brother [Matt] in Chicago. My brother told them about me. They were looking for a guitar player to have. My brother told them about me. And so, then I came here with him. Yeah. That's how it got started.

What was the name of the hit record that they had?

"Spring." It was like rock and roll. Yeah, it was on the juke boxes . . .

How did the record with Birdlegs and Pauline, how did that happen?

Well, that was their idea. I just lay down some chord changes for them and arranged it.

Where was it cut?

Cuca label, which was based in Wisconsin.

Do you have any notion of around what year that was?

That was way back. Had to have been in the '60s?

Also, somebody told me to ask about a record, The Major and the Lieutenants. Is that the name of the group or the name of a record?

That's the name of the group—The Major and The Lieutenants . . .

Tell me, if you will, what that one was about.

It was mostly instrumental—no singing just instrumental piece. One side is "Love, Peace and Soul." The flip side was "Communicating." Those are more soul records. Yeah. Early '70s—somewhere in there.

I'm told you were responsible for teaching Guitar Junior how to play.

Yeah, well, I showed him some things. But he is pretty fast. You know? He don't need too much. He was playing drums. He was a drummer, and then later on, he came to me and asked me to show him a few things. How do I do this, how to do this and how to do that. I guess he made a connection for all he needed. He can play.

Were you down in Memphis when that happened?

No, that was up here . . .

He just said that you were responsible for getting him started. And the other thing he told me, he said that you've got some big rock star that admires you.

Well, somebody told me that Jimi Hendrix was influenced by me. Well, I don't know for sure. But somebody read a statement that said that Jimi Hendrix was influenced by the Blue Flames, you know?

What do you think of the notion that Sam Phillips is still down there in Memphis with the Sun studio?

He doesn't have that anymore. No, but he's still got *a* studio down there. He's got another studio, yeah, across from it—that's right.

You just cut a record down there in the last couple of years. Did you go to the historic Sun Studios or to where he is working now?

I went to the first one, yeah. That's the one I went to.

And who did you record with?

Geneva Red.

Is that something that continues today?

Yeah, I still play once in a while, yeah, but we don't play that regular.

Johnny Heartsman

This interview was made possible by Dick Shurman. I had no idea who Johnny Heartsman was, but Dick had a great deal of knowledge regarding blues and R&B from the West Coast. Dick was shepherding him around town and asked if I wanted to interview him. If Dick was promoting him, I knew it would be worth following up. He brought Johnny up to the combo studio at the station transmitter for the following conversation. Johnny was a multi-instrumentalist from the Bay Area in Oakland, and worked a great many of the recording sessions in this area.

■ ■ ■

When I was about fifteen and a half weighing about 195 pounds on the football team, looking like I was 20, my mom's boyfriend one evening took me to a club called Woody's in Oakland on Seventh Street. And they had a drummer and a guitar player there. And they were looking kind of weird on the bandstand, it seems that their piano player had just joined a guy named Chuck Higgins, a saxophone player. And they had no piano player. So, at the time, I tried to play Fats Domino's stuff. We, as kids in high school, as a football player, I didn't care. But my mom's boyfriend kept saying, "Hey, my little son-in-law here, he plays piano." There was about four people in the place, so they got me up there to play my Lloyd Glenn song that I had learned how to play—Old Time Shuffle. I played that and the guys asked me, "Can you sing?" and I sang. I sang a Fats Domino song—I think it was, "If You See Rose Mary," something like that—or maybe "They Call Me The Fat Man." And they hired me for seven dollars a night, which completely blew my mind. The guy, Fred, the guitar player, showed me changes, blues changes, and I had been listening to all kinds of music from my mother, who was a show business hanger-oner. She used to make clothes for different singers and stuff. So, I learned. Then, Lafayette Thomas, they called him Thing, a guitar player, would play that club whenever he wasn't working with Jimmy McCracklin. He would be down there, he had a girlfriend that worked there at the bar, Linda. All of this is over my head—I was so thrilled playing with these guys. They were in their late 20s and 30s, even early 40s. So, in those circumstances, I really had very rich beginnings. Professionally, I didn't make any money, so to speak, but it was more you know, I played with grown men for that short while. Subsequently, I had my own little band in high school, and we played off the door for like sixty-five cents or a dollar and a quarter and we bought some Thunderbird wine and partied and had a good time. It was a marvelous feeling. Every now and then you get it playing as an adult, you know? And, through Lafayette Thomas, I was introduced to Jimmy McCracklin. I used to go out and watch them play. And so—I was playing. I finally bought myself an electric bass. And I got a chance to play a number or two with Jimmy—and Jimmy recognized the fact that, I was a youngster, but I could learn and keep my mouth shut and listen. You know, we musicians, we like to talk. Just about all musicians were teachers to me. Everybody's always trying to show somebody something. So, I was the youngest person on the scene and they all took a liking to me—Lowell Fulson, Jimmy McCracklin, Earl Brown, the people in Ray Charles's band, you know. They would come through and Charles Brown—just all kinds of people, and I learned from them. And subsequently, I met Bob Geddins, who was the father of the blues recording industry in Oakland. And he found out that I would stay in the studio all day for nothing, just to be around that, you know, because I wasn't doing anything else. And I'd play and I'd listened and any kind of way they wanted, I'd play, if I could do it. The stuff was really simple. And there was no problem, just play—I just had that consuming desire to be around this music. You know, never mind the twenty bucks they'd give me for the recording sessions, but I did a lot of recording with Bob Geddins. I'm talking around the mid-1950s—about 1953 or '54, I'm not quite sure, something like that. What I was recording, well, that was my DooWop period, where I recorded with DooWop groups and I was in the Music City Soul Brothers, the Rovers, who had "WPLJ" [White Port Lemon Juice], the GayLarks, the Crystals—I don't remember the whole list. The only reason I remember these groups is because they did an article on me in Goldmine magazine and the guy came up with about twelve different groups that I'm playing on. I recorded a lot of 45s, most of them are very forgettable. The DooWop period. Of course, there were a couple of tunes that were kind of cute little songs, but most of them were ghastly—out of tune, and it's just some data for a person who collects and say, "Oh, these were done for Ray Dobard at Music City records." And the ones I did with Bob Geddins on the blues scene were Willie B Huff, Johnny Fuller, Joe Simon, Big Mama Thornton, Jimmy Wilson, Sugar Pie Desanto—Oh, Sugar Pie, we did that for Ray Dobard—"Slip-In Mules." I did. Yeah. And there probably more people that I can't remember we bought. What's his name? Eddie Boyd. "Five Long Years" by Eddie Boyd. Yeah. And Jimmy McCracklin stuff, you know, I did a lot of Jimmy McCracklins, Al King, Tiny Powell, Allen Nettie. I even did some things with Vernon Garrett and Jill and Vernon Jewel. I think that was for Modern though. But I did a lot of sessions around there for different people.

What was the first session? Do you recall that?

My very first session? Yeah, was for Jimmy McCracklin. Ironically, my very first session was one of my biggest paid sessions. I recorded for the Bihari Brothers and Modern Records. On that they used a studio over in San Francisco with Jimmy McCracklin. I remember I was going to high school. And I went over there I was just thrilled because I got up to a big high point. I was making fifteen bucks a night. I did this session for the Biharis, we did an album thing and we recorded all day. But anyway, at the end of the session I got $300—and I had never had $300 of my own money for nothing. I didn't even know where to start spending it. All of a sudden there were all these different choices to me. I could now buy a complete wardrobe, instead of some shoes and socks. Anyway, it was amazing. I went to school, I held on to a couple 100 bucks for just days and days and discretely flashed them when I was buying a soda or a hamburger for somebody.

Being on the scene we were you interested in buying records? Did you buy the records that came out?

Oh yeah, I bought records. I'll tell you what we bought. As far as the singers were concerned, we bought Percy Mayfield because he had a song called "Loose Lips" and [*sings*] "Down in Louisiana . . ." He had that tune out and Maxwell Davis was doing the arranging. Maxwell was our favorite arranger. We could recognize his stuff. He was doing stuff with B.B. King. He was doing Percy Mayfield and Jimmy Nelson, you know, and Maxwell had a very identifiable sound. He was by far my favorite blues arranger. And we were kind of into arrangers and stuff like that—blues arrangers. But we bought Percy Mayfield songs. And then we had an organo. Have you ever heard of an organo? You take a piano, then you take this long bar and put it on top of the piano keys close to the back of the keys and you put it down, Okay? Each key has a little peg. When you depress the key on the piano, that peg comes down and makes a contact into the amplifier and it gives an organ sound. So theoretically, if you got a nice piano, you can put this thing on and tighten it up and adjust the pegs and "boom," wherever you go, you've got an organ sound. But in practice, when you go to these different clubs that got a key broken off club or got the, the ivory knocked off and there's none but the wood. So, you put your organic thing on the keyboard and then it goes [*makes a series of crazy buzz tones*] because the keys are all messed up or broken—or non-existent—it was wild! We got turned on to Bill Doggett, you know, it was before he had "Honky Tonk" out. He had all these tunes out, "Honey Boy" and you know, all these nice organ grooves. And we'd hear Billy Butler. We were into that stuff. We'd buy Bill Doggett and we'd buy Percy Mayfield stuff, and then we'd buy Shirley & Lee. I would buy Willie Mabon, "I'm Mad" and "I Don't Know." And things like Preacher Stephens, he had a song called "Whoopin' and a Hollerin'." But we liked all of that kind of stuff. And then we'd buy some of the Coasters before they were the Coasters, when they were The Robins, before they formed the Coasters. And you know, just the various DooWops. We liked the Dells—they've been around forever—them and the Spaniels. [*Sings*:] "Doo, doo, doo, doo," was that the Spaniels? [*Sings:*] "Good night, my love . . ." We'd buy that stuff—and then the Dinah Washington stuff. I love Dinah, and the Johnny Otis stuff with Little Esther, and Big Mama Thornton, "Hound Dog." That was, that was the anthem. Pete Lewis was another one of my favorite guitars, mainly on the strength of that guitar performance on "Hound Dog." But T-Bone, I would get anything T-Bone ever had. My Mom liked T-Bone too. So, she had a lot of those records. And then we would have a saxophone in the band and we listened to a lot of Gene Ammons and Sonny Stitt's stuff—especially their blues stuff. We couldn't really get with the standards—you know, when they do "All The Things You Are," and all that kind of stuff—we didn't understand that too much, but when they do that just good old blowing you know, we were there. Gate Mouth Brown, "Okie Dokie Stomp" and "Gate Walks To Board," I had all those. Another guy I used to have records by was Amos Milburn. Yeah, I had all Amos Milburn stuff, and Nat Cole, I had a lot of his stuff. I was always aware of the Los Angeles people like Jack McVea and all the people on the Specialty Label, Roy Milton, Camille Howard. I had a very diverse record collection. Because I never was real crazy about the trendy things but I liked Little Willie Littlefield and especially Charles Brown. We had records by them and we'd see them whenever they were in Oakland. There was a place called the Sweet's Ballroom. It was the most beautiful ballroom I've ever seen in my life. I've traveled to different countries, different continents. I've never seen anything like that. It was completely circular—completely round. It seated about 5000 people. It was completely round and when you walked into the ballroom and you look straight ahead, in that there was a bandshell about twenty-five feet before you get to the back of that circle. And that band shell had a big stage. And all around the sides of the room, there were couches—beautiful nice couches. Upstairs, it was like auditorium seating with rising seats. It was just a great place. On Wednesday nights the promoter that owned the Fillmore auditorium, Charles Sullivan, would buy dates. He'd book these people and he'd work them in different cities around the area. He'd bring them into Oakland on the weekends. And, Wednesday night was kind of a bad night. So, they'd play in Oakland a second time, at Sweets Ballroom and I got a chance to see Sonny Thompson and Lulu Reed, who I fell in love with when I was 16, and Ray Charles all the time, Fats Domino, James Brown, just everybody that was doing any touring in the area.

How much of an opportunity did you have to see all these folks?

At the time Jimmy McCracklin was by far the biggest name from around the Bay Area, particularly on the blues scene. Jimmy Wilson, Big Mama Thornton lived around there for a good while. And I worked with them, you know. But Charles Sullivan used to buy acts from Texas. Arizona. Yeah, Southern California bearing in mind. And we would get in free. Most of the times we take our instruments along and our uniforms and walk in *en masse*—four guys. And Ivory Joe Hunter, I got a chance to see Ivory Joe, and meet him a little bit. And that's just a few of the people. I never got a chance to see Saunders King because he was in jail. Saunders King was Black—and the mayor of San Francisco was white. Saunders King was very flamboyant. And he was going out with the mayor's daughter—and he had her on the streets. Whatever he did, it had to have been more than that, because he was in jail a long time, I mean, he was in jail when I was 12 or 13 years old, and he was still in jail when I was in my 20s. People who played with him say he was a good-looking guy and that was happening to a lot of chicks. And he never really recovered from that incarceration or recovered musically.

Who was your band at that time? You talked about working with some of the top blues guys, but you had a younger band?

Yeah, with my high school buddies. I had a guy named Fred Casey. He was on drums. Fred Casey toured with Bill Withers. Very good drummer, but emotionally, he's a nine to five person. And he was never into the nightclubs or the touring scene. He missed it badly. That guy, when we first went on the road on tour, he was eighteen years old. He had never spent the night even over at a friend's house. So, the first two weeks man, he never even went to the bathroom for two weeks [*laughs*]. We thought we were gonna have to put him in the hospital. He overcame that, needless to say, and he's a good player around the bay doing a day job. I had Albury on sax, who was definitely a nine to five person and he ended up he's been working at the post office for like about twenty years now. He just quit playing. Then, on organ. I had a guy named General Chalmers. And it was so funny because he was twenty-two years old. And he was weird in the sense that he was into buildings, he liked buildings. He'd go to City Planning Commission meetings. I mean, can you imagine anybody going to City Planning Commission meetings? "Where are you going?" "I'm going to the city planning meetings!"—and they'd send him these big beautiful books with estimates on city redevelopment and everything. The books got to cost like 100 bucks or so. And they got General Allen Chalmers on the list. They just thought he was a retired general and something. We haven't been able to find him. They gave me a party at the club where I work in Sacramento, for my fiftieth birthday. And they dug up all of these guys I haven't seen in 20 or 25 years, but we couldn't find General. I saw my old saxophone players—and all the good old guys, who had long pretty hair and stuff like that—they're getting bald and fat now. See, I've been bald so I'm good with that—I'm cool. Now they've caught up with me, and they're not handling it very well.

Who would you call your main influence in terms of your guitar playing?

It's evolved. In the beginning, my main influence, the things I was listening to on guitar before I met Lafayette Thomas were Pete Guitar Lewis and T-Bone Walker. Those are the two guys that I really like. But my main influence stylistically is T-Bone. I like his playing and his different records, and I wanted to be a bass player with T-Bone. I also had, you know, Barney Kessel albums. I pick like Barney Kessel because at the time Barney Kessel was only doing downstroke picking and that made him so fast with the finger thing. But T-Bone Walker was the big influence with Barney Kessel—and a little shout out to Kenny Burrell, who we just love to death. Then Lafayette Thomas came along.

Who was the main influence on Lafayette Thomas? Who was his main man?

When you talk to Lafayette, it all depends on what sign the moon was in [*laughs*]. One time he would say Charlie Christian, the next time he would tell you T-Bone. And so, I don't know who his influence was. Dick Shurman was telling me Lafayette's biggest influence was his uncle, Jesse Thomas.

Would you tell the story about the "do" cream that you made?

I had this real good friend whose name was Byron Morrow. And Byron was a big guy—bigger than me, but the thing is, his mother was sanctified, one of the mothers of the church, a good strong woman. She was six feet tall and about 300 plus pounds. And very firm—but very nice. So, I used to go to their house to eat. Byron and I were like brothers, but Byron was very bad. Like we'd break into washing machines, you know? They had just come out with coin operated washing machines—you put quarters in. And, I've never been a very good accomplice to any kind of crime—I get so stressed. So, he would be breaking in the thing and I'm a block down the street—I'm supposed to be watching out. And I can hear him "Boom!" and it's got me scared to death. Anyway, we decided we were going to make ourselves some conk, that's what they called it. Black people have real curly hair and conk is a straightener—that's what it is. We found out how to make it. The basic ingredients of the straightener are potatoes. We boiled our potatoes, and then whipped them up. And we put some oil in there. And you're supposed to put some soap powder in there, you know, and then you put in some lye. Then you put it on your hair, leave it awhile, and it relaxes the curl. So, we made the concoction, but we forgot to put the soap powder in. The soap powder is what lets you wash the conk out. When you put water on it, it makes it easy to come out and get that lye out. Boy, I'm telling you, we put that conk on there. We put that stuff on and when it started burning, then you know it's time to rinse the stuff out. But we put that stuff on our head and because we had no soap, we couldn't get it out! When we finally got it washed out, it was beautifully straight man and look really great. But when it dried, it was all stuck to our head and all scabbed and everything because we had burned off the surface of the skin. The only thing I can think of more painful than that—15 years ago I decided to shave my head. I'd wanted to do it for about twenty years. So, I decided to do it one day. When you do it, you're not supposed to shave against the grain, just with the grain because when you shave against the grain, you shave off the little tops of the follicles. If you shave those little things off, then when the hair grows out, it doesn't have a chance to grow out enough, it grows out and then back in, and it causes bumps. When it grows out, it grows out at little angles, and it irritates all the little nerves all over your head. And man, I'm telling you, I couldn't lay down, I couldn't go to sleep, I had to sit up for about three nights, I just had to sit up in a chair with a fan on my head [*laughs*]. Eventually, what you do is oil and massage your scalp. So, I finally went to a barber. He put a lot of stuff on it. He just told me to massage it and let it grow out and then come back in. I saw guys with shaved heads and it was like that cue ball effect, you know, billiard ball, just real smooth. And when I went at it, what I did, essentially, was I skinned myself. And that was really cool when you first do it, it's sensitive. When women walked by their skirts rustle, you can feel the breeze.

I was looking through the Bob Geddins section. I didn't realize that Trilon was a Bob Geddins label.

I didn't either. Bob had two or three labels. And then, when I did the San Francisco Blues Festival the first time, they had this page on Bob Geddins. And they have about eight to ten labels that he was affiliated with us. The Trilon label really wasn't his company. Trilon, essentially, was a scam to get a bunch of Bob's masters. What they did was send him on the road. And while he was gone, they told him they would take care of his bills—and they didn't. So, they seized a lot of his assets and held an auction and then arranged that one of their people would be the only bidder. So, when he came back, he found out all these bills have piled up, and they had a bunch of the stuff that he had done for them. So, yeah, they hired him to work for them.

Vivian Green, I think is the name that I have on Trilon and had no idea where it came from at all.

I think, maybe he did the Lowell Fulson stuff, too. I don't know.

When we talked about the Jimmy McCracklins, you're on the Jimmy McCracklins. Were those on another label before they showed up on Imperial? Are we talking about two different versions of the Jimmy McCracklins? Would there be a title for Bob Geddins and then he'd go and re-record it for Imperial?

I don't know. I really don't know. Didn't some of Jimmy's stuff come out on Bob's label? You know, like "The Walk"—and "I Want To Know"? Also, "Club Savoy," and "Fare-Well," "Take A Chance," and "My Love For You." I think some were done on Art-Tone—and also on his label called Geddinson's. He did a lot of licensing—he did a lot of stuff, because I remember we did this thing with Johnny Fuller, [*sings*] "I just moved into my new house today . . ." that "Haunted House." And then didn't some rock group do it? And he got about twenty-five grand. I know we were kind of upset because we only got session pay. Bob Geddins—did you ever get to hear him talk? Oh my God! You got to get the violins out when he's talking. [*Talks like Bob Geddins:*] "Well, I don't know, you boys. I don't have a whole lot of money. But you know, y'all been doing a good job for me—I think I'll give you $25." [*Laughs.*] And we'd say, "Okay—okay . . ." But then he got about twenty-five grand for the tune that we recorded. We were kind of upset but his little son was driving this convertible white Cadillac—and he was such a dummy. He had Cadillac and had the hydraulic shocks extended as far as they could go. The car was up about nine feet off the ground, driving down the street with this white Cadillac with the shocks extended. I think he got up there and couldn't get it down. [*Laughs.*] So that dissipated all the anger. We said, "That's so stupid, we're not gonna even be pissed. The heck with it." Bob was fair, he was decent, he would always pay us. We loved Bob. We could never really get angry. Now, we could get angry at Ray Dobard—because he was really secretive about his stuff. He would just record stuff and record and he'd sell the masters off; you know. And he made money—and he was just a tightwad. We would do twenty takes on a song, and he would use the first take—eventually. He was very, very tight—and could have been the Barry Gordy of the West—or whatever big-time person you want to make a comparison to. He had action on having Johnny Mathis, Etta James, Richard Berry, a lot of different people and he just turned them down.

Let's talk about the actual logistics of a session that you would do with Geddins. How would you find out that there was a session coming up, and who it was with? How long would you rehearse? Would it all be done in the studio that same day?

Bob Geddins's sessions were long and arduous, extremely boring sessions for the most part. For the other part, it was always exciting on the way to the studio, "I'm going to record." But when you get a session it would involve doing a lot of stuff over and over again. They weren't as boring as Ray Dobard sessions. With Bob Geddins, we would get more accomplished. Bob was into the theory, if you got the musicians here, you got four hours. And if you got two songs done, and two songs to do, let's do two more songs. And let's do as many songs as we can—and sometimes it would go like that. At some of Joe Simon sessions, we had a set amount of stuff to do and we did it. With Bob Geddins, going to his studio was different because he had about seven different studios during the time that I recorded with him, seven at least, and then he would lease or he would use other facilities for a session. He would be in one place and if you didn't record with him or see him for two months, we're going over to Bob's and do a session, we'd be on the other side of town somewhere—and he's just putting stuff in and just nailing egg crates to the wall and stuff like that. And stuff was forever breaking down—forever. We'd wait there for an hour and a half for the engineer to come over to fix the stuff. It was always breaking down but, you know, you're not gonna go home, because you haven't gotten paid—and you haven't done the job yet!

Were his sessions on tape?

On tape. We recorded for a guy named Wayne—an old guy in San Francisco had a studio in his basement, a good studio. He also had a disk machine. He would tape and put it on disk. Why? I don't know. But anyway, Bob's stuff, started with a two-track. He had a two-track machine. I think the last time I recorded for Bob he might have had a four track. But we've done things in monaural, we did things on single-track for him. We did things two-track. We did a couple of sessions in three-track with Joe Simon.

Was that all worked out in the studio? You never had any prior knowledge of what was the material to be covered?

No. The only time we knew in advance with Joe Simon, was when I wrote the tunes. When I wrote the tunes, Joe would come over and I worked the arrangements out. And, when we did things with Ray Agee, because we had horns—anything we had horns on, we'd work them out. But most of Bob Geddins stuff, Bob didn't care about horns unless it was just one sax doing the soloing. So that we didn't have to really work anything out because generally they were all straight-ahead blues.

Can we run down a checklist of people from out in the Bay Area? Maybe you can give me some reminiscence on how you met them or recorded with them. Let's start out with Jimmy McCracklin . . .

Well, as I said, I met Jimmy McCracklin, when I was sixteen years old. I met him by hanging around with Lafayette "Thing" Thomas. Lafayette was working for him. And when they were off, Lafayette would come down and then play at Woody's, where I was playing. Then I would play bass and he would play guitar. And when he thought I was ready, and I could play well enough, they invited me over to McCracklin's Club. I started sitting in and I got a chance to work with McCracklin. And I subsequently played on his albums—either bass or guitar or piano or something. But Jimmy was very particular about how he wanted his stuff. I've always had great respect for his musical integrity as far as what he was doing. Because no matter how simple it was, he wanted it like that. Traditionally your blues are eight bars or twelve bars. He'd do songs that ended up having a 13-bar blues and stuff like that. Like "I Want to Know" is one of these songs. We did it, but just the way it falls in the timing is real messed up—and he would always mess up drummers. I've done some festivals with him within the last four or five years. And the count is awkward—but there's precedent for that on the record, you know? [*Laughs.*]

How about Lowell Fulson?

I met Lowell at one of Jimmy's clubs. Then I talked to him a couple of times when he and Earl Brown played together at Minnie Lou's, but I didn't really get a chance to know Lowell until he played with my band several years later. About three or four years later, I was about 20, I worked at a place called the Timeout Club and then Lowell would come down and we'd back him up on stuff, since he knew I had all of his records. In fact, I used to try to get him to do this Lowell Fulson and two guitars. Lowell was a hell of an inspiration for me because he was always extremely sharp at the time. He would have pink silk suits and always had a Cadillac and plenty of ladies, you know? So, all of these people that have the stereotype about blues man with the overalls and straw hat, I wasn't exposed to those kinds of guys. I was exposed to Guitar Slim, Lowell Fulson and Saunders King—you know, people like that. These guys liked big fine cars, fine women, fine food, plush accommodations—everything like that.

Maybe in their youth they might have done some that back-in-the-country stuff, but when I met Lowell, he was on the top of the heap then—and I mean, he was drinking the best whiskey. So, when I met him and played with him, he had "Reconsider Baby" at that time when I really worked with him and inter-related with him on a personal level. I could play his guitar solo note-for-note just like him. I was that enthused about what he did on it—I loved it but I used to ask him to do that two-guitar thing. He would never do it. He would act like he didn't even remember but it was great stuff, kind of like the Mississippi delta stuff you know? [*Sings.*] "Lord have mercy" or "Ain't gonna pick no more cotton. Oh, Lord, I done got tired." Stuff like that, he didn't want any part of those kind of songs . . .

Did I hear you mentioned Guitar Slim?

Yeah, Guitar Slim used to come through there. Boy, he had a red suit on, white shoes and a green car! [*Laughs.*] He had that tune, "Things That I Used To Do"—but the song that we liked was the flip side—"I Done Got Over" [*Sings:*] "Doo-da-doo-da-doo-do-doo." Yeah, we liked to do that, it sounded like my song "Cockroach Run" that Lafayette Thomas recorded. Our heroes in the blues were guys like that. My aunt used to like things like "You're One Black Rat, One day I'm gonna find your trail"—Memphis Minnie! My aunt would play that and I would walk—I couldn't deal with that. And, Charles Brown and stuff like that, I didn't really pay too much attention to stuff like that until a friend of mine in Seattle used to play me some Doctor Clayton. He was an older Black guy, and I was teaching him guitar. But I ended up getting him to show me some of these old licks, because I wasn't playing stuff like that. My people I loved were Billy Butler, and blues guy—like me and Wayne Bennett. We've always had a mutual admiration society. I love Wayne's playing, and he'd come up to me and say, "I love your playing!" And I'd say, "You love my playing? How can you love my playing when I love your playing?" As a kid I bought all the Barney Kessel albums, you know, all Barney Kessel stuff, Charlie Christian stuff. And I play blues because they needed a guitar player. And I could play that. It was easy for me to play. So, it didn't seem like it was going to demand anything from me.

How about Jimmy Wilson?

Jimmy Wilson. Jimmy Wilson was about 6'3" tall, and he was thin. And just his clothes, the way he dressed was impeccable. And he, well, we all know he had just the most beautiful voice. I mean, his voice would send chills—he could sing. The guy was just a nice, good-looking man—his whole appearance, the way he carried himself. I was about nineteen. And I think Jimmy was in his thirties and his woman was about thirty years. I was madly in love with her, but she was madly in love with Jimmy Wilson. I worked with him. We did this tune called "The Strangest Blues." And it came out under someone else's name—Jimmy Nolen. And I'm playing bass on that, Lafayette's playing guitar. Ray Kahn's on drums. It was a great song. I didn't work with Jimmy Wilson too much; except I did some stuff in the studio. And I worked about two jobs with him. He was between Dallas or Houston or wherever he was living in Texas—and the Bay Area. He didn't work around the Bay Area very much, even though he had this big record, "Tin Pan Alley," he never did work around the area. And we would only see him occasionally. He'd be in town man two or three weeks and the only way I would find out is the lady upstairs from my aunt Lucille was one of his girlfriends. He'd go visit her. So, I don't know too much about him.

So, you're on a number of the records though?

Yeah . . .

How about Ray Agee?

I worked jobs with Ray Agee—a beautiful guy. He's a very sweet man. He had polio. And a good singer, good singer. We worked and we recorded, but he didn't get a lot of work. At that particular time, blues singers like Ray Agee, unless he really had a nice/big name, weren't being hired too much in the clubs around there. The best place to play was when Jimmy McCracklin had his club. He was hiring different blues acts but generally where we worked—I worked at the Showcase Lounge—and they'd bring in Clyde McPhatter, B.B. King, and Laverne Baker. They'd bring in people like Etta James and Louis Jordan—we played behind them. But other than that, people like Ray Agee, we worked a few jobs around town with him. I'd spend more time in studio with him. But I know he's a beautiful man. He's the kind of guy who would do anything for you. He was nice in the studio . . .

Was that for Bob Geddins?

Ray Agee recorded for Ron Badger, at Sahara Records. "Red Fire" on Sahara. We did that. That was Ron Badger and Bob Geddins—they were partners on some stuff.

How about Roy Hawkins?

Roy Hawkins, man, now we worked with Roy Hawkins. From when I was 18, I worked with Roy Hawkins a good deal. The thing I remember about Roy is he drank a lot. And he was a sweetheart of a guy and he played piano with one hand because one was messed up. And he had a fine old lady—with about eight kids. And we used to wonder, you get all the scuttlebutt—Roy was older than us. So, we young guys, see this guy and this woman's bringing him drinks and she's gorgeous, and everything. We'd say, "Gosh, I wish . . ." But you never know what's going on—it could be complete hell with the relationship. We never stopped to say, "Wait a minute, I don't want to have only one hand, even if I'm going to have this fox and eight kids, too." I had my daughter try to find this woman because nobody knows what ever happened to Roy Hawkins. George Hearst told me though, is that Roy went down to LA with a model called Precious. The only other thing I had heard was from a record collector Dick Bass. There was a record store in Richmond and a guy there told Dick in late 1970, when "The Thrill Is Gone" was a real big hit for B.B. King, that Roy Hawkins had come into the store looking for a copy of his original record so that he could sue for his money. That's the only thing I ever heard. I wrote to the state and asked if they had a death certificate and they just told me that they wouldn't tell me so I never pursued it.

Well, wasn't he in a car crash?

Yeah, he was in a serious car accident and his one arm was paralyzed. Isn't this weird? I've forgotten which hand it was. How could I forget that?

So, the accident happened before you actually knew him?

Before I knew him. The only thing I heard is that he was a vacuum cleaner salesman in LA for a while.

You talk about some moody records; those are some beautiful moody records . . .

You better believe it—like that "Strange Land"—I love that. "I Walk Alone," "The Condition I'm In"—all those things. Yeah.

Who are we forgetting to talk about?

Oh, yeah—Jimmy Nelson. Now I worked with Jimmy Nelson only one time. And during the time that I work with him, it was so hectic. I think we did a fashion show or something, and he never got there to rehearse. And I was all nervous. My favorite record that he did was "Meet Me With Your Black Dress On." His biggie was "T99"—but I loved "Meet Me With Your Black Dress On." In fact, that's another one—I got to get the words to that one, that's a great record. But he didn't work around the Bay Area very much at all he recorded around there. There was a guy named Chick Morris who wrote some stuff for him and Chick Morris also was one of the co-writers of "Please Send Me Someone To Love" with Percy Mayfield—although I don't know if he got credit. Chick was very talented. He did a lot of writing, a lot of tunes with Percy Mayfield. And he was kind of bitter about something. I don't know what it was, you know, I didn't want to hear. He was always real bitter when we would do a session. We did some sessions with him for Ray Dobard.

I guess then the next name on the list is Johnny Fuller.

Oh boy. Johnny Fuller. He just died about a couple of years ago. Johnny Fuller had a record out called "Johnny Ace's Last Letter" that was big. He had a lot of songs out. He was a good singer, a really good singer and played some good piano and guitar. There were three brothers—the Fuller Brothers. They were all real good, but Johnny was the one that really sparkled. He was deaf in one ear. He would always play with one ear toward the band. An occupational hazard for bluesmen was booze. Johnny did a lot of drinking. He would drink a lot. I played a lot of little $10, $15 jobs with Johnny when I first started playing. I don't mean for it to sound like I'm putting the money down, that's just what the money was. But the enjoyment was, like $100 a night, because I was playing and working with guys older than me and working for adults and people liked what I was doing. And so, I was getting this nice good rush all the time—that thing that you give out to the audience—and they give it back to you in another way. So, I had a good time. Then I kind of outgrew my music, the things that I needed musically in that form of expression. I was young and I was listening to a lot of other things. And there were a lot of things I wanted to play. So, as a consequence, I didn't work with Johnny Fuller, too much. We still maintained our ties with the strictly blues musicians by doing recording sessions with everybody, but it was just really, it got almost impossible around the East Bay in the Bay Area on the West Coast, to make any money just playing blues.

Maybe tell me a bit about Tiny Powell.

Tiny Powell used to be with the Five Blind Boys of Mississippi for a while—and just an intense, an intense singer. I mean, he would be singing and shaking his right hand [*sings an intense note*] and his shoulder and his face would be shaking. And while you'd be looking at him, he'd be turning red and everything. But he was a really, really good singer. He had a timing problem where you'd have to watch him and kind of tell him when to come in on stuff. But he could sell us on a song. He was a great person. He was a skycap at the airport for years. And he would always call me and say, "I got a session for you. We're gonna do this session. I gotta get me a record." He'd always call me. And I was kind of looking forward to it. Because I know if we got him together, he was always comfortable with me. Because I would get the band together. And I would say, "Don't worry about Tiny—just do your part. And if he comes in wrong, don't worry, we'll fix it in the studio." And so, he was a good, good singer and a good person—a really good person. I was very saddened to hear that he passed a few years ago.

It's amazing to me that somebody who was in gospel would have a timing problem. I wonder if that's common?

Yeah, you know, Joe Simon had a timing problem. If you sing long enough, you can recognize the signs. Music is just like on a highway, you know your entrance. You know your exits. After a while, you find out, okay, that I'm supposed to start here, I'm supposed to get off there. So, it's a matter of showing them the signs and then them getting their signs together so they'll recognize them. Joe Simon has got his stuff together now. But when I worked with Joe, I used to be in the control room. I would just point to him to come in. The same way with Al King from the Bay Area. Al King had this great voice, man, kind of a Lowell Fulson—just a great voice. But he would blatantly look at me like I'm his mother when he was in the studio. "Where am I? Where am I?" [*Laughs.*] The other guys really didn't care for it too much, but they knew that they were kind of off. But Al would have no idea what was going on. And I'd have to point to him to come in, [*sings*] "So long. Oh, I hate to see you go . . ." Otherwise, he would wait man about two minutes. [*Laughs.*] But, that comes from people having a good voice and concentrating on the pitch—on their emotional delivery, and not really concentrating on the music's time. Some people have a kind of a natural affinity for knowing where they are in the song.

Was K.C. Douglas around when you were there?

Yeah, K.C. Douglas was around—he sure was. I worked with K.C. Yeah. I don't really remember K.C. that much because I think he was quite a bit older. We worked for K.C. And we work with L.C. Good Rocking Robinson and different people like that. But they were in another groove from us, and they had their established groove. And we, I mean, we just worked with them. They were never any of our favorites. Like L.C. Robinson, boy, he'd come on your gig ready to kick ass. I mean, he had his long cord, like Albert Collins's and he had this guitar lick, a stroke [*sings*] "chucka-chucka-chuck." He had that stroke, you know, long before Isaac Hayes and Shaft came out. L.C. was doing that years ago. And he had this big, very nice, hollow-body guitar. I was into Stratocasters—I wasn't interested in no big, fat, old-timey looking guitar. And then he always had a bunch of old chicks around him too, you know—which was cool, now that I done got old [*laughs*]. And I've gained a lot of respect for him—I had respect for him, but he wasn't a guitar player that I cared that much about. And, I'm really embarrassed to say that, I feel terrible. It's a loss on my part, because the man was there. And after his death, I got a chance to hear stuff that he did that I fell in love with. His violin playing is amazing. I mean, God, he just brings tears to my eyes. He's so good, you know, and his playing, his singing, his playing, his whole thing. I just wasn't into it. I'm real glad that we've got tapes and records on him. Because I could have completely missed out on it. I heard him play violin, at the time, we would've had a barn dance, you know, play country stuff. And he just played a lot of violin like Gatemouth Brown. They played country stuff. But then I heard him play some blues on a violin—and I had never really heard him play blues on the violin. And then I heard him at the barn dances playing country & western stuff. It's not that I didn't like it. But it wasn't anything that made me say, "Wow!"—until I heard this album he was on. I said, "Who is that on the violin?" So, there's things that I didn't do that I should have done. And but I'm really sad that I didn't listen to L.C. more. I mean, I used to really love to hear him play that guitar and do that "chunka-chucka" thing. And L.C., bless his heart, was a very good cat, but he was a very jealous hearted guy as far as you play. He would come on your set and brings his guitar and his long cord and he would do a show on your set—and he go out and do a 20-minute song. And then he get his steel guitar and play everything. Now that's what he would do on your set, but if you came on his set, he'd have you sit around and he just didn't make you feel welcome. L.C. didn't really care for us sitting in.

So, we didn't go around. We invited him to come on down on ours. And you know, we said, "Yeah, we're fine."

In that same vein, was Mercy Dee Walton out there?

Mercy Dee was out there too. And he had [*sings*] "Sittin' here—a thousand miles from nowhere—in my little one-room country shack . . ." I never did work with Mercy. Mercy worked with L.C. He only worked with L.C. when he was in town at IU—and they worked at a little place, and we never really would go to that place. I was working at the Showcase Lounge and I was working uptown you know, and this place, The Main Event, was down on Seventh Street—like in Chicago, it would be a great place. You go in and it was a really rough crowd—good people, good people, good hard-working people. But they'd go down there and get juiced and get thrown out, man, and every now and then somebody would turn the whole joint out, when everybody would leave about 12 o'clock. The police would come. They had a jam session on Sundays and sometimes we'd pass by there. I went down a couple of times to see Mercy Dee, you know, and every time I'd get down there, he'd be on a break. We'd be out in the car getting drunk, man, and sit around and I finally end up getting me something to eat and going home.

Honeyboy Edwards

David "Honeyboy" Edwards was an interesting figure in blues history. He recorded both before WWII for the Library of Congress and after the war with six commercial recordings listed during the 1950s, a couple of them quite good. But, I've always felt that his true value was greater as a witness to history than as a musician. Over the course of his travels, he met and interacted with a Who's Who list of blues notables including Charley Patton, Son House, Tommy Johnson, Robert Johnson, Little Walter, and Sonny Boy Williamson II (!). Honeyboy was around the blues scene forever. I first interviewed him in 1972 and then again with the interview that follows, done twenty years later, in September of 1992. He died in 2011 at the ripe old age of 96 (!), unheard of for a bluesman.

■ ■ ■

I was born in a little town in the Mississippi delta called Shaw, Mississippi. That's about sixty miles out of Clarksdale, west outta 61 Highway. 1915—the twenty-eighth day of June. My mother had seven kids—three girls and four boys—but I got a lotta relations, cousins, first cousins, things like that—my mother's brother's kids. There's seventy-five or eighty of us in all. There's about seventy-five out on the Westside right now—right on Cicero and Harrison! They hang right there every Friday and Saturday—right on the corner about twenty-five or thirty of 'em be hangin' around.

Were you all together down south?

Yeah—they was down there but their mother and father moved here and they were small, before they growed up, you know. They got kids—you know what I mean? I got a first cousin over there—she had fifteen [kids] and she got a daughter got thirteen. And they all over there on the Westside.

How did you get the name Honeyboy?

My mother and them told me when I was a little better than a year old and I was tryin' to walk—I was standin' on the floor tryin' to walk. I was standin' up tryin' to make a step but I was scared to make a step. And my older sister said, "Come here baby. Come here baby!" So I started runnin' to her and I fell and she said, "Mama, look at little old Honeyboy!" And they started to call me Honey. All the white people down south start to call me Honey and when I start to recordin', I said Honeyboy—when I start to recordin'. But they did call me Honey first. That's all everybody know—Honey. My father, he played violin and guitar—and my mother played a harp. I learned some from my father and I remember when I was fourteen years old—that was 1929—and we lived on a plantation. My father was a sharecropper. And a man stayed in the country there. Had a guitar ordered from Sears Roebuck, I think he paid twelve dollars for it. That was a good guitar. And we used to go to his house every evening when they come outta the field from work we'd go to his house and he'd play the guitar for us and we'd stomp and dance—called ourselves dancin'. And I wanted to play the guitar and my father bought that guitar from him. He sold it to my father for me. He was playin' some of that old style stuff like some old ragtime stuff, you know—"Bring it down to my house baby—Ain't nobody here but me." "Nickle is a nickel—Dime is a dime, got a house full a children ain't nairn mine!" [*Laughs.*] Something to make you shuffle across the floor with—I started playin' right when my father bought the guitar from this man. And he would teach me some chords on the guitar. He'd show me how to make G and C and D you know, like that—my chords. And I 'member in '29 after three/four months after I bought the guitar, I was hittin' some pretty good strokes. And some people lived back behind us in the field and they give a dance with one of them old wind-up Graphophones. That Saturday night they broke the spring in it—so they didn't have no music. They said, "What we gonna do now?" They said, "Let's get little old Honeyboy— He can play!" And they come got me. I had never played for a party before. I guess I was singin' a hundred different songs and playin' the same number all night long! [*Laughs.*] But they was dancin'. Well I played for the party and just got busy then tryin' to learn all I could. Then in 1930—that was in the Depression—I was fifteen and I kept my guitar until '31. And we was in Greenwood, Mississippi. I was raised around Greenwood. On Christmas Day me and some boys was playin' in the street on Johnson Street. And they knocked the guitar offa my arm—offa my shoulder. I had a little cord string. Tore my guitar up all to pieces. I didn't have nothin' to play on. And that was '31. '31 my sister married a man with a guitar. And I start to playin' pretty good in '31. I was hittin' some good strokes. And Joe Williams came to the country—Big Joe Williams. He was playin' for a country dance that Saturday night and I went over there where he's playin'. He had a red handkerchief around his neck and he was playin' "Highway 49." He was playin' the Blues and I was lookin' at him so hard. He said, "What you lookin' at me son? Can you play?" I said, "I can play a little." He said, "Here's my guitar—hit me a little lump." So I taken hold to his guitar and hit a couple chords. He said, "I can learn you how to play." So that Sunday morning he come home with me and my father and played for us as we eat breakfast. He ask my father could he take me off in the winter time—he could learn me how to play. My father want me to learn. He said, "I don't care—Honey ain't doin' anything. It's the winter time—you can't work on the farm. Go head on!" So I took my brother-in-law's guitar with Joe Williams and he carried me to New Orleans. He carried me to Greenwood, Vicksburg, and I stayed with Joe about six or seven months till I learnt pretty good.

Did Big Joe Williams have nine strings on his guitar at that time?

When I met Joe he had nine strings on his guitar then. It was just something he invented hisself. He'd bore three holes up there on the top of the neck of his guitar. The guitar was made a little different then—they had a flat pegheads then. And he'd put two B's together and he'd put two little E's together. Sometimes he'd put two G's together. Most of the time he'd put two B's and two little E's together. But when he put the two G's together then he had nine strings on him. But that's the way he played all the time—his guitar sounded mostly like a mandolin.

The two of you were in unusual tunings together. Can you explain how you tuned together?

He taught me this because I really didn't know at the time. He was older than I was and had experienced more about the guitar than I did. And Joe would play with a capo on his guitar in Spanish. That was cross keys in Spanish. And would put his capo about second fret or third fret and that guitar would be so high it sound just like a mandolin. He would put me in E in natural and I would tune down low in natural but I'd be leveled off with the Spanish—how I tune—but I'd be low but I'd be in natural. And when he played the Blues in that Spanish high key, I'd be in that low key with the bass roarin' just like I was playin' a bass guitar behind him—had the same tone but I was low in natural. We would play on the streets for nickels and dimes and quarters. I was glad to get away from home, you know, outta the country. And he give me sometimes, thirty cents, forty cents—back then that was a lotta money—me just a boy. At that time I wasn't large—I was kinda skinny. And I liked to play with balls at that time. I loved my guitar but I still had childish ways, you know. And Joe would be in some rooming house somewhere with a woman drinkin' getting drunk and I'd be out shootin' marbles somewhere with the boys [*laughs*]. And then he go and get drunk somewhere to get broke. He'd say, "C'mon Honey, get your guitar, get your guitar!" He wanted to make some more money then [*laughs*]. Joe learnt me a whole lot—Joe learnt me everything! And the man couldn't read or write. He didn't know his name hardly when he see it. That's right! He could go to New York, stand there on the street on the corner, go all over New York and come right back there to that same corner. And that'd be the corner where he left—he's just like that! He had recorded back in the '30s—on RCA with Sonny Boy—Sonny Boy #1. He record some with him too—out of Jackson, Tennessee? He'd come back down there and his little record'd be sellin' down there and everybody thought he was a big man. I wanted to play with him cause his name was Joe Williams. And by him havin' recorded a little bit on wax, he *did* get a chance to make more money than regular Blues players in the country because he had a name—you know what I mean.

Would he ever carry any of his records with him?

He's carry some every once in a while—take around and sell 'em for a little amount of money. When he had recorded and his name got a little down south there, he'd come down there get somebody to give a dance or party and he'd charge at the door, you know. He was Joe Williams. He'd charge fifteen to twenty-five cents at the door. Sometimes make $25 to $30. You know what I mean. That was a lotta money then! When we got down to New Orleans Joe started drinkin' so much he wanted to fight and clown goin' you know. So I slipped off and left Joe—left him in New Orleans. And I come down number 90 Highway—right down the coast—come back into Biloxi. And I had my guitar on my shoulder. I didn't know what to do 'cause I had never played by myself. So I stopped on the bridge—people catchin' crabs in nets you know. Say, "Boy—can you play that guitar?" I say, "I can play a little." So I started to playin' the Blues by myself. They started to givin' me nickels and dimes. I say, "I can make it by myself now!" So, I just kept a playin' till I got better 'n' better—meet more musicians. When I went out on my own, I picked up my harp—I always could play harmonica. And I practiced around the house with my harp and guitar. I seen how to make my strokes with my harp and guitar together. And I went out on my own then. I was playing on the streets with my harp and guitar. Then I played like Joe Williams a long time. I played in Spanish and I played a lotta high note harp—like in F and E's, you know, 'cause I play tuned up high with a capo and I played a lotta high note harp to correspond with that high Spanish you know. When I got to Memphis I knowed the Memphis Jug Band—some of them. When I got there I played pretty good. And I was a stranger in Handy Park. Old Dewey played the can—played the bass can—he grabbed me, cause I was just a young boy and could play pretty good. And he got me cause he could make some nickels and some quarters with me. I was young. He played the can—like a tub. I played with the Memphis Jug Band awhile. He hooked me up with his step-daughter. So all the money I make I had to give it to them [*laughs*]. I quit playin' with them and went to playin' with Big Walter Horton. We was pretty close together—I'm two years older 'n Walter. So Walter's playin' with them too but when I come to Memphis we started playin' together in the park and I went home with him. Walter's mother say, "This boy's about the same age you is. Y'all get out there on the streets and y'all make you some nickels and dimes and come back. I'll keep your money for y'all and cook for y'all. Y'all let them old mens alone—they ain't doin' nothin' but takin' your money." [*Laughs.*] That's what they were doin', you know. We had a kitty, you know, you play for the kitty—cigar box you put nickels, dimes, quarters in there. Well—some tryin' to steal, some tryin' to count. There was always something up—'cause they wouldn't break fair. So, when me and Walter got together we'd go down to the Peabody Hotel on the river there, Hotel LaClairs, and we'd go down there in the lobby and play for the white people. They'd give us quarters and dimes, we'd make our money and come home to Miss Emma—she'd count it and she keep it. So we stayed away from those old musicians for a long time.

Who were the members of the Memphis Jug Band? Was Will Shade there?

Yeah. Will Shade, Charlie Simms.

How about Casey Bill Weldon—Was he there at that time?

No—but I remember Frank Stokes. I knowed old man Stokes—and I knowed his son, Little Frank too. I knowed both of them. And I knowed Sleepy John Estes—I knowed him.

How about Dan Sane who used to play with Frank Stokes?

Yeah. I remember him. He come from Mississippi—round Hunniana [Hernando], somewhere down in there. He was livin' in Memphis but that's where he came from. And Son Brimmer, he played guitar with the jug band. I knowed most all of 'em around there—Bubba, Raymond Paines—all of 'em played in the Beale Street Park there. That was about '35, somethin' like that. Up until the '40s they all would hang around the park. But they had me playin'. They had been playin' there way before then but that's when I come into the picture round '34 or '35 but that's when they were still playin' in the Beale Street Handy Park.

How about Robert Wilkins? Was he around?

Yeah—he was around. He hadn't joined the church yet. No, he was playin' I remember him. I believe he was playin' banjo or somethin'. Robert Wilkins—I remember him.

Wasn't Gus Cannon the main banjo player in Memphis?

I heard of him—never met him but I heard of him.

But it was Robert Wilkins playing banjo?

At the time. He played both of 'em, banjo and guitar.

How about Furry Lewis?

I never met Furry Lewis. He come outta Mississippi too down there. But he came into Memphis but I never met him. I met a lot of people but I never met Furry Lewis. I was in Memphis in and out. I met Sleepy John Estes, I met Yank Rachel—all personally I knowed them. I knowed Son Bonds, Hammie Nixon—he was outta Tennessee. I knowed all them! And Allen Shaw, his son Tango Shaw. I used to go down to Jackson, Mississippi. Tommy Johnson!—I used to go to his house. Hang around with Tommy Johnson and Clarence and Major—his brothers.

What kind of shape was Tommy in at that point?

Oh boy! Tommy drinked a whole lot a canned heat. I went to his house one time. His wife worked all the time but Tommy didn't work too much—he mostly played. He'd like play for Friday night, Saturday night parties—make his little money. She worked for white people. Rent was real cheap there in Jackson, Mississippi. Rent was $20 a month for a whole house—know what I mean? So Tommy made enough in a couple a nights to pay the rent and she bought the food. I used to go there with Tommy. I know once I stayed a whole week with him and he was using canned heat. He'd get that canned heat, called it Sterno. Women used to dress their hair with it. Stuff be's in a can—looks like jelly. And he would strike a match and burn that acid off. When you strike a match there'd be a blue blaze, flame up. When the whole can flame up you blow it out. Then you take that and put it in a thin rag, get that jelly and squeeze it down in a pan till all the alcohol comes out that thin rag. Then you put about three orange pops in on that alcohol. Then you got about a pint or a fifth you sit there drinkin' and get drunk—Whew! Then you start yellin', "Canned heat is killin' me!" [*Laughs.*]

What was he like to get along with?

Tommy was pretty nice to get along with. He was easy goin'. Most he liked to do was drink—that's all. He liked his canned heat. He didn't drink too much corn whiskey. He drink his canned heat and alcohol—grain alcohol? He'd drink corn whiskey but he really wasn't crazy about it. He just like them made-up drinks—and home-brew beer. He used to make a lotta home-brew beer down there.

Had you run across anybody that played like Tommy Johnson?

Tommy and his brothers, Mager and Clarence, played like him, played just alike. Used to be a fellow here in Chicago, I don't know if he's livin' now, Pegleg Sam Norton. He used to play in Jewtown [Maxwell Street in Chicago]. He played with Tommy and them too. He played like 'em too. And he used to play the streets over there in Jewtown. He had one leg—called him Sam Norton.

Was Houston Stackhouse the same age as Tommy Johnson?

I really don't know—but they was pretty close together. Now Stackhouse was pretty close to Tommy Johnson a lotta time. When he played "Called For Water, Gave Me Gasoline" he played that just like Tommy Johnson. I knowed Stackhouse.

Wasn't that the style known as the Crystal Springs Style?

I know where Crystal Springs is too! Crystal Springs, Hazelhurst, Brookhaven, all them right there together on 51 Highway goin' out to New Orleans . . .

But when you ran across him it was in Jackson, Mississippi?

It was in Jackson. When I first met him, he was in the Mississippi delta. Pickin' cotton—Tommy Johnson and them was. See there used to be a whole lotta cotton in the Mississippi delta—wasn't nothin' in the hills where they come from. But the people would come out the hills to the Delta to make a livin' in the fall and they bring their guitars and drums with 'em, get that big house on the plantation and give those country dances. And that's where I met him at—out from Greenwood—him and his brother—him and Clarence—playin' the same stuff then.

Who else did you meet?

I knowed Tommy McClennen good. When I first saw Tommy back in 1928, I was thirteen. He come out on the plantation and played for a country band. He was tryin' to play piano then—but he couldn't play no piano. He had a guitar and piano and he bumbled the piano while he grab his guitar to feed him offa whiskey out there—give him about three dollars a night [*laughs*]. From then on, I'd go to Greenwood. He'd be playin' in Greenwood. Finally my father moved around Greenwood in '30 and '31. I was right at Tommy then. I'd go to town—I'd go to Tommy's house all the time. I know Tommy's wife Ophilia. He had two kids—that's all they had, a girl and a boy—Bubba and Camay. They're here somewhere—I don't know where. Tommy—he was little *and* short. Him and Robert Petway used to play together. Robert Petway built the same size. Robert was a just a little bit bigger than Tommy. Same size—same height. Maybe five foot four I reckon—and small. His hat would be down over his ears! [*Laughs.*] But he had a big mouth—he had a big voice, little as he was! Yeah—I knowed Tommy real well. And Rube Lacey—he come from Greenwood too.

I'm familiar with his record. Was he very popular?

At the time. He had come up here and cut a few numbers but he come back down and his name was popular a little bit down through there. He didn't last too long—his—didn't last too long and it soon got kinda slow. Rube Lacey went to California and he got to be a preacher, you know. He wind up a preacher. Oh, I know Charley Patton too. I know Charley—hhmm—1931. I knowed Charley in 1931. Matter of fact, I met him in Marigold, Mississippi. I was down there with my cousin. Marigold, that's where he used to stay in Marigold and Dockery. He stayed on a farm betwixt Cleveland and Ruleville called Dockery Plantation. And he come off Dockery. When he left Dockery, he come over to Marigold. When he left Marigold, he come over to Holly Ridge where he died at. That's where he'd record for old man Speir [H.C. Speir] in Jackson, Mississippi. Charley died in 1934, March. The reason I know so good—I didn't know that he was sick but I was comin' over to my uncle's house and I had my guitar on my shoulder. I was playin' then and I come by that store at Holly Ridge and bought me some bologna, sat down to eat it and bought me a pop and I met some more young boys about my age. They say, "Did you know Charley Patton?" I say, "Yeah—I know Charley." She say, "Charley died last week. See that first grave down the street—that's where he's buried at." And I went down there by the graveyard and I looked. His uncle lived over in the field about a quarter mile from the store. That's where Charley Patton was livin'—with his uncle, Sherman. Sherman was a big bootlegger. He made whiskey. And I went over to Sherman's house. Sherman say, "Yeah—we lose Charley last week." Bertha was still over there—Charley's wife Bertha? Charley was some twenty years older than Bertha, so Bertha was right at my age. Charley was in his forties when he died. So, I stayed down there with Sherman pretty close to a week. I played for Sherman—he was a bootlegger, give dances. He say, "There ain't nothin' we can do. Charley's gone." Every once in a while, I'd meet him [Charley] in Ruleville. We'd play on the streets a little bit together. Then he cut out to a country dance somewhere. I never really was a partner to play with him but I have played with him. Just like Son House and Willie Brown. I never was a partner to play with 'em but I have played with 'em. When I first met Son House, I was in Memphis. That was 'round about '36. I left outta Memphis one Saturday evening. I got tired hangin' round the park. I said, "I'm gonna go down to Tunica, Mississippi." And I caught a ride hitchhikin'. I caught the ride about ten or fifteen miles outta Memphis. I met a fella at a little old store aside the road there. The little store was off side the road and he said, "Do you know Son House?" I say, "I really don't know him—but I hear talk about him." He said, "Well him and Willie Brown are playin' outside of Flower tonight." A place called Flower Plantation. It was about four or five o'clock then. It didn't look like I was gonna get on the streets in Tunica in time to make no money. I just went on out to the country where they was playin' at out there. When I got out there they was sittin' up playin' and drinkin' white whiskey. A big crowd around there. Big old plantation—Big barn, tractor barn had a big store and big barrelhouse off the barn where they could play music and have fun. I went in there and I saw them play some and drink whiskey. That's when I first met them. Willie Brown was a better guitar player than Son House. He died early. He was chubby—kind of fat. But that man had some beautiful chords he made in A—beautiful chords he made! Son House was mostly a rough guitar player—rugged guitar player, rough slide player you know. What I mean by rough—wouldn't nothin' be clear sometimes of day. Now you take Robert Johnson. He had some the beautifullest clear chords of anybody you want to hear. Everywhere he set them fingers it was right clear. He didn't make no bobble or nothin'—no bulge—what it is, that's what it was! Man had some nice chords to make! I met Robert in nineteen and thirty-seven, in the fall of the year. Early fall—something like September. I met him on the streets on a Saturday evening. He was stand up on the streets and I come down the street on Johnson Street in Greenwood. I come from the South end walkin'. He was on the North end standin' up a little alley there with his guitar on his shoulder—just standin' there. I come walkin' up and when I walked up there to him I stopped and wanted to talk to some more people. I wanted to hear how he played—I want to hear some myself. So a lady come there and say, "Mister, can you play 'Terraplane Blues'?" He just had made them records over in Austin, Texas. He had been over in Austin, wasn't over in Austin long. He recorded in Austin and come right back to Mississippi wasn't two or three months, he recorded and those people release that stuff right away. That stuff was right out on the jukebox just that quick. He said, "Miss—that's my record." She said, "If you play it I'll give you a dime." [*Laughs.*] That's a lotta money then! And Robert Started playin' that "Terraplane Blues" and standin' and shakin' goin' on. She said, "I believe that *is* that man. That sound just like that record." Then he started playin' "Hellhound on My Trail," "Come On in My Kitchen," all them different numbers he recorded. Then I walked up to him and I spoke to him. And he used to go with my cousin in Tunica, Mississippi. She's still livin'—Willie Mae Powell. That was his girlfriend. She had done told me 'bout Robert but I hadn't met Robert. And that's the way I got talkin' to him. I said, "You from around—" He said, "Yeah." "You been to Tunica?" He say, "Yeah." "You know Willie Mae Powell?" He said, "That's my girlfriend!" I say, "That's my first cousin." Then we started talkin' and we got kinda close together. By me knowin' so many people and so many bootleggers, people in Greenwood, bein' raised around Greenwood, I took him to all those bootleggers' houses. [*Laughs.*] I took him to Otis Spee's house, Rolla's house, Big Emma's house—all them big bootleggers on a Saturday. Feel just like we sit down and hear music, you know. We get two or three dollars apiece off them country people comin' out the country to the bootleggers, you know. And I carried him 'round. He met this man at the Three Forks where he got poisoned at. He had been playin' for this man. He start playin' for him then. He played for him all the fall, I was with him all the fall of '37. It was at the place they call Three Forks out in Greenwood. Robert played for this man all the fall. That winter I left—pulled out and left. I went down to Vicksburg. I had friends down in Vicksburg. And I went to New Orleans and I come back in March of '38. I hooked back up with him again. And I stayed with him until August in '38. He died in August—around the seventeenth of August. The night he got poisoned—on a Saturday night—we all was in Greenwood, walkin' the streets and playin' music. This man come in and got Robert and carried him out before somebody else pick him up and take him out. Cause a lotta country jukes they come in town and find the good musicians. Say, "Come on." Say, "I been playin' for so and so." "How much he pay ya? I'll pay ya so and so." If you come in and bid for more, he'll go with this man, you know. So that's the way this man come and got Robert, carried him out first 'fore somebody else come in and beat 'em for him. Me and Sonny Boy [II]—his name Alex Miller but everyone call him Rice. He'd stayed around Greenwood—wore harps around his waist, belt was rubbin' with harps all around his waist, you know. He could play! When we got through hustlin' the streets we went out there where Robert's playin' at. Everybody's drinkin' havin' a nice time probably hook up with him and have a big time. I got out there first. I went out there about eleven o'clock—Robert was sick then. He was sittin' around the corner with his guitar around his arm. About twenty minutes later Sonny Boy come in woofin'—talkin' a lotta trash. Drinkin' half high. After a few more minutes a truck come in with a gangload of peoples to hear him play. So they say, "C'mon play some Blues—play some Blues!" This woman had give him some whiskey then—it was poisoned! I know he was poisoned! I was there the night when it happened. But she had give him whiskey. I didn't see her give it to him. But he was crazy 'bout whiskey and he had been drinkin'. And Robert had been goin' with this man's wife—and this man didn't wanna do nothin' to him. But I guess he just got his waitress to put somethin' in the whiskey. It wasn't a deadly poison because Robert lived from Sunday until Tuesday. I went over there Monday and he was sick, crawlin' on the floor, heavin' up and goin' on. If he coulda got a doctor like times is now they coulda pumped that little stuff outta him and he'd a been alright. But at that time, if you didn't work for some of those white folks down there, somebody speak up for ya or get you a doctor—you just died! And Robert was just a stranger in there just playin' music, hustlin' and he got so sick. Mostly Black people didn't have too much money to get a doctor at the time—you had to pay for the doctor. And he just died. He died for [lack of at] tention. He died for 'tention. After then I started to get from around Greenwood. Then I come over around Coahoma, Mississippi River, Clarksdale in '38 and '39. I'd start to playin' around Coahoma and Clarksdale and I'd go back to Greenwood every once in a while—then go over to Helena, Arkansas. I start to mess around in Helena over there—on the street different places and in the jukehouse in Helena. In '42 I record for the Library of Congress. Somebody knowed me—I really don't know. Alan Lomax come from Washington [DC] and he had record Son House and Willie Brown. And he come on down to Coahoma and asked about Honeyboy. And who told 'em about me I don't know. But one Monday mornin' he drove in the yard. I had been playin' over in Jonestown, Mississippi that Saturday, that Sunday night. Jonestown, Mississippi that's right over from Coahoma bout four or five miles—over there around Marks, Mississippi—but a little town called Jonestown. I'd come in that Sunday—I was 'bout half drunk. I lived with a woman out there. Got to bed and went to sleep. I didn't wake up no more till that Monday mornin'. That Monday mornin' Alan Lomax had drove in the yard with a brand-new Hudson. A '42 Hudson Super Six—dark green—I'll never forget! And he drove up in the yard, he said, "Do Honeyboy live here—that boy who plays guitar?" This girl's Auntie, she saw him out there but she was scared to tell him yes—'cause she didn't know *who* he was. She say, "I don't know, he come here sometime—I'm gonna see if he's around." [*Laughs.*] So then he said, "I'm Mr. Alan Lomax. I'm from the Library of Congress in Washington DC and I want him to make some records for me." I say, "Tell him yes I'm here." So, she went back out "Yeah—He's in there!" [*Laughs.*] I come out and talk to him. We went to Clarksdale and he rent me a room at a little place Holiday Inn longside the 49 Highway—rent me a little room, carry me to the restaurant, bought my dinner. And we went out—out there where Muddy Waters used to live, around King [Cain] and Anderson, where Muddy Waters come from there in Clarksdale. And he rented a place in the Rolling Wall School—that was in July. July the twentieth. We rent the place and man—up come a bad storm! In the middle of the session, like a tornado. He was recordin' me about middle way in the session. He had to cut off everything for about a hour. When it all blowed over, we started back. I done seventeen cuts for him—seventeen numbers. He gave me twenty dollars—that's more money than I ever had in my life!

Did the fact that the storm came up in the middle of your session have any bearing on your tune "The Howlin' Wind Blues"?

No, I used to play "The Howlin' Wind Blues." I think that storm came up—and we stopped. He HAD to stop—the lights went all to blinkin' with the electricity goin' on you know. We just had to stop. I was young then—I could think faster 'n a monkey could then! [*Laughs.*] I was thinkin' of the songs just like that. I done seventeen numbers! In about an hour and a half—seventeen! '43 then I started on to St. Louis. Started back to playin' with Big Joe and Yank again. They was livin' in St. Louis then. And James DuShay, Jelly Jaw Short, we all mess around and play up in St. Louis. I had a steel guitar then, a nice one—a National.

What was your style like at this point? You played with Big Joe, Charley Patton, Robert Johnson, Tommy Johnson. What was your style like?

Well—I used to play like Joe Williams, like I said. I really was dead on his style but I liked Robert Johnson's playin' too. But I started with Joe Williams first—and I liked it cause Joe could make some hellava chords in Spanish. You think he's in Natural. You know you can get a lot out of Spanish—if you know how. You can get Rock & Roll outta Spanish if you know how—but you got to know how. Spanish is a hard key to play in cause all the keys is open. You got to skip play 'em—skip! It just hard to play it if you don't know how but a lotta people done play there and you think he's in Natural. When I started thinkin' really about music for myself—I really thought about it—I tried to come in on my own style—you know what I mean? Like if you say, "I'm playin' like so and so." I got to be over average to get better than he is—he's already good. So, I went on and try some of my own style. I make up my different chords don't nobody else got and I can take some chords outta his number that he was playin'—and put 'em together with mine! Connect 'em up. As long as they come out right. So I got my own style—but I can play like a lotta people! Well—I was there with my Auntie there in Coahoma, playin'—and they start to draftin' there. I went to Friar's Point—that's three miles from Coahoma over the riverside. And they sent us all there to Friars Point to the [Draft] Board. I had a Social Security card. I went into the army at Camp Sheridan—right down by Collins, Mississippi, way down the line! Camp Sheridan! I went down there and I just had got hitched up there and I got in an accident—some woman had hit me. And the doctor looked at that place. Man I was takin' soap pills and everything to make my heart beat fast—I didn't want to go in the army. Old Hitler and Mussolini was shootin' 'em down like flies over there then! [*Laughs.*] I didn't wanna go in the army! When I went down to Camp Sheridan, when I got down to the last doctor, he took a look at that sewed up place. He say, "That's a bad scar! Do that ever bother you?" I didn't have to say 'em but one word, "No it never bothers me," and I'd have shot right through. I told 'em I have spells, I say I have fits. [*Laughs.*] I didn't wanna go. Man, that was a bad war. And we had to go to the Board every week. And we would take shots—just like you had bad blood or what-so-ever—till they clean you out. I taken shots—they had to clean me out. I taken about twenty shots, get about one a week. When you get cleared out with that doctor—you're ready to go. You didn't go into the army nasty! They all told me I better not go nowhere. Say if I go anywhere anytime they pick me up, they're gonna ship me right straight in the army. They wasn't gonna hesitate—just put me right on in there. So that keep me playin' around a few little jobs but I always came back to Coahoma to the Board. I go to Jonestown, I play—I leave Jonestown, I go to Marks, I go to Belen. I'd go down to Clarksdale. I'd go to Shaw, come right back to Coahoma to the Board, you know. All around 30 or 40 miles in the hub and go right back, you know. So, they give me a Class 1. That's they're liable to call you anytime. Class 1. Then they gave me a B—that's to sit there and see what they gonna do with ya. Then they give me that 4F—they're through with me. When I got the 4F I wasn't fittin' for nothin'—I hit the road again! [*Laughs.*] That took a whole year—better 'n a year. I was handicapped for a year about. I came here a few times and didn't stay too long—and went right back out! I don't know, I just wouldn't stay nowhere long. And then when I came back here in '45—me and Little Walter Jacobs—we started in Memphis. He left me in Memphis and he come to St. Louis. He said, "I'm goin' to St. Louis." I said, "I'll be there next week." When I got to St. Louis—he told me where he was gonna be—somewhere around Franklin and Delmar. He had been playin' his harp on the streets and when I come in I had a National [guitar]. When I come in and went over where he's s'posed to be hangin' out at, I start to playin' on the streets. The people started gangin' around me sayin', "Ooohhh man—you can play that guitar!" They say, "There's a little old boy here—I sure do wish you could meet him." That's who I'm lookin' for, Walter, but they don't know it. Say, "Man he's workin' at the laundry cross the bridge over on Paraphane Avenue. I sure wish you could meet him! He'll be off work after while. Man, he sure can play harps—Y'all need to get together!" I'm lookin' for him anyway. At four o'clock I saw Walter come across the bridge swingin' his head. Walter, he say, "Sonovabitch, when'd you get here?" "I just got here early this mornin'." They all say, "Oh—they know each other!" [*Laughs.*] So we hooked up and played around St. Louis about a week. Walter would work at the laundry. He'd steal me a shirt—put on two shirts. Bring me a shirt back. We both were ragged as a can of kraut [*laughs*]. So, we lit out one Saturday mornin'. Course we come to East St. Louis and come to Breckema [Beckemeyer]. And we caught a ride from Breckema to Decatur. We hung around Decatur—we didn't have too much money then. We played on the streets in Decatur. And then about train time—the train that came to Chicago here—We come to the train station and went in the train station. The depot agent just kept a lookin' at us so. Walter had his harps around his waist like Sonny Boy used to wear his'n. He kept lookin' at us and said, "Can y'all play those things like that?" We say, "We play a little." He said, "Hit me a tune over there!" So we started playin' Blues in the depot and we made enough money to ride on the cushion here in Chicago—right at the train station. He give us some money as we catchin' the train. Fares was cheap then! Think about three or four dollars apiece from here to there. We come in to Maxwell Street—It was three o'clock. Saturday night—Sunday mornin'. And Maxwell Street, at the time the people was still workin' steel mills. And the steel mills were workin' three or four shifts at the time. Plenty of people workin'—right after the war and people still workin'. And Maxwell Street was just like this. Cause the people come in from work in the mornin'. They have three shifts sleep in the same bed. They get up and wanna make the bed up for the next shift to go to bed. And they'd come in and have a drink and walk the streets and we'd be playin' in the streets! They'd stay out two or three hours, get drunk, go home and go to bed—and get ready for their shift. So Maxwell Street never was closed—we used to play it all the time! We get up about nine o'clock out there people still walkin' the streets. Drinkin' whiskey and folks shovin' nickels and dimes and quarters to ya.

Who else did you see on Maxwell Street?

Porkchop [Eddie Hines] used to play down there. Stovepipe [Johnny Watson]. Stovepipe used to play harp down there. He used to follow the old minstrel shows. Porkchop played the drums. Jimmy Rogers just had come out the army—he was playin' on the streets. Floyd Jones played on the streets. Workin' at night in the steel mill—playin' the daytime on the streets, Floyd was. Snooky Pryor was playin' on the streets. Snooky and Elgin [Evans, a.k.a. Elga Edmonds] was playin' on the streets. Robert Nighthawk—he wanted to be a little too much to play on the streets. He would play. He would come and set in—but he wouldn't sit out there like we'd sit out. He would come and play a couple numbers and walk, you know. He thought he was above the streets then, you know. Robert had a little thing goin' on then all the time. His little band would come up and break up, break up and get back together like that. Robert run—he never stay nowhere long, no way. He'd come up here and stay two or three months, go back down to Clarksdale—then come back here. He had a sister over there on Wabash had a music store over there one time—and that's where he got all his instruments—from his sister. He'd never work nowhere but play. He had some good instruments—but he got 'em from his sister. Otha [Othum] Brown used to play in the streets—you never knowed him too much. Otha Brown—good guitar player. He come from Marks, Mississippi.

Whatever happened to Othum Brown?

Otha Brown went to Detroit where his sister was and he start to havin' seizures. He died from seizures. This was in the '60s. He went to Detroit with his sister—Otha was always a funny type. I knowed Otha real well. He come from Marks, Mississippi. I used to go down to Marks with him before he started playin' with Little Walter. We went to Marks together—just me and him one time! Good guitar player!

Where did Ora Nelle Blues come from?

That's Otha's own song. Otha was a pretty good singer, he was pretty good. A country boy. That was Otha's own song. I never heard anybody do it 'cept Otha. He done Hard Time too. "Hard Time Blues killin' me, put me on the killin' floor, ain't gonna be bad no more." He was a good friend of mine—I knowed him.

Did any of you guys have any club gigs?

The musicians made more money in the streets than they did in the clubs. That's why they were flockin' the streets. They made more money in the streets. Club would only be about seven or eight dollars a night—somethin' like that. I was on the Southside there around 47th Street. I was there playin' in the streets and one night I come in. This Italian run this joint and he want to give me six or seven dollars to play that night and I was makin' ten and fifteen in the streets and I wouldn't stay there—I went and was playin' on the street corner. I was young like I say and I'd rather play on the street corner than play in one place all night. I got—out there it look like. Club gigs wasn't payin' nothin' . . .

Did you ever see the artists who worked and recorded for Lester Melrose? Did they ever work the streets?

I didn't see 'em but I've heard that Tampa Red and them used to play out on the streets.

Were you accepted by the older, more established Blues players in town?

Well—sometimes they had things goin' to theyself and they want to keep things to theyself. They were kinda scared that you might come in and take their little jobs, you know. You could go to a club where they was playin' at—they wouldn't hardly let you sit in. 'Cause they were afraid of you sittin' in.

Was Sonny Boy I that same way?

He didn't care too much. He used to play at 31st and Giles—right over there where he got killed at. I forget the name of the club—Sunnyland always used to play over there. Plantation, I believe it was. He would play over there—play all night. But Sonny Boy had a different harp style from any of the harp blowers—I'm talkin' bout John Lee Williamson. He had his own style—really a country Blues harp player he was. Like Little Walter Jacob had his own style of playin'. Now—all of those guys has their own style of playin' just about. Little Walter had the best style of any of 'em! Now Big Walter could play more harp than Little Walter play. Big Walter could play all over the harmonica—take one harp and play in four or five different keys. Little Walter couldn't—but the keys Little Walter played in—it was cooked so good, it sound so good—that you couldn't turn it down. And the style that he played on—he played in that 'cordian [accordian] [chromatic] style. Like they play in Loosiana. They play the 'cordian in Loosiana—that's the style he played on. He played that harp just about like you play them 'cordians! And it sound just about like those 'cordians. Then he turn around and make it like some sax. See that's where he got his break playin' harmonica.

Somebody told me that Walter spoke French—Did you ever hear him speak French?

He was a Frenchman! He come from Marksville, a little town twelve miles from Alexandria. I've been to his hometown with him. He's a Frenchman—he's from Marksville, Louisiana. There's some of his people down there now. He's a Frenchman—he really was! He would start talkin' that old funny talk and I didn't understand him. See, he left down there when he was young. He ran away from home. Walter left when he was something about fourteen or fifteen, something like that. 'Cause when I met Walter, Walter was about eighteen years old when I first met him, he wasn't quite twenty. He was a good harp player then. I could never get him to talk none of that stuff—I used to hear him try and talk it and I'd laugh at him. Then he got away from a lot of it too after he stayed out, out in the Delta among the people. He got away from a lot of that—but he really was a Frenchman. I knowed that because I been there and met his people. He played harmonica on the Cajun sound style—that's why it sound so different from the other harmonica players. He had the Cajun sound. But the Cajun sound mean that's the 'cordian sound. Sometime I tell ya when I was hitch-hikin' lots—if hitch-hikin' got bad and I couldn't get no ride on the highway I'd catch a freight train. I'd hobo. I'd catch a freight—it was faster. Like I used to be in Cairo, Illinois. After I get through Cairo—I'd probably come from Memphis into Cairo—then I'd come North of Cairo in the yard. I'd find out what time a manifest is comin' here to Chicago. Some of the brakemen would say, "Well we got one leavin' 'bout four o'clock this evening." The brakeman around the yard—they make up the train. They'd make up—sometimes be a hundred cars! They'd run around on the side track, makin' up, you know. When they make up and everything they say, "We leavin' out about—." I walked out of the yard about fifteen or twenty feet something like that—seventy-five feet somewhere where I can get in the bushes. 'Cause the special agents were bad then—they were called the Dicks! They would pull you off there and put you on those P-Farms. They had a P-Farm [penal farm] in Cairo.

What's a P-Farm?

They put you out there and make you work—give you about thirty days out there to punish you for tryin' to catch the train. I used to catch the trains when I was in my early twenties and come here to Chicago. Stop in Effingham—sometimes Carbondale. Get put off in Carbondale and somewhere up in there. I know every stop clean to Mississippi!

It amazed me that the brakeman would tell you the schedule.

They didn't care! Sometimes the engineers didn't care. It was the special agents that kept you off the trains—The Dicks! That was the high law that would ride the trains like policemen.

Would they ride the trains?

They'd ride the trains too sometimes. They'd ride the trains and put you off—sometimes they'd catch you on the train and they'd say, "When you get to this next town you better get off here." In that next town he had that big .45 on him and everything, he'd put you off—and you had to lay and catch the next one—and dodge the next special agent that came in. They'd come in at Halsted, Blue Island. That's the train come in at Halsted down there come from the South. We'd come in at Halsted into Blue Island—We'd get off down there, get off at Halsted and catch the bus—C'mon down to Jewtown and start playin' on the streets!

Did you ever get put off the trains?

Yeah!—Many times! I remember once we was up in Hope, Arkansas—comin' in Idebel, Oklahoma—me and Walter. We got on the train and when we got to this town this special agent saw us. He had on Blue serge pants and white shirt. He say, "Where you boys think y'all goin'? Y'all gotta get off this train. The next stop we get to if y'all don't get off—I'm gonna shoot ya' off." We said, "Okeh—Yassuh!" So when we got there to take on water—you know the trains used to take on water and coal. They don't do it no more 'cause they got diesel motors. At that time, they had the coal burners. They were takin' on water and coal—we put it down. We didn't get on there. Lay over till the next one come—come through the next day. We didn't see a dick. We catch it and come on in. We just had to dodge 'em—come in by time comin' in!

What cars would you ride on?

Well, if we get on before the special agent see us, we'd get in the boxcar. Then we'd pull the door closed. Get a spike—know what a railroad spike is? That was to spike your ties with—you know spike your rails to the cross-ties? We'd get one of them spikes, pull the door to and put it down betwixt the door and bar where you shut the door up—where you can't do nothin' but roll against the spike. You can't shove it up not less you pull the spike up inside. We got to pull it from the inside. He can holler all he wanna holler—we ain't comin' out. See we spiked the door on 'em. Sometimes he know we're in there. "Come on out there!" We'd just stay in there—he can't open the door—not unless we let 'em in there. 'Cause we got it spiked from the inside. And every time you shove the door the spike gonna catch it. He can't do nothin'. We got to pull the spike out. I have ridden on gondolas too. We get on line it wasn't too bad, all the hobos talk to the other ones . . . "if you goin' to Chicago or comin' back to St. Louis—watch it in such and such a town. They'll pull you off there," or "Nothin' will happen." So, we know where we're goin' cause we all would get the message. And then we'd get on a flatcar or gondola. But if it was bad we'd get in a boxcar—and spike the door. If we run up on one, we don't care cause we ain't gonna let 'em in. And they can't make you open it.

Have you ever ridden the Rods—the suspension under the train car?

Once or twice. The Rods—I rode the Rods. But them rocks would whup you *so bad* you come out from under there. [*Laughs.*] I remember once right here when I blind a passenger train from here to St. Louis—passenger (!). I got so good I'd blind a passenger!

What do you mean by "blind"?

Mail car—a passenger train carries two mail cars. They're black cars—don't nobody ride in them. Call 'em baggage cars. That's just for mail. I'd get in the second one. The first mail car is right next to the engine. And the cars are right together—so I'd get in here, right in the middle between the first and the second. There's enough hole to get back in there, stand back there and ride the rods. Ride the rods stand there and hold the stirrups. And get in the blind side. And every time they—in St. Louis, you'd be on the blind side. If the police walk he got to walk on the depot side, the station side. I'm on the blind side right there.

How did you manage to make it down to Texas?

I heard so much talk of Lightning Hopkins and Candy Harris and Lowell Fulson and all those guys—T-Bone and all those was up in there. Gatemouth Brown and Willie Mae Thornton. I said, "I believe I'll go down there. I probably may do a little better down there." I went out there and I had a different style than the Texas style. And the people went for it. I went in there one Sunday mornin'. I drove in there about eleven o'clock and this guy open the tavern at twelve—in Houston. I drove up in an old Ford and I went in this tavern and I asked the guy about one thirty or two o'clock—the people was thirsty for a drink. It was Sunday mornin' and the people come in and goin' on and everything around the bar you know—big crowd. And I ask the guy could I play a couple a numbers. He say, "Yeah—Sure go head on—play!" I start to playin' the Blues then and folks lookin' at me say, "Where'd this guy come from? [*Laughs.*] Man—he's good!" And they called Ms. Cullom—she had the Artist Label— Anna Cullom, she's the first one that record Lightning Hopkins and Thunder Smith. She give 'em that name. She come and she put me with a band—a sax player and drummer. And she recorded me. That's the number I made "Who May Your Lover Be" and "Build Myself A Cave." She sold the masters to Chris Strachwicz in Berkeley, California. That was in '52. I'll tell you who else I recorded for out there too—Old man Bill Quinn, Gold Star—you hear talk of him? I record for him too. He's a—man, has his own manufacturing and everything. He recorded a lot of Lightning and them too! I don't know if he released it or not but I know Ms. Cullom released hers. Old man Bill—he might not have released it.

Didn't you have some sort of run in with Don Robey?

Oh yeah, yeah—yeah. Yeah—you right! See I was young—well I say that all the time. I was drinkin' heavy. I used to drink pretty heavy. I had cut a dub and carried it out to Don Robey. He lived in a suburb of Houston. I went out there for him—carried the dub and listened at it. By me bein' drinkin' he said, "Yeah—I like your style. It sounds good. But I don't understand nothin' you say." On some of my words and verses—cause I was drinkin'—I wasn't sayin' 'em clear. Like when you say, "My baby gone and she won't be home no more!" I said 'em in a way so you couldn't understand 'em you know. Don's tellin' me "Yeah—you know what you say, but I don't know what you're sayin'!" And we got to arguin' you know. *You don't know everything and sometimes you got to go along with people—I mean, I don't care how good you is!* They can take somebody who can't play nothin' and make somethin' outta 'em—did you know that? You can take a guy can't play nothin', push him and make somethin' outta 'em. I had to find that out, 'cause I know that I can play and I had a pretty good little sound then—but that wasn't everything though. A lot of guys was playin' triflin' to where I been—I *know* they wasn't playin'! But they was doin' alright. And I know they wasn't playin' nothin'. So I didn't go back to him. We had a little 'spute. See Don Robey—he's Black! His daddy's a Jew, his mama's a Black woman. He used to be a peddler all through Texas—sell clothes on his back—so they told me. You know how peddlers used to go through the country sellin' clothes? Peddlers have clothes in a suitcase on their back. Somethin' like a gypsy! See he used to be somethin' like a gypsy. He pulled up and made some money and opened up him a studio. Clarence Gatemouth and a few others helped got him started. Just like Muddy—Muddy made Chess a lotta money. But Muddy was livin' good—got 'em a home, a house and car and things. Livin' better than he ever lived in his life! But still he didn't have the money he shoulda got—Chess had the money! You can take some but don't take it all! Muddy didn't care how much Chess made long as he could live good. I don't blame him 'bout that—you ain't got nothin' from the get-go—put you in a new car, bought you a home, somethin' you ain't never had in your life—you can't blame the man!

I think I read in an article that you used to have a hot temper—is that right?

Well like I say—I used to drink and clown some—but I soon come out of that though.

Did you carry weapons with you at all?

Never did. When I was in the country—before I left the country I did. I'd go to Greenwood, get a pistol there for $3. Wasn't no gun laws. Wasn't nothin' like this—like now. We'd go to a gun shop and buy ya order for two or three dollars then. You could order a brand-new special from here. I kept a pocket of old guns all the time. We wouldn't do nothin' with 'em but shoot birds and rabbits, hunt with 'em. We didn't fight or nothin' like that.

So you didn't really have any kind of trouble?

No! No—you know one thing, somethin' I believe right now. The more guns the people had, the quieter they was. They wasn't violent—the quieter that they was. 'Cause they could get 'em they wasn't shout about 'em. But when they be's hard to get they wanna do somethin' with' em. Think about it sometime—If everybody had a gun, an old pistol or somethin', they wouldn't say nothin' 'bout it—go hunt a rabbit and hang it up over the door somewhere—they wouldn't study 'bout no guns or nothin' like that.

How about rules of conduct for the bandstand? I've heard it said there were certain ways you'd carry yourself—certain things you didn't do. Did you ever have any problems with this issue?

Yeah—I had a lotta that. That's how a lot of musicians used to get hurt, you know. A woman will come where you're playin' at, got their husband or man with 'em and wanna flirt with the musicians. Well—her man don't want that. He's sittin' over there with rocks all in his jaw. A lot of mens have got hurt like that. So, after I found that out in my playin'—a woman will come up smilin', pullin' on me, and rubbin' up against me. I say, "Look—I'll play your request but go right back over there where your man at." You take a man that's workin' hard, got a good job, he's not a musician—he don't do nothin' out in the public but work every day and got a good lookin' woman. And he don't want to lose that good lookin' woman cause if he find out he'll kill ya about it. He'd rather be dead than lose her. So, you better leave that woman alone. That's the way it used to be. But now there ain't too much of that happenin'. Man say, "What's the reason of me killin' that man 'bout a woman. I'm goin' to the penitentiary and she out got everybody else that she want. Let her go!" He let her go now—but people didn't used to be like that! I know a man used to kill ya 'bout his woman. I know a time down south if you said a cuss word 'fore his wife, he'd wanna kill ya. Say, "You cussin' front my wife I'll kill you!" He would do it too! She try to hold 'em. She ain't got no business in that kinda company.

How could you tell the women that were available from the ones that weren't?

Sometimes they'd come out—Their boyfriends'd be on a bust or spat or somethin' like that. Some of 'em were pretty square. They'd come to you and say, "I got a boyfriend but we not together—we're on a bust. We ain't doin' too good together." So, we may talk and he come in, walk out—say, "Well we're separated." Then you'd probably have a chance at her—you know, something like that. I remember my wife, what I got these kids by her in Chicago now, she was twenty years old. She had married a boy in Helena, Arkansas. And he was drivin' a truck, a log truck over there in Tunica, Mississippi. But he come to Helena every weekend. He stayed a week over there where he was workin' and in the weekend he come in. And somebody had told him that I was goin' with his wife. But he thought I was playin' with Robert Nighthawk's band. But I was with Sonny Boy and them at the time. I just had come up here—I was dressed up. I come up here and gotta lotta old clothes. I come in that Saturday evening with my coat all cocked up and my hat broke down and I come in the restaurant. The woman what I was goin' with was sittin' with this girl, sittin' in the restaurant eatin'. When I walked in the door, he looked straight at me like this. He said, "There that son-of-a-bitch is right there!" She said, "I don't know nothin' 'bout him." He say, "Oh yeah—that's one of them Nighthawks." He thought I was playin' with Robert Nighthawk. He said, "That's one of them Nighthawks there!" So, I heard the conversation but I just flew on by like I didn't hear it. I went in the back and got me a drink, you know. So, what he done—he fooled both of us that night. We were playin' at the Hole in the Wall, Arthur Crawford's place. He told her, "Well, I'm goin' back on the job. I'm goin' back to pick up my truck." He had to go back 'cross the river to get his truck. And he went across the river—But he came back! About two o'clock that night everything was over. Two thirty that morning we're walkin' home behind Helena's Grocery Company. They had a big grocery company. We had to come by the grocery house and then come up behind the grocery house. When we come up *behind* the grocery house walkin', there was a big wholesale company. When we got back there walkin' he jumped out with a big long knife.

He said, "Yeah—I caught ya!" She said, "That ain't him!" He say, "Yes it is!" And she held him for me to run. And she kept holdin' him and I seen that knife so I turned the fan on! [*Laughs.*] I got outta the way. She give me a chance to get away! The next Saturday night we played there in Helena, here come the baddest rain and snow that ever been down there. We played—we made three dollars apiece. The man turned the crappot boxes over to us and said, "Now y'all see I ain't made no money." So, I went to Memphis with my sister. My sister lived in Memphis. So, this guy, what my wife was livin' with then—he put her out on account of me. So, she come here Sunday mornin' to my cousin's. She said, "Honey—" I didn't want no wife. I didn't want nobody not to take care of. She said, "Jake put me out and I ain't got nowhere to go." And I felt bad, if I was the one busted them up, I didn't look out for her. So, I went and got me a little old job there in Memphis. And I played on weekends and pawned my guitar out. And I sent her a ticket and she came where I was. And we stayed together a couple of years—had another kid. He died. She had married this guy. I didn't marry her then. I married her in Houston, Texas. 'Cause we wouldn't a been legal cause they didn't get a divorce but I married her in Texas. Then we started getting' them babies—all them children. And they here in Chicago now. I have two girls and a boy here. My son's forty. My daughter Betty's thirty-eight and Edna's forty-one. They're right here in Chicago! Come and see me all the time. Call me every day!

Tell me about recording for the Sun Record Label.

Betty was two years old so it would be in '53. I was out from Hughes, Arkansas. I lived over there about three years. Sun was recordin' everybody then. I got hold to the word that Sam Phillips was recordin'—I went in there one Monday mornin'—we left Hughes—I got there about eleven o'clock. I taken Blue with me—a harmonica player named Blue. And they was settin' up stuff in the studio and everything and Sam Phillips recorded me. He already had heard talk of me. I recorded "Sweet Home Chicago" and a couple more numbers. He recorded about four or five of us that day. What I was tryin' to do—I had been bummin' along so long and I had a lot of fret recordin'. I had a little name out there and when you get a little name out there you can make some money—you know what I mean? I was tryin' to get to the point where I could make myself some money without hustlin' too hard. When you got a name, you got a little followin'. Somebody know somethin' about ya. You ain't got no name—it's hard. I don't care how good you play, you got to have a name. What he done, he released that number and put somebody else's name on there—Albert Joiner Williams. Now I know the time I recorded. I know my song. I know my changes in my guitar and

I know my voice. I know that's me! But he put this man's name on there—I guess to keep from payin' me. But I know he done that! 'Cause I know my playin'—I know every break in my guitar. Every note—I know it! People can get close to ya' with the voice but you watch real close, there's somethin' that they ain't got.

So the original 78s came out with somebody else's name on them?

Yeah!

How did you find that out?

Well a company of people found it out 'cause I know Sam Phillips and I know some people that talked to him about it, ya know. A lotta people know that.

Did you hear the record when it first came out?

Once or twice I heard it. But after he put that name on it like that there wasn't too much I could do about it—you know what I mean?

Did you have a permanent home base that you'd come back to at that time?

I'd come back to Memphis where my sister and them was sometime. I was around them until they moved up here—and they moved here about '54. I was in Houston then. See I went back to Houston about three or four times back there. I sent them a paper where I was on the show with Charles Brown. My brother said, "Honey, you come on to Chicago. You run around everywhere and done everything—if there's anything for you, you'll get it right here in Chicago!" By the time I got here my brother told Big Walter I was here. Walter ran over to the house. Say, "I got a job for us!" I had to go to 40th and State and join the Local 208 [musician's union]. I had to get in that Local 208. It wasn't but $75 to join and I got a little job. And my wife, she went down there and got me a union card Local 208. 'Cause they were kinda strict about playin' the clubs then. They'd come in and pull you out. Somebody had to have a card then! The leader, at least, had to have one. [*Laughs.*] But now the whole band can play and ain't got none! But somebody had to have a union card then because Doby and them would pull you off that bandstand. "Come here, come here—have you got your union card nowhere?" And after I got my union card, I had a little band then, Doby and them come in, had his briefcase under his arm, lookin', rollin' his eyes around—that's the steward, you know. I look at him. He say, "Come here. I know you straight—What about your boys?" I say, "You know how it is. Let us make some bread man!" I give him a pint of whiskey and give him $5 and he'd gone on down the street to the next little old somebody else playin'. Pint of whiskey and $5 *and he gone!* Every Saturday night I have that pint waitin' for him and Brother, *he gone!*

Were the musicians unions segregated then?

Well the union I was in, Local 208, I saw a few white musicians comin' in every once in a while. Me and Howlin' Wolf and Muddy Waters too—We all belong to 208! All us on the Southside belong cause it was on 40th and State—right on the old "El" used to go over to Halsted to the stockyard.

I find it interesting that you recorded for the Library of Congress—you never got to hear those. Those were never issued as records. They were simply put on file. Then you recorded in Houston. Then for Bill Quinn and Gold Star—again nothing issued. Then you recorded for Sun and somebody else's name was put on them. . . .

I was having a hard time there, wasn't I . . .?

So how about the records for the Chess Brothers—how did those happen?

After I come out of Dallas, Texas—See I was playin' in Dallas—and I come into Shreveport, Louisiana. I was playin' down the Black quarter neighborhood that Saturday night. This boy walked in—he worked for Jewel record company, Stan Lewis. He heard me and say, "Man—you good! You can play that thing. You sure is good! I like to hear you play that. I want you to check with my boss-man Monday mornin'." I said, "Who's your boss?" He say, "Stan Lewis is my boss—up on Texas Avenue. Come up there and talk to my boss." He was the stockboy there. So I went up and talked to Stan and Stan say, "Yes—I like your style and everything but I'm not usin' no blues. I'm usin' all gospel. I'm gonna send you to my cousin Chess." And so that Tuesday he put me on a bus. I left my car there. My wife was pregnant then. I left my car there and I come here to Chicago. Chess and them picked me up. When I got in the studio there sat Muddy Waters. There sat Willie Nix, Jimmy Rogers . . .

Had you known Willie Nix from Memphis?

Yeah! I knowed Jimmy Rogers from before then too. I knowed all of 'em! I didn't know Muddy too much but I had met Muddy once or twice in Rollin' Fork when he was down there in the country. Chess said, "Do you know him Muddy?" "Oh yeah—oh yeah!" He didn't know too much about me, you know. He *heard* lots about me and I met him once or twice in Rollin' Fork but he didn't know nothing about me. But I went to record—an' I was usin' the slide *real* good. And I put the slide down and every time I made one of them bad chords Jimmy Rogers 'd point at Muddy Waters like this—Walter'd laugh and Muddy'd go like this—he didn't wanna hear that! Him and Chess like to got to fightin' back there. They argue so much that Chess got mad. That's why that "Drop Down Mama" is the shortest number on that album. Chess got mad and cut that number off and never gave me credit for it. Still didn't give me credit for it. Muddy say, "You know I recorded something like that?" Chess said, "The man don't even sing like you. The man ain't got nothin' like you." See Muddy didn't care too much for me 'cause I was too close to his style. If Chess had released some of that stuff—at that time—I'd have pushed Muddy way back! I'd have slowed him down—that's what they know! I'd have slowed him down. But once he had everything goin' like he wanna—he wanna keep it like that. He didn't want no competition. If I'd a done it—he'd had some competition! I got sense to understand what's been happenin'. And Muddy didn't say nothin' to me in a long time. He didn't care too much about me—my style was too close to his. When Muddy started talkin' to me we played at the Palladium Club in New York City. He was gettin' sick then—in the '80s—a little before he died. John Lee Hooker played that night at the Palladium—and Johnny Winter. Eddie Kirkland played there that night.

This was thirty years later?

Yeah. Well after he saw that the people recognized me so much, he hate to be a dragger behind. He hate to be a sag. I was sittin' up and they had two big tables for the musicians. All sorts of food and I was sittin' back there. Muddy had loosed his hair then. Muddy come in, I had my hair pretty. Muddy say, "Looky here. Here's this son-of-a-gun got all his hair. Looky here—look at this—I'm baldheaded now!" [*Laughs.*] But he never did used to say too much to me—he didn't care much about me. I never was like that about musicians. It's just one of them things. Some musicians jealous—I'm not jealous. What you do is your business!

How did the session happen with Fleetwood Mac?

I didn't know anything about them. Willie Dixon come got me. Say, "Hey man—I got a job for ya. I got a band here from overseas want you to record." Now Fleetwood Mac and them heard talk of me somehow or another—I don't know. But Willie Dixon know where I was. So he come got me. He got Big Walter Horton and J.T. Brown and Homesick. And Spann—and we had a big thing. We all recorded. It was pretty nice.

When did things start picking up for you?

'75.

Tell me some of the countries you've been in.

I've been to Sweden. I've been to Belgium, Germany. I've been in Holland. Scotland, Ireland. I'm goin' back this year—last of next month! When I first went to Japan and got back with six thousand dollars—that's more money than I ever made in my life! I never thought the guitar would bring me this much money! [*Laughs.*]

Part Three **Blues Esoterica**

Jimmy "T-99" Nelson

I remember early in my record collecting days I bought an LP, an anthology of recording artists that were issued on the Chess label. The LP had two artists who, at that time, were unknown to me—and who immediately became my favorites, Percy Mayfield and Jimmy "T-99" Nelson. Both of these singers caught my ear because they sang way back "in the pocket"—their phrasing had them delivering lyrics way behind the melody. That wasn't an unusual style for singers from Louisiana like Percy Mayfield, where everybody does everything "way back in the pocket"—but it was quite unusual for a singer from Philadelphia where Jimmy Nelson was born and raised. Hearing them on the LP sent me in search of other recordings by each artist. Finding records by Jimmy "T-99" Nelson in those days was "slim pickins." Jimmy had hits with his classic recording, "T-99," a famous highway in Texas, and a later follow-up, "Meet Me with Your Black Dress On," but, little had been reissued. Eventually reissues of his records became available first on LP, and then on CD. I was also excited to learn that Jimmy was still alive, living in Houston, and had recently come out of retirement and was performing once again. I got his telephone number and we did an extended phone interview. Jimmy stayed in touch for many years, often sending me Christmas cards and his latest CDs. Jimmy passed away in July 2007.

■ ■ ■

Well, I was born in Philadelphia, Pennsylvania, April 7th, 1919. My mother sang and my father played the saxophone many years ago, but I've never met my father. Well, my mother, and my father didn't get along. It was just one of those things. He met her at the dance and here I come. He didn't want to take care of me. And he wouldn't buy milk and nothing like that, you know, when I was a kid. And as I got a little older, I went out to South Philadelphia. I read this ad in the paper about a clarinet—four dollars and fifty cents. I walked from North Philly to South Philly to this Italian barber shop. And this guy said, Yeah, you can have it. So, I paid him and brought the clarinet home, and I walked all the way—and it's something to walk in Philadelphia because it's a long way. There was a little pussy cat I saw at the corner, you know, the drugstore at 13th, and Mastic and I picked the little thing up and took it home. And my mother saw that cat—that little kitty and the clarinet and she opened up that second story window and threw them both out the second story window, out in the street. Oh man, that hurt—that hurt me. But I didn't know her feelings toward my father, you see. Her feelings were different from mine toward my father, and she didn't want me in show business at all. And that was one of the main reasons I left home.

Did you ever make contact with your father?

No, no, I think my father passed away, I'm not sure. My father played tenor in Doc Hodges's band many years ago in Philadelphia—and he never did contact us. Now, he was a much older man and by the time I turned sixteen, something like that, he was out of my life all together. So that was a chapter in my life I forgot all about. My mother didn't want me in show business. So, one of the reasons why I left home was because I wanted to do my own thing, you can understand that.

I was a young man—and wild and I wanted to get out. A good friend of mine and I, we blinded [stole away in the train car suspension] a passenger train out of Philly. And I came through Chicago one night. All I remember about Chicago was the great big broad streets with a whole lot of lights. Well, my reason for walking that boulevard was because we had to leap—jump off the freight train and get around to the other side of the train yard to catch a train to Dallas. That was my only time being in Chicago. We were left there and caught a freight train to Dallas, Oklahoma and Dallas. And then I went out to California and I started listening to different guys out there. And then the band came to town, Harlan Leonard's Kansas City Rockets. And the powerhouse behind that was the band—and Big Joe Turner. And that's how I started in listening to that man sing the blues, I fell in love with his voice and all that he was singing. And I started to do my thing behind Joe, and he and I turned out to be very good friends over the years. We gigged together in Stockton, in Richmond, California, I used to work at Tapper's Inn out there and I stayed out there a long time. And that's how I got into the business. That was in the late '40s. Gosh, man, it was easy for me to sing the blues because I felt like it, you know, I felt lonely all my life anyway. And with Joe's stuff and then I wrote some things on my own. And I stayed at Tapper's Inn in Richmond, California, oh, God, three years. And then we worked around Oakland at the Clef Club and then between the Clef Club Richmond and San Francisco, we had a thing going, you know. We went to the Long Bar Showboat in San Francisco and worked there. That thing was a block long bar! That bar was a block long! They had every kind of bartender you can find in there—and had a stage in the middle of the dance floor. Crip Heard worked there—I think he's from Chicago, the one legged, one armed dancer. He worked there. And Billie Holiday worked there. And Louis Armstrong worked there. Who else worked there? A boy out of New Orleans, Larry Darnell, worked there. And during that time, I stayed at S.W. Collette. He kept me there—he wouldn't let me go. And when I made "T-99" over in Oakland. Gosh, man, I thought he would let me go. But that enhanced his business.

Was that your first record?

No, I made some dubs. Wish I hadn't made them—"Baby Child," which I hope nobody would ever play. And a few other small things that I didn't feel.

How did you make the dubs to begin with?

Oh, well. Two guys, they were enthusiasts when it comes to the blues and they had machines. Over a bank at 7th and Kirkham, 7th and Peralta, 7th right over the bank—right across from the Black and White liquor store. We rehearsed a bit with a girl. I had "T-99" in my little brown book and I met this man, he had a tune called "Please Send Me Someone to Love"—it was Percy Mayfield. So, Percy and I went up there. We got a couple of beers and we went up there and did this thing with a wonderful band. Johnny Ingram band. He had a uniform band—I mean the guys were sharp—shoes shined, uniforms, you know. They had a kind of guy called Big Windy Morgan, a trumpet man that could blow your wig off! [*Laughs.*] Man, he's a big Black dude and he could blow that horn. God—that man was powerful. And we did "Baby Child," we did "Big Hunk of Man." And we did some other little things I wish to the devil I could burn—just get a hold of and destroy. But you have to start somewhere in this business.

Was that for any specific label?

Yeah, that was on the Trilon label.

Was that Ray Dobard or Bob Geddins?

Yeah, well, I didn't want to mess with those guys too much. Because I've been kind of warned about those guys. They were the type of guys who would cut you in and take all the money.

So how did the "T-99" session actually come about?

Well, I had three sides to cut and they called me to come over to the Clef Club on Seventh and Henry. And it was a nightclub, and they said, "Well, there's two guys over there set up by RPM records. They want some stuff on you and they want you to make a dub." I said okay. So, in my little book, I had "White Drops of Rain," "T-99," and a few other things. I cut four sides. But the things that stood out was "White Drops of Rain," which is backed by "T-99." And we cut that one night when the joint was closed—with all the waitresses cleaning up the glasses, sweeping the floors and carrying on. We did "T-99" with the Peter Rabbit Trio—a uniform trio. They were a jazz outfit. They didn't like the blues, but they liked me, so they played the blues for me.

Who was Peter Rabbit?

Walter Graham's. I don't know where Peter Rabbit came from but that was a stage name, Peter Rabbit. He plays squeezebox, he played vibes, he played piano but he had a trio. During that time they were the "In" thing. And Peter Rabbit gave me this chant for "T-99"—[*sings the background vocals*] "T90–99, T90–99." They really knocked me out—you know? I can see and hear them now doing that thing.

What is "T-99"?

Texas Highway 99. It was just a chant behind the blues. You see, that just enhanced that tune.

I mean, anyone can sing the blues—but if you have a chant behind "T-99"—or if you have the band chant behind you on [*sings*]: "Meet me with your black dress on . . ." and everybody's singing that in unison—that offers some novelty to the song, you see. There's nothing like having the musicians come out in front, stand beside you on the microphone on stage and run through that chant thing—slow and easy.

I've seen a number of different years listed for "T-99" and the rest of your RPM records. Can you give us a specific date, a year for these records?

Well, "T-99" was recorded in Oakland, California, 1951. August the eighth, I believe.

Okay, so you had four songs in that particular session?

Yeah, I had four songs on that thing.

How did you know that "T-99" had turned into any kind of a hit? What were your first indications that it had made some noise?

Well, I was working in the Longbar Showboat in San Francisco, and the guys would come through and ask me "You're Jimmy Nelson?" "Uh, yeah." He said, "Well, you know, your record is moving in different parts of the country." I said, "Oh, that's nice. Maybe I can get some gigs behind that," you know? So, finally, it dawned on me—and even at the club, I was working. The box had "Sixty Minute Man" and Nat Cole had "Mona Lisa"—and then they had "T-99." Oh, man, that was nice. Was that nice? And I heard that and I said, "Oh, man . . ."

So, I got the arrangement on "T-99." And my copyright came back and I was in full bloom then. And then Ben Waller sent for me. I went to LA along with Pee Wee Crayton. We went down and did a gig with Fats Domino. And Ben Waller took me to this tailor and bought me about seven suits! He set me up, man! He said, "Well, this is where you start. I'll put you with either Joe Liggins and his band," or he had another cat—I've forgotten. But he wanted to put me with a nice band. I said, Okay, I'll go with Joe Liggins. So, he put me with Joe Liggins. And guess what—right into the Apollo Theater we went! [*Laughs.*] From there, we went to the Howard Theater in Washington, DC.

Who was in the Joe Liggins show in the package besides you?

Oh, there was Joe Liggins. And there was China Doll—she was a dancer. I remember China.

Hmm, I can't recall the other guys who were there. I wanted to get back and make more records. But the company wouldn't send for me because Ben Waller had me all hooked up with these one-nighters all down through the Weinberg tour—that's eighty-one one-nighters, you know, that's a long time.

When was the next session that you did?

The next session was "Meet Me with Your Black Dress On."

Can you give me some idea of when that was recorded—what year, what month?

That was done in 1953 because I left the Howard Theater and I wrote that on my way to LA. I wrote "Meet Me with Your Black Dress On" and I had "Big-Eyed, Brown-Eyed Girl of Mine." And I had two other tunes.

Was there any specific inspiration for "Meet Me with Your Black Dress On"?

No, it was a novelty. It was a novelty tune that just came to me. And then I sang it and said, "Well now let's try some voice behind this." And it came out of my own little head . . . [*Laughs.*]

So there was no incident that . . .

No—no, no, no incident. Gosh, if half of us live the way we sing the blues and the things that we talked about. Gosh, there wouldn't be any need to live—just blow your brains out [*laughs*]. I couldn't live like that. I mean, I just think about it. You know—take another drink and be somebody. Sad, so I couldn't live like that.

How much of your stuff did Maxwell Davis do?

Maxwell Davis. You can hear the album. "Meet Me with The Black Dress On"—he did "Big-Eyed, Brown-Eyed Girl of Mine." He did the majority of the rest of it. I used to go down to LA and he would say, "Well now, you sing that stuff that you would tell me about it." He made notes at the piano, at the hotel, you know, for all those tunes that I have, he said, "Okay, I'll be back at two o'clock and pick you up. Let me go to my garage . . ." which was a studio. I said, "For what?" He said, "I'll have all this stuff ready . . ."—and he had them all ready—he was wonderful. Max would never blow. He didn't blow his tenor, he was more or less a director and a writer and arranger. There's a lot of studios out there in Hollywood, he did wonderful. And then when I went on the road, why I left Maxwell behind, and he passed away but I couldn't get away from his sound. "I Sat and Cried," I did that at the same time I made "Black Dress." And then Joe Bihari said, "Well, don't worry about it. Now. You go back out on tour and we're going to put voices behind it. [*Sings*] "I sat and cried. I sat and cried." I said okay. And lo and behold, I go back out on the road, and I hear this thing, and I forget where I was, somewhere in Louisiana. And that record came on a jukebox—and I said, "What the hell happened to the voices?" And that was one of the many reasons we fell out, I fell out with that company. "I Sat and Cried." Gosh, I wanted voices behind that.

Who did you record for after you left RPM?

I came to Texas and did something for Steve Ponzio. I did a few things for Steve. Steve had a record distributing thing here, and he wasn't all into making distributions on any of our stuff. And Percy Mayfield did some things with me here. And they hadn't been released—they're somewhere. And guys, like Ames would buy them up and put them out. And they're not mixed. They're more or less dubs, and you can't put an unpolished dub out at market. You can't make a market out of unpolished stuff because it just doesn't sound right. It has to be polished. It has to be mixed.

Are those the things that ended up on the Chess label?

Yeah, yeah. And "Her Last Bye-Bye" now listen, guys, some voices were supposed to have been behind that and after we cut "Her Last Bye-Bye" I said, "Well, my god, no more of that." They said, "Okay, we'll just throw that away and do something else." I said okay. And lo and behold, Chess got it out.

How did you finally get off the road? And what did you do when you got off the road?

Well, I finally got off because it hit me that now's the time to write. Because out on the road, I couldn't write. I was making money and all those one-nighters, I couldn't concentrate on my stuff. And I'm the type of person if I write a song, I have to get into this the lyrics and the music. You know, I just don't want to throw something together and think the public's gonna buy it. I want to give the public something for their money. You know what I mean? "Black Dress" and "Big Mouth Blues," and "T-99." When I made "T-99" and "Meet Me with Your Black Dress On," I was just getting into myself. Can you understand what

I'm saying? I can just feel myself doing these things, you know. I felt so much alive when I do "T-99" and "Black Dress." Because, well, I just dropped it—and I quit the road. I said, "Now this is the time to write." Because when I was in Oakland I had a chance to go with Lionel Hampton's band. He and Gladys said, "Well, we're going to LA to do a gig and when we come back through meet us at the North Pole . . ."—that was at Eighth and Kirkham—"Meet us at the North Pole and we'll hear what you got. If you sound good to us, you can cut with us and then we'll take you on the road." And I said okay. Man, listen. I got pencil and paper and I couldn't write anything, because the pressure was so great. It was tremendous amount of pressure and everything I did just didn't come out right. So, I said, well, I finally found me. I say I've got to study these lyrics. I got to study the background. I don't want to use the same riffs other guys are using put behind the blues and it's the same old thing. And so, I said, "Let me stop for a while"—and I stopped. And I went to New Orleans, stayed around there with Frank Pangaea. He booked me out through Mississippi, Georgia and places like that. In the meantime, I'm still writing. I got to Houston and got married and I'm still writing. So, I said, it isn't luck in this business, it's being prepared. That is the luck in show business. If you don't have the material to put on record, you're not prepared. Well, this is what Lionel Hampton taught me. And that's what I taught myself. Be prepared, which is the key word here. Be prepared for anything. So now I'm prepared. I got my songs—all those songs I've been writing all those years. I got them under my bed and I'm bringing them out right now.

You've been quite active the last couple of years, haven't you?

Yeah, I've been over in Utrecht, Holland, with Joe Houston, he's a Texas blues man, and Blues Boy Hubbard and the Jets, H-bomb Ferguson & the Bluesmen, and Sherman Robertson band. William Clark's West Coast band. Yeah. And also Robert Cray from Chicago, Grady Gaines, Texas Upsetters, Peppermint Harris, Otis Clay and his Chicago band—yeah, Big Ed Compton and also Big Daddy Kinsey with the Kinsey Report. Terrific band, nice people.

What kind of a band do you like to play with today? Do you like horns or guitars?

Well, you've heard my sound on "Black Dress On"? Sure. Why you hear that? That background? Okay, that's my shot.

So you like a tenor in your band? You like horns?

I like the horns. Yeah. Okay. I like the horns because it's a hell of a feeling, and I like a baritone, tenor and alto—and four rhythm.

It must have been somewhat of a loss for you when Arnett Cobb died.

Oh God, yes. Because I said to myself, well, this is what I need. When Arnett passed away that did it . . .

Slim Gaillard

Slim Gaillard came to town when he was booked by the Jazz Institute of Chicago. I made arrangements to interview him at the Blackstone Hotel. I remember he told me to come on over and that I didn't even need to bring a tape recorder—that he was an audiophile and he traveled with all the recording equipment we'd need. That sounded good but I brought my cassette recorder with me—just in case. When I got there, he had a Montgomery Ward 7' reel-to-reel with bundles of color-coded wires running from out of the deck in every direction. Slim pressed the on-button and the meters lit up but, what a surprise—the reels wouldn't turn. He pulled the plug so the smoke wouldn't trip the alarms and we used my recorder. He performed the following night and I brought my girlfriend along. Slim was greeting all attendees, in-person at the front door and saved his extra special greeting for my girlfriend, turning his handshake into a two-handed clasp, and overwhelmed with feelings of friendship pressed her hand against his crotch, saying repeatedly in melodic island brogue, "It's so good—it's so good!" The girlfriend finally asked if she could have her hand back and we found seats for the performance.

■ ■ ■

The starting of the music era was the Mills Brothers and I listened to them. That was really a starter right there. They were really big—and I listened to them. The world wouldn't exist without listening to them because their theme song sounds like a band and just for the inspiration. It was really some sound that they made with their close harmony. When they came through on a tour and they came into Detroit, I was a typical fellow just looking at celebrities. Like they used to come into the pool hall and shoot pool and everybody would crowd around and say, ". . . that's one of the Mills Brothers!" And I'd look and I saw them shooting pool even. I'd say, "Oh, this is great." I used to play a little four string guitar like they had and then I played a tipple, 10-stringer, then I got into guitar. I used to sing in a quartet. I started singing in a quartet around Detroit as a boy and there was a show that came on WXYZ. And this show was named the *Lone Ranger*. [*Laughs*.] I sang on the *Lone Ranger* when they started, Brace Beamer on WXYZ in the Maccabees Building in Detroit. They asked what I was doing—I was singing "Home On The Range" or something. I was traveling and Tonto was coming loose. Fats Waller was one of my big inspirations on the piano, I played his style, I just think it was super. I studied quite a bit of music. I used to teach lots of piano and guitar lessons. And I wrote a lot of stuff. It was in the Middle West mostly around Detroit. And then I began to like other piano players, like Duke Ellington, Count Basie and Claude Thornhill—and different piano players and bands—I liked big bands. These big bands and small groups, also Ink Spots. And Cab Calloway, Cab was later—he came in later and he was not too much of an influence on my type of work. I enjoyed his work. We worked together, too, many times in places. I enjoyed his work very much. Well—Detroit to New York. I was doing a little touring—not booked, but you go from one town to another, working your way into New York. I left Detroit and came into, I think, it was Fort Wayne, Indiana. I stayed around and came on an amateur show with Ted Lewis. He was touring east doing amateur shows, and I came on his show. And Fort Wayne, then I came to Pittsburgh, Pennsylvania. They had shows. I'd find out where they had amateur shows. I'd go there and win an amateur contest and keep going. So, I came up to Gus Greenie's on Wiley Avenue. There was another place, I forget the street it was on, but I came in there. I went upstairs and played and there was a little boy playing I've never forgotten, Errol Garner. He was playing and he came up to see me. I would listen to him play. And then from Pittsburgh, I came into Columbus, Ohio, I think it was. Most places I went I had my little guitar and my tap shoes. I used to wear them, travel with plates on [*laughs*]. I'd walk in ready to work. I think you won about ten dollars or something like that—but ten dollars back then now's worth about fifty or sixty dollars. I'd get on the bus or train, it was cheap money, it cost nothing. Then sometime I would get rides. Somebody would say, "Where you're going?" to me. I'd say Philadelphia. Baltimore—I worked in Baltimore area and to a place down on Pennsylvania Avenue. And then this place there was a little girl singing named Billie Holiday. I saw her there but this place that I worked there on Pennsylvania Avenue, they would take movies in there on a Monday night—then, on Friday they showed them to people. Everybody wanted to be in the movie. That was a nice idea. Everybody wanted to be on that film. I would do things like "Nagasaki." "You Are My Lucky Star" was my big hit there. I made a big hit with that song, I would stroll around the room singing with the band playing, but I was strolling around the room. The people would keep the rhythm—the club gave out little round hammers on each table. They knocked on the table with little hammers. I remember on New Year's Day; they gave all of the customers those little hammers at the table—they kept rhythm but they had lots of broken glasses—the people were beating on the tables and their glasses. And then I left Philadelphia and I came into New York and did the amateur shows. There they had booking agents for the Major Bowes Show. You had to do auditions. They had agents that brought you down and you had to do an audition. Everybody got $17 apiece. I did some shows with Frank Sinatra on Major Bowes amateur shows. We all got $17 and ate at Big Foot's Restaurant, they'd give you food—one meal. And you get there on the subway. So, I was on Major Bowe's many weeks. I'd go on every two or three weeks. Because it was radio, they gave me a different name each time I'd go on—this week I'd go tap dance, the next week I'd play the guitar, and next week I'd sing and play the guitar and whatever—it all changed around. I remember when they had me on—they called me Bobo [*laughs*]. "We're gonna name you Bobo this week!" It didn't matter—$17 looked good. It was worth about $112 back then I guess—sure. You go buy half a dozen bananas, a quart of milk, a loaf of bread, and make banana sandwiches [*laughs*].

Tell me how you first got on record. Wasn't that with Frankie Newton?

That was the first one. I wish I had a copy of that. The only thing about that record—I just sang on that record—just a solo vocal. I don't know how they got me there. Well, he had listened to my singing in New York. And then he came to the club one time up in Harlem—and he asked me if I'd be interested in singing on a record. I said I'd never sung on a record before. He said he liked my voice and to come on down. I don't even remember the name of the record . . . ["There's No Two Ways about It," 1937]

How did Slim and Slam get started?

When I came down to Harlem and got Slam. He was sitting down in a place called the Big Apple. I think it was down in the basement. He was playing his bass down there and I came over and asked him. Martin Block [a pioneering radio host] listened to us on the amateur show and then he said, "I think I can get you fellas a recording date over at Decca." So, he brought us over to Decca and he introduced us to the people—and they said, "Sure—you're okay." So then after we recorded for Decca they didn't get together on a contract—Martin Block and Decca. No, they didn't get together—and so that was a waste of recording time. Then he brought us over to Columbia with him, to come out on the Vocalion label, and that was the release of "Flat Foot Floogie" and "Tippy-Tippy-Tin" and "Ferdinand the Bull." And we did "Tutti-Frutti,"

"Flatfoot Floogie." It came out and made a big hit, number one on the hit parade, every week for about eight weeks. So, it was nice. "Flatfoot Floogie" has gone down in history—they put it in a time capsule at the World's Fair in New York—Westinghouse put it down there. So, in the future many people will hear it and say, "What were they doing back in those days? They were way out there!"

We came from New York to Los Angeles to work in a club and show the people what we do. The show business people said, "We'd like to put you guys in a movie." We said, "Okay—we'll go." And that was *Hellzapoppin'* and we were supposed to do the movie *Stormy Weather* together, but I got my greeting at that time—my greeting from Uncle Sam [*laughs*]. [It was his draft notice for WWII.] So, I had to leave and Slam did *Stormy Weather*. They wanted Slim and Slam together, but I had to leave so Slam had to do it. So, they put him with Cab Calloway and Ethel Waters and different groups.

So, you actually did get drafted?

Oh, it was really some fun because I was in the Air Corps and not the Air Force. I was in the plane department. It used to be the Army Air Corps but they changed it to the Air Force. So now of course there is no more Army Air Corps. But I came in and they tried to get me in special services with music but I wasn't even interested. I used to practice Morse code before I came into the service. So, when I first came in for basic training, they said, "You know the code well enough that you could teach the code"—so they made a teacher out of me and I taught Morse code. And I taught DFCT1 code—that's what they call it. I have a book, you read what's in the book, but you don't know what it means—you don't know what you're sending. Like you send C5072M3—but it's code you know, so maybe it means "Move the troops forty-four degrees this way"—whatever, you don't know what it says. So, I was seeing about thirty-five words a minute on it. So, I was a radio operator before I started training for planes. Then, I had 133 IQ test. And they figured that I would be qualified for flight school. So, I got into planes. I studied B-25s and B-26s. We had training on the plane. We had to study the plane—both planes. And as a mechanic you had to learn how to be able to repair it and the whole thing—and at the end of the course, you go through all of the gyro instruments, every instrument in the plane. You had to disassemble, assemble, and repair the whole thing—and read schematics of a whole electrical hydraulic system, every part of the plane, you had a strong heavy course to go through. You had to be pretty heavy with the mathematics on the course. On the last day of the inspection, you take the engine from the plane—you couldn't call it a motor because you'd be disqualified. You had to disconnect the engine from the firewall completely and you had to make a tripod with a pulley and they gave you about four tools and a flashlight. That was the final test—walk through and show them, show the inspector that the engine is not connected to the rest of the fuselage. Then he'd say, "Okay . . ." and before daylight you had got to put the engine back on with these instruments connected, all the hydraulic, electric, put everything up, get in the plane, start the plane up, rev it up, watch the magnetos and see how much drop you got on both sides and if you get your mercury up to what you want on the plane, then you got to take the plane off and they troubleshoot in air—because if you don't put it back together, it's your fault. That was the test in Sheppard's Field, that was what we had to go through, you had to learn that plane. We rushed—but we took our time. We used to make tripods out of trees. They'd give you trees you know, practice that so when you were in combat and you didn't have all the facilities in a hangar you knew you could pull that thing out. But on the test, when we were in flight on the final test, the instructor would fly with you. So, then he would go back in the fuselage while you were up front and he would turn some kind of valve off, to keep from feathering the prop because some were electric and some were hydraulic prop. It was Pratt and Whitney Wright engine so they would go back and cut a faucet off, one of the shutoff valves, and you looked at your pressure on the hydraulics and go back and find out where the problem is. So, you go right back and you look to find it out and they grade you on it. Then they give you a certificate of completion. You would be able to fly a plane but you're not a crew chief. You could be a crew chief on plane because you know more about the plane than a pilot who knows the instruments but he doesn't know all the problems in a plane. With my training, I could go look in the cockpit and pull up papers, Form 41B, look at it and place a red diagonal on certain things in the plane and they can't move it. I saw it happen—"Look, we gotta go—this plane has got to fly." Well, he can't move it. It's marked with a red diagonal—you've gotta walk away from it no matter what. You can be a general—anybody—but with the red diagonal, he can't touch it. He can get angry, but it's too bad. We trained in the desert to go to Alaska. It was 135 out in Rice, California. We trained in Marshfield, also—that was hot there. And then we had taken off to Alaska cold country. [*Laughs.*] Well, there was nothing wrong with that. So cold up there, their words even turn to icicles—wait until it thawed out to see what they were saying. I met one of my buddies, Percy Heath—we were in the service together and he's still in the field because he studied. We all went to the same school—he's a jazz bass player AND he was in the Army Air Corps too—and he's a pilot, too.

When I went in the service, Slam went back to New York—he lived in the New York area. And then when I got out of the service, I came to California, in Los Angeles and then I was discharged in Presidio Monterey in California. So, I got my mustering out pay and came to Harlem and started sitting in with Lester Young, Lee Young and Billie Holiday, whoever was up there. I'd sit in with them and I got a job as a drummer. I was a drummer when I first got out—I worked in my uniform [*laughs*] and I stayed in California while Slam was in New York and we just divided up—I went this way and he went that way. I worked for Billy Berg's Swing Club there. Then I worked for Billy Berg's on Vine Street. And then a fellow—Mike Riley was his name—came in and asked me would I be interested in recording again? Sure—absolutely! I just got out—I'm ready. So, he said okay, he was a musician and played vibes. And he was a little broker than me. He didn't have *any* funds, you know. If you make a recording session, they give you two weeks to pay the musicians—you get two weeks to pay. So, he had to go out and play his vibes and work a job and get money to pay us through the union. So, we cut four sides. We had three sides all rehearsed, down, timed and everything. And the fourth tune we didn't have. The engineer said, "What are you gonna do next?" We said, "Why don't you take a little break and when we come back, we'll be ready to do the next one." So, we go outside on Sunset Boulevard where we were recording. The sun was shining and sitting there was a cement mixer in the middle of the street going "putt-putt-putt-putt-putt" like this, filling a hole in the street with some cement, you know, repairing the hole in the street. And then we came back inside. The engineer says, "Ready? Let's go!" I say, "Everybody on three—'Cement Mixer'—puttee, puttee!" Everybody looked at each other [*laughs*]. No lyrics, nothing—and that's the one that hit. The other side was the A side—that was called "Scotchin' with the Soda." I recorded that. That was his number. He wrote it and that's what he wanted to plug—his number. So, I put my number on the other side and the record was carried by that—"Cement Mixer." Okay, now we get paid for the date. And they had all of these different radio stations with different types of music going on. So, it costs him money to get it plugged over the air. He'd go around—they call it Payola. He got his old piece of station wagon loaded down with records. He'd peddled them around and it kept going on and on. "Cement Mixer—Number One!"—oh, he was happy—he made lots of funds—he bought two-thirds of Las Vegas . . . We had the Slim Gaillard Trio—it was Slim Gaillard, Bam Brown on bass, and Scatman Crothers, he was my drummer. He worked with me on recordings also, we toured around together as a trio. We worked the theater in downtown in Los Angeles, with the Buddy Rich Big Band and my trio. Yeah Scatman—he worked with me and he was my drummer, for three years, I guess—something like that. I remember that I bought uniforms, the ones that are on the cover. What they have is I bought the uniforms for a $3,000 wardrobe, which at that time was worth maybe nine or ten thousand dollars, because when I bought the uniforms, he said he was gonna pay me, you know, everybody's gonna pay for their own things—fine! Yeah, well, he paid me—when a grape got as big as a pumpkin. [*Laughs.*] Nobody paid! I'm not complaining about it, I'm not knocking it because he's my friend. I was out to his house in the valley. And we were gonna go out and play golf together, but I had to leave and go back up north.

I took a taxi cab from San Francisco to Los Angeles. I was working at a place, at The Say When in San Francisco—Erroll Garner and myself—he had a trio and I have my trio up there. They say Slim Gaillard is gonna open tonight in San Francisco? I said, "Well, I got to call the airport"—no planes available. I try to get a bus—a bus would never make it in time. And I tried to charter an ambulance—and they said, "We can't cross counties and states lines. You need to get more than one—like from one to another to another." They couldn't make it—and the train would never have made it in time. So, I got a yellow cab and asked the driver. "Well, I never did hear of that place. Can you tell me how to get there?" "It's in Los Angeles." "Oh—that's a different story." So, he says, "Well, I gotta call my boss and find out find out what my boss says." I say, "Okay—call him!" He says, "Well, what will we charge? $250? Is $250 okay?" Okay—yeah, let's go—I gotta make the job because Lionel Hampton's Big Band was on the stage and I had to follow him. The driver went by his home and picked up a little overnight bag and he drove. So here I go tearing down the highway in a yellow cab—we just continued riding until we got into Los Angeles. I'm scheduled to go on at nine o'clock. I got in about two minutes to nine I walked in the door. It was awesome. "We're glad you're here—so glad you're here!" I got my guitar walked up on the stage and said, "Take care of the cab . . . ". He said, "How much is it?" "Two-fifty!" He gave the guy $3 and said, "Keep the change!" [*Laughs.*]

I remember—I can make this very clear statement—is that working in Hollywood when I had "Cement Mixer," my big song, Frankie Laine used to come in and sing. He asked Illinois Jacquet and his band to play for him—and Jacquet refused to play for him because he said Frank sang off-key. I told Frankie, what you do is just tell me what you're going to sing and my trio would play for you—with Zutty Singleton, Bam Brown and myself. He said, "I wanna do 'Black & Blue' . . ." and then some other numbers. He sang good, got over—and then sitting in the audience was the president of Mercury Records and Hoagy Carmichael—sitting at a table. They said, "We want to meet him." I said to Frankie, "They want to meet you." So, I brought him over and introduced him to the people there. And the president of Mercury Records says, "I would love to make a recording session with you." Oh man—he didn't know what to say or what to do—because he used to sing from one place to another around in Los Angeles, free, trying to get a break. And he will tell you in all of his interviews, radio, television, magazine, anything—he will say, "Slim Gaillard gave me my break. Thank Slim Gaillard—he gave me my start." And I said he started the whole thing. And he always said it, see—my record were just fading away and Frankie was right on top doing "Mule Train" and all of those different things. Big Records! Frankie Laine—Frankie Laine—making big funds every day. Whoa. Making very big money.

So, he got a job playing in a little cocktail lounge down in El Cajon, California. It was a bowling alley and then the man who built the bowling alley had a chain of restaurants called the Chuck Wagons—I think it was worth about 200 million, something like that. But he built this bowling alley out in this valley out there and it was really hot out there—beautiful place. He built a duplicate of one of the hotels in Vegas. They built a room with chandeliers that was unbelievable for a bowling alley. He put everything you can think of in that place. It seated about 400 in that room—that's in a bowling alley yet! Very first class, I mean plush on everything was plush—velvet booths and the whole thing. Everything he made was very first class because he had the money to do it with. He invested in everything you know—he had pools there and everything else. So, I was playing in the room still sticking around San Diego area and he was booking shows, big packages, big productions—that's how big the place was. He had about a thirty-piece band and that's how swinging it was, okay? And Milton Berle played there—he was big doing the *Texaco Hour*, you know—and he's still big to me, you know? Well Frankie was booked in. Okay, now I'm still in my little room playing, when I play in my little room there it was a kind of little lounge there—very intimate, people right close on you. You could shake hands with everybody in the place. See, my room is prior to the big show. People come in and get a little drinky and some entertainment with what I do and sing. Then they go in the big room for the show, for the real show. The big room is loaded—packed. Frankie Laine, he did his thing with harps and violins and everything you can think of—the whole shot. Then he says, "Ladies and gentlemen, I'd like to acknowledge the presence of a man that gave me my start—my break. He looked out for me. He used to give me gasoline when I had no gas for my car." He had a little piece of Pontiac convertible near the top was rotted away and he had no gas and I helped him out because I was swinging with lotsa funds from my "Cement Mixer" and so forth. So, Frankie says, ". . . he's been my friend and he's still my friend. He gave me my start and thanks to him—Ladies and Gentleman, Slim Gaillard."

In Los Angeles, the Go-Go rock and roll was the type of music thing was a little too strong for the type of music that I was playing. And I backed away from it because then a lot of the companies wouldn't pay you. But then when I got out of music field, I got into movies and started making movies. I had played a date someplace around in Hollywood, the Haven, that's what they called it. And after I get through in the morning, there's a little place called Theatres—we used to go in and get breakfast. People, musicians and singers and dancers and everybody went there—the meeting place. I used to see all the stars like Danny Thomas, Milton Berle and Joey Bishop. They all met at one table and exchange jokes together. And I walked in and there was an agent. He was walking around saying, "Hey look, are you working in movies? What movie are you in?" "I'm not an actor—I'm a musician." He says, "Would you like to read a script for me?" I say, "Well, I don't know . . ." He said, "You look like just what I would want for this part. You have a chance to get this if you go and read for me." So, "Okay—I'm not a pro." He says, "That's alright." I went out to MGM and read for the part. They said, "That's alright—you got the part. Yeah, you leave for Phoenix tomorrow. The plane's at so-and-so time." We leave with the crew, everybody's going to Phoenix, Arizona. It was a TV show called *Then Came Bronson* with Michael Parks and I got the part in that, working with Robert Hooks. He's a champion, pro actor, so he kind of quotes me a little, he says, "You're doing great. You did fine." And when I got back from Phoenix, the agent had submitted me to *Marcus Welby, MD*, so I got those segments in there. And before I finished that one, I had *Medical Center*, all were feature parts. In *Medical Center* I was a musician in there and that was the only one. I had a featured part in *Roots*. I worked in *Roots: The Second Generation*. I was Sam Wesley, the baseball expert down at the train station. I knew everything about baseball. I knew so much I talked about the Red Stockings and those guys. I had a lot of work in that part—and a screen credit. I have a Screen Actors Guild card—I can't play extras. And then I did *Love's Savage Fury* with Raymond Burr. I did that on location. It was a Movie of the Week. They've rerun it already. I keep watching *TV Guide* for reruns. I like reruns. I get the residual. I look through *TV Guides* to get residuals. And I worked in *What's Happening*, a little comedy thing, Rerun. I worked in two or three of those. I made a movie called *Willie Dynamite* and that was in Universal Studios and did quite a few movie and TV things. Some people have approached me to do a kid show thing, you know, because they said I would look like an Uncle Remus type thing—but that wouldn't be accepted today. It would be kind of put the Blacks down. My movie agent in Hollywood asked me if I would go down and read for part at Disney, an Uncle Remus type thing—but this was a not for a movie. They wanted me in the parade, to lead in the summer parade for all of all the Disney characters, Mickey Mouse and all of the Disney characters, they wanted me as Uncle Remus—because I look like him. I told them I don't think it'd be accepted. I just started back, not too long ago, I worked in Seattle getting back in the music field with Dizzy Gillespie. I've worked with different groups who come in to the area there. They would play the set and then I would play my set and so forth—I wouldn't be working in the band with them. I played piano sometime with a group and maybe five pieces.

Norvel Taborn

Over the years I've always referred to my radio program, *Blues Before Sunrise,* not as a blues show, but as a blues-heritage showcase—because I've always presented several different genres of Black music. Perhaps the most influential record in helping me define which different genres I included was a two-record set on the Columbia label called *Stars of the Apollo.* In addition to blues and rhythm and blues were big band vocals and a genre I refer to as hep harmony—quartet harmony singing. This genre included groups like the Mills Brothers, the Ink Spots, the Charioteers, the Jubalaires, and many others. One group I discovered was the Four Vagabonds, who did wonderful four-part harmony. I was surprised to discover that a surviving member of this group, Norvel Taborn, lived in Chicago and made arrangements to invite him to the station to talk about the group and their records.

■ ■ ■

I was born 1916. I was born in East St. Louis, Illinois. But I was raised in St. Louis. I had ten brothers and sisters.

Just out of curiosity, how do you pronounce your first name?

Nor-vell Tay-born . . .

Were you named after anybody—your father or a grandfather? Or did they just they just came up with that one out of . . .

. . . out of left field! [*Laughs.*] Yeah, you could say that. And, as I understand, it was a tossup between the name my mother wanted, as my mother would tell me, and the doctor gave me the name. And it struck her fancy. There wasn't so much of a musical background in the family. My father, he was about the only musical one you could find in the family. He sang with a group.

Where did you go to high school?

In St. Louis, at Vashon High School. And we started in the Glee Club in the school. They had a Glee Club, and the four of us were in this Glee Club, and we were supposed to have had the best voices in the Glee Club. So, at one time, they organized about four quartets out of the Glee Club. And the quartets competed against each other in a contest on the stage in the school—and we lost the competition. But the other kids, they didn't last as groups or go anywhere. We were the only quartet that stayed together and made something out of it.

Can you tell me the names of the members of your quartet?

Well now, they're John Jordan, the lead singer—he's the one that organized the group at the time. And Ray Grant, Jr., he's the bass in our group. And Robert O'Neal, he was first tenor. And myself, I was a baritone.

Were you all in the same grade?

No, we weren't. John Jordan, he was a year older. Then two of us, Ray Grant and myself were the same class and we graduated together. And the other boy, Robert, was a year younger. While we waited for him to graduate, we all had little jobs after school, you know. I worked at an ice cream company. In St. Louis they have a lot of affairs, you know, like picnics. And they had to hire people to work late at night—and that was good for kids who were in school, and weren't on vacation anything, they could get these jobs wrapping ice cream bars, and making those little Dixie cups and things? And it was nice. But I worked there from the age of nine, until I graduated from high school. Part time, you know . . .

You started out in Glee Club in school. What did you do after everybody graduated?

Well, we just kept singing. And somebody took a liking to us on a radio station in St. Louis, WIL, which was in the Melbourne Hotel. There was a show on that particular station every Sunday. And they heard us on the free station WEW, which happened to be in St. Louis University. They had a free station, and they featured free talent then, and so we stayed on that station quite a while until finally this commercial station heard us. And this was a commercial program that was on WIL. So, they called us over and we happen to be right across the street from each other. And they hired us and we stayed with them, I guess for about eight years—regular! It was on for half an hour. And it was on every Sunday evening around about six. And as I recall it was for the Missouri Insurance Company. This was a regular thing for us. That's the way our popularity began to grow, from this particular thing.

What kind of wages would you get for doing that?

Well, it was a lot to us, still being in school, you know? And I can't recall how much it was, but it was pretty good.

What kind of things were you singing?

Popular song, spirituals, everything—we could sing everything.

Did you guys have any influences at that point?

The Mills Brothers were our influence. We loved what they did. And they were very popular back there in those days. And this is one reason that we lost the Glee Club contest—because the teachers felt like they didn't want our group to influence others, you know? But the Mills Brothers were the hottest thing going and the kids were just wild about them—and that was the first time in the history of the school that the kids booed the principle, you know, for giving first place to the other group.

Where did the name the Four Vagabonds come in? Were you always the Four Vagabonds?

Yeah, always. At the time, we were picking a name for our group, and we couldn't come to a conclusion. There was a club in St. Louis that were very popular, and this particular club was named The Vagabond. We kind of liked that name, and we said we'll be the Four Vagabonds. There was another group known as the Four Vagabonds at the same time. And we had to prove that we were first—and that's the way it was—although they were very popular. But we were first, it was confusing. They tried to make a lawsuit but it wasn't necessary. We proved that we were first. So, both of us, both groups, met down the road after that, and worked cross streets from each other in nightclubs. And we met together and it was fun. Most people remembered us from the *Breakfast Club* [*Don McNeil's Breakfast Club* on the NBC Blue radio network/later as ABC Network in Chicago], most of our work was radio, especially on the Breakfast Club. But this other group, they remembered them from the theaters. Later we were singing on one side of the street and they were singing on other side. So in between sets we'd get together and just have fun. We'd get up on stage and sing together and sing. As to the routine, it was so many things happening at the time. We were doing different shows on station KSZ and KMOX. The station called us to fill in—at the time the Mills Brothers were supposed to do a show—and they missed it, so the station called us to fill in. They had heard us on the network over WIL. And they remembered the popularity and the group, so they called us in and we fill the spot, you know. So, when the chance came here in Chicago, there was a group that used to be on NBC here in Chicago—and they were leaving. So, a fellow who was on the Edgar Guest show on a regular basis, he became our manager. And he was also managing a group in St. Louis—that's where he met us. He came to St. Louis and saw us on the show on WIL. And he never did forget—he said we did such a beautiful job commercial way. And he said, "I won't forget when I get back to Chicago.

So yeah, if anything happens, I'm gonna let you know—get your bags ready because when I call, I want you to come." So sure enough, it happened just like that. These fellows, the group that was going to leave, they were going with Duke Ellington. And just like the man promised, he called us—and we grabbed our bags—we didn't take much. But we were anxious, hoping that something would happen. We grabbed our bags and came up here. At the time, there were other groups that were trying to get on the show, to audition to get the spot on NBC. One group was called the Harmony Hounds, back then in Chicago. They were very popular. And another group was Darnell Williams, who came out of the Earl Hines band. He had a trio, musical trio. And then there was Nat King Cole and two other guys, but he wasn't singing—it was just a trio. And do you know we won out over them—a three-year contract? And from then on it was a three-year contract every three years [*laughs*]. And we stayed on there eighteen years.

How long would you be on each day—and were you on in a regular time slot?

Well, we were contracted for sustaining shows. "Sustaining" shows were programs that were produced without a sponsor. And they were to be used anytime—day or night—in spot that was not commercial. And we had one particular show at 4:30 every afternoon. And this spot made us very popular in the city, you know, with the kids especially. They raced home to listen to us on the radio.

So, you're doing a live show at 4:30 in addition to the* Breakfast Club*?

Yeah, yeah. See, that was in the morning. And then sometime we'd have one late in the evening called *Jamboree*. And that was Don McNeil's idea, too. He was head of the *Breakfast Club*. And these other spots were sustaining shows—they weren't commercial. We were used anywhere we were needed; you know. But we did have one particular time that was ours, which was 4:30 in the evening—every evening.

Did that play just in Chicago—or did that play across the nation, the network?

It wasn't a regular network program, but it was available to any station that needed it, and in any time slot they needed it. We did quite a few shows that were sold to small stations out west.

Walk me through the schedule of your typical work day at the radio station.

We were scheduled every evening, so we had to have an arranger to help us keep material, music for all the show. We knew what we wanted, which tunes, but he would arrange it for us. We would write our programs and they had to be handed in a week ahead of time, because all the songs had to be cleared by New York ahead of time before we could do them. And that how we kept up with our program—we always knew which tunes four or five days ahead. We had a regular announcer that would put us on the air—there were several different announcers that worked with us—but that was the way we went on the air. We had skits, and each one of us had names on the air; one of us was named "Security," another was named "Pappy," another was named "Aloysius"—and I was called "Contagious" [*laughs*]. The names and the skits kept the listeners' interest—it was a lot of fun.

How many songs on an average would you do on one of these programs?

. . . about five songs. I guess they each ran about 2:30.

Was the Four Vagabonds' program on five nights a week?

Yeah, yeah. Five nights a week.

And how about the* Jamboree *program?

Well, that was a big show in the evening, in primetime. And it had a big band and people with talent from the studio on the show. And it was really nice.

So, you'd only do like a guest spot, like maybe do one number an evening?

Yeah, or a couple. Very seldom we'd do two, and they'd have a live audience in studio.

What about* Don McNeil's Breakfast Club*? How would the Four Vagabonds be used on one of those programs?

Well, that wasn't a hard thing because we were scheduled on that show. So, they'd taken the song that we were going to sing to be cleared in New York. And when our time to sing came up the announcer would talk us in to our tune.

What years were you on the* Breakfast Club*?

From 1936 to 1951.

Was this a living for all four of you?

Yeah, that was our living—and, this is where the booking came in. We had someone to book and that happened to be through NBC, they had their own booking. And whenever it was possible for us to do a show outside, like when we were on *The Vaughn Monroe Show*, we were booked through NBC. So, we would go to New York and do the show, and fly back and be ready for the *Breakfast Club* the next morning. It was nice, though. It was no problem because we got a kick out of it. We were doing what we wanted to do. And we loved what we were doing. And it was a thrill. And we were on *The Perry Como Show* and did the same thing. We had to fly to New York, and come back the same night, flying back to be on the *Breakfast Club*. A lot of time, they would book us to appear in the nightclub or a theater but wherever we went, wherever we were, we'd still do our fifteen minutes show at some station—the nearest NBC station.

In getting all this material prepared, did you rehearse?

Oh, yeah, we had certain time that we would get together in the evening. Sometimes we'd go down studio earlier before our program and rehearse. But most of the time, it was done at one of our homes, after work hours, and we'd spend three or four hours rehearsing. That way we kept up with our programs and with the different songs. Otherwise, it would have been a pretty tough thing. Our arranger had the music ready to be taught to us. And that kept us moving much faster.

How many songs would you say you had in your repertoire?

It's hard to say—I would guess about two thousand songs. We were out there so many years and we had so many because we memorized everything. All our songs were memorized—after we learned them from the sheet music. You can't have music in front of when you're on the stage presenting a show. You've got to know that music—you can't stand there read it. It's not a show if you do.

Did the war have any effect on your performance routine?

Well, no, no, not really. Because we were doing shows during the war. We would go to Great Lakes Naval Station [suburban Chicago] to entertain the guys in different places. Savanna Ordinance [Savanna Army Depot, NW Illinois]—we would go out there and entertain the soldiers.

How did you make records?

I think our first records were for the Bluebird Record Company. They heard us and liked what we did. That was our first chance to make records. They called us in and we made our first records.

Were those sides cut in New York?

No—right here in Chicago.

Was Lester Melrose the recording director?

Well, it's been quite a while but the name sounds very familiar. The record company was on the Outer Drive, just as you go across the bridge, and it turned north. Out there on the Outer Drive, there was a big building—not the Furniture Mart, not quite that far, but it was close to the river there. And I think that place is still there.

Where did the record "Roseanne of Charring Cross" come from?

Charring Cross was a hospital in England—and Roseanne was a nurse. So, the wounded soldiers were being brought in. And this particular soldier was falling in love with the nurse. And that was what it's all about.

What about the records for Apollo? How did they happen?

Yeah, I think we made those in New York? I know at one time we made some records in New York. I don't know if it was for Apollo, but we made records in

Carnegie Hall which had really beautiful sound—and nobody was there but the group to make the record. On that one tune, "The Lazy Countryside," that was me whistling.

What happened, this goes way back to when we were in school. And in sports in school, Ray, liked to box. And he was hit in the kidneys—he didn't think anything of it but this caused a problem for him many years later. He started going blind and there was no cure. We were on stage in New York when it really got serious. We finished our show and we sent him back to the doctor in Chicago. And that left us out there without him. But we got lucky because our arranger, Bill Sanford, who prepared our tunes, was a musician all the way. He played four or five different instruments. And he also sang bass. So, he stepped right in with the guitar—that's the only instrument we used—and sang bass with us, and that kept us going, hoping that Ray would get well, you know. But Ray didn't get better, he died. And it turned out that Bill couldn't just devote his full-time to our group. He was doing arrangement for other people, and other bands and because Bill Sanford wanted to attend Juilliard School of Music in New York. So, this was the beginning of the end of the group. We tried to continue. We had two or three different guys come in and try to replace Ray but it just didn't work. Their attitudes were different than what we had always done. The replacements we tried all seemed to be free and easy, you know? Come what may—and we weren't like that. When we decided to do something, we did it—and stuck to it. But these guys were the kind that come in anytime. And we'd call a rehearsal, and they'd come in high. And that wasn't our way, we never drank. Everything was business with us. And we loved what we did—and we didn't want any interference. And these people, they just didn't care, you make an appointment, they're going to be late—things like that. We just couldn't tolerate it because the house notes were still coming due—and you've got to have something coming in. So, we came to the conclusion we've got to find jobs *right now*. I decided to do what I'm doing now—my artwork. I have a diploma for commercial art. I had no idea that this would be my next living. But it's beautiful. It's something I knew, and I was doing it when we were singing—a bit here and a little bit there. My artwork never did leave me. I use all the mediums. I make pictures for the home, oil painting, watercolor, pastel or whatever, charcoal, I do the whole thing. But you don't get enough of that. There're too many artists. So, I went to the commercial side where you do sign work, truck lettering and things like that. And this is the type of work that brings in the money.

Art Sheridan

Art Sheridan was the owner of the Chance label, and one of a handful of white folks involved in recording and distributing Black music in Chicago in the late 1940s–early 1950s. His years in the record business were just an early chapter in an extended life arc. By the early 1970s Art had moved on to new fields of interest—investing in petroleum and chemistry. Three decades later, Art Sheridan was still knocking around the Chicago suburbs and I sounded him out for an interview. He agreed and we conducted the interview in his north suburban home. He was very easy to talk to but warned me in advance that he retained few detailed memories of his years in the music business.

■ ■ ■

I was born in Chicago on July 16, 1925. And lived on the north side of Chicago, went to Grammar School public school out there and also to Senn High School. My father had a little factory on the south side of Chicago, that manufactured small electrical appliances like toasters and coffee makers and table stoves and things. And it was on South State Street right across the street from what was Armour Institute, which is now ITT. And my father thought I'd be good as an electrical engineer, which I really didn't want to do. But I couldn't do much about not following the wishes of my father at that time. So, I enrolled in Armour Institute. And after about two or three months, I realized it wasn't for me. I was not very good at math. And it just didn't grab my interest. I'd been in the ROTC in high school, so I thought, well, I might as well join the army. All my buddies were gone. So, I talked to my dad until I was seventeen. And I finally convinced him to allow me to enlist. I joined the army, went to basic training at Fort Benning, Georgia. Somewhere along the line, I took some kind of a test, and apparently, I did well. And they sent me along with a lot of other soldiers to Indiana University, at a program that existed then call the ASTP, which I think was the Army Student Training Program. It was very nice. We lived in the girls' dorm; we had great food that was carried on by the normal kitchen of the university. It was not a bad life—except can you imagine what the course was? Engineering. Very fortunately, the course program busted out after about a month or so. But it was the kind of thing that if you dropped the pencil, you might be a day behind. And you didn't dare get ill because you might get kicked out of the program. But that was not the way you wanted to exit it. When the program ended, I went to Camp Campbell, Kentucky, and the 20th Armored Division and became part of the armored infantry. I was trained as an infantry man, a sniper and a scout. I was a pretty skinny little guy and weighed maybe 117 or 118 pounds, and I could move around pretty good. So, I became a sniper. And I was backed up by my friend, Charlie Bean. Charlie was an interesting guy, he was a big fellow, we call him the Elk because he was so big even his ears stood up. I was a skinny little guy, and I would be marching in front of him when we were in a column. But he became my backup when I had scouting or sniper responsibilities. We were allowed to forage pretty well on our own because of what our duties were, and not have as much discipline when we got back into the enclave. Though we came late to the war, we wound up going through a great portion of it, and then had some battles later on. As an armored division we were involved in almost every army in the Second World War, because they would move it around pretty good. We went through France, Germany, Belgium, Holland. I remember when we were involved with General Patton. And I remember some of the orders that came down to us and which were a little more difficult than we got from other people. Our group was part of the group that liberated Dachau. And that was a very interesting experience, but more so later in my life. And at that time, because that keep in mind, I was a seventeen-eighteen-year-old punk—and the issue of genocide, we didn't know very much about that, nor did it have the impact back then that it has on me today. That was pretty interesting. We were on our way to capture Munich, when we stumbled on this camp. We didn't know it existed. And then when we saw those folks in the condition they were in. It was horrible with dead bodies and things like that. We've seen dead bodies, but not in the stacks over there. And wound up at the end of the war on the border of Austria.

And then I came back home being prepared to invade Japan. We were sent to California, to camp there. We were doing the basic things we had done before. A little more mine-sweeping because we knew that would be a tremendous problem. And the war ended. When they announced that the bombs had been dropped, we were very, very cheerful. We didn't understand it, but we felt that that would save us from going there. And then ultimately, it was announced that we wouldn't have to go there. And I had sufficient points, you know, you got discharged based on your points.

What were the points based on—just basically time served?

Yes, time served. And I came back to the states and had my forty-five-day leave, which I enjoyed and came back to this area and got my discharge at Camp McCoy.

I went to work for my dad for a while and his factory had grown quite a bit, it was called Sheridan Electronics Corporation. It was then on 29th Street and Michigan Avenue in Chicago, I became his sales manager, but I didn't know anything about it. Very fortunately, the previous sales manager's secretary was a very bright woman. So, she, in fact, actually became the sales manager. And the funny part of that is, when I would go out in the countryside in other parts of the country to visit our distributors, they would complement me on being such a young fellow and writing such good letters, when actually it was this woman who was doing that. But I accepted the compliment. My father, somehow, had met a gentleman named Syd Nathan who owned King records, and Syd was saying he needed to get phonograph records made. And that was difficult because phonographic records weren't being pressed right after the war. My father was an interesting entrepreneur because he liked to make everything himself within his factory—molding, machining, tool and die making—when other people would farm that out. So, he found an engineer and we began building the presses that made phonograph records. Those were the old compression molding machines, where you bought the shellac, you heated it in like a book mold, which contained the tracks of the record and began making phonograph records. Then we began to put up a couple of those plants for other people around the country. In order to do that, we would take on local pressing for other people in order to demonstrate how the plant worked, and also to keep it operating. And that's how I met the people who, at that time, owned Aristocrat Records, Evelyn and Chuck Aron, and began pressing their records—and a couple of other companies like the Apollo Label, and Rondo Records. In doing that, I met Leonard and Phil Chess, who at that time, worked for their father, who had a junkyard on the south side of Chicago. They subsequently bought a nightclub called the Macomba and they ultimately bought out Evelyn and Chuck Aron. Subsequent to that, I went into business with Evelyn and started a record distributing company. And we located that in the 2000 block of South Michigan Avenue and what ultimately became Record Row. We were there with American Record Distributing, next to us was the Mercury distributor, down the block was King Records, and then the Chess Brothers opened an office there on South Michigan Avenue. And at our record distributing company, we represented a lot of the old rhythm and blues labels.

Subsequent to that, I started Chance Records, I decided, well, people are coming to me about getting recordings done. A lot of the rhythm and blues artists, the Black artists in there would come in and ask about this and that so I had already become involved with Bill Putnam and Bernie Clapper who owned Universal Recording. They were an interesting pair because they had a background as communication sergeants during the Second World War—and the Civic Opera Building was the headquarters of the Fifth Army at that time, so, they knew every bit of wire in the place. When the war was over, they rented the penthouse of the Civic Opera Building and started Universal Recording. And that became their studio up there. And in fact, I believe that the first echo chamber was developed there. They turned the lady's washroom into their echo chamber. It was kind of an industrial washroom with tile all over the place. They put a speaker at one end and a microphone at the other and a guard on the door and wouldn't let anybody in there during the recording sessions. So, I started Chance Records. I just picked up various artists that came in on the south side. I had a little bit of reputation, because of having been in the record distributing business I knew most record distributors across the country. So, it was easy for me to get distribution—and that was the key. Then I met Vivian Carter and Jimmy Bracken. During the time that I had the pressing plant, and then the distributing company, I met a young Black fellow named Ewart Abner, who had graduated college as an accountant. And at that time, it was difficult for Black people to get jobs in that kind of discipline. So, we hired Abner. We never called him by his first name—and he became the accountant of the pressing plant, and also, then subsequently into the distributing company. And then he became involved with Vee-Jay Records, with Jimmy and Vivian Bracken, as I did. I became kind of a consultant to them. Actually, it was really a Black company, and they wanted to continue that operation in that fashion, so I was somewhat of a consultant, kind of off the record. I then opened another label called Sabre just to have some other artists on it to expand the distribution. And that's basically how I got into the record business.

As blues collectors, we've heard all about the Chess Brothers—that they had these partners in the Aristocrat Label, and the partners soon disappeared. Was that a friendly transaction between the Chess Brothers and the Arons?

I understood it to be friendly, the Arons split up, they got divorced. And I guess that's when they wanted to get out of the record business, and they sold it to Chess. Subsequently, having met the Arons when I was pressing their records, I became personally acquainted with Evelyn. We ultimately married and opened a distributing company because she knew so many other people in the business that I didn't know. Basically, I think I got my original education through the Arons—not particularly the Chess Brothers, because at that time, they were pretty green in the record business.

The popular version of the "takeover story" implied that the Chess Brothers were ruthless and forced their partners out . . .

I don't think that they were partners with the Arons. I don't remember it that way—let's put it that way. In their dealings in the business, they were innovative and aggressive. They became very good friends of mine; I pressed their records. And even when I had my own label, we were still friends. I would travel as I did with Ernie Leaner; I would travel with Phil Chess in the south to visit our distributors and pressing plants. It's been a long time since I've seen Phil, but you know, we would spend time with the families. That sort of thing.

Tell me about the Chess Brothers, if you were good friends with them.

Well, the Chesses came out of the junk business that their father had and somehow got involved and had this nightclub on the south side and then ultimately the record business. Leonard in my mind was the more aggressive and business minded of the two. Phil was no dummy, but he was not the same as Leonard. They just built their business and reached out into the Black community, much more than many local people, and found these artists because of their distribution and their ability to get things played—and this was before they had WVON. They understood how to deal with artists in a better fashion than most people. They were difficult, but they were fair in the best degree in those days. And their idea of building their own studio within their building was interesting to us, at that time. I didn't do that, I used Universal Recording—or if I traveled the country, wherever I was, where there was a recording studio. That's really what I mean—and that, ultimately buying WVON. You know, that's rather unique for a record label guy to have—particularly a guy in the rhythm and blues business.

I always thought that the King label was based in Cincinnati. And yet you say that Sid Nathan was here in Chicago. Was he based here in Chicago?

He was in Cincinnati, that was his home base. But he had a distributing office in Chicago, on Michigan Avenue. He was the kind of manufacturer that wanted his own distributing. And so instead of giving it to myself or Milt Saulstone, who had the Mercury or Ernie Leaner, who had a distribution company to some degree, Nathan had his own office on Michigan Avenue. I think, but I'm not positive, that when King closed his office in Chicago, that's where Chess moved his office. That was in the 2000 block of South Michigan Avenue, that was Record Row. And our favorite restaurant was around the corner on 22nd Street—Batt's Restaurant. It was basically an enlarged delicatessen. They had everything.

Who was involved in the Mercury label?

A fellow named Green. I don't remember the rest of them. But Mercury was a pretty well-established label. It had some history to it. Milt Saulstone was the distributor in Chicago and he had the store and distribution center right next to ours. Milt was a good friend of Evelyn and Chuck Aron. He was basically a south sider and they [the Arons] lived on the south side. I assume that's how they got to know each other. Mercury had their own pressing facilities and their own places. Most of their records might have been pressed at RCA. But I'm not sure of that.

Between 1950 and 1954, were you recording directly to platter or were you recording to tape?

The early stages were to platter. I do think near the end they were recording to tape. But I always thought it was interesting in the control room at Universal Recording record studios. Bill Putnam was married to a lady. I think her name was Belinda. And when they were recording, Bill might be running the control board and Belinda was at the lathe that was cutting the record—brushing off the excess shaving, things like that. So, it was in the early stages. That's how it was done. Yeah, the base was metal, but they would have the acetate on. The acetate was what you brushed the shavings off. And the acetates were plated to make the metal master. And then from the master, you would re-plate and you get the mother. The mother is what you put into the mold. This was what we call compression molding. It's a very simple, elemental process. The machinery you had to have in order to do it, the fact that you had to create this steam and so forth, requires a pretty big boiler. The presses had to withstand some reasonable pressure. But they're pretty rudimentary. The shellac came in square, a piece about four by four. And you put that on the press.

How do the two halves of the mold come together? Are they horizontal?

They're vertical like a book—hinged. You place the piece of plastic manually and the steam heats the compound. You have two vents. There are two because one feeds it in, the other one takes it out.

Would you put labels actually inside the mold?

Yes, there is a place to put the labels inside the mold. So, you put the actual substance in there and then it closed, like a book and heated it.

How long does the platter actually stay in the mold—and if it was still hot, was it malleable and how did it cool off.

It stayed in the mold for about two or three minutes. And then it would cool off because we take the other end of the book out, let it set for a few minutes. And it went through a cycle of heating and cooling in the mold. So that would keep it in decent condition that we'd strip it out of the mold.

I know there was a recording ban during the war [WWII], and during the war it was difficult to get shellac. Did you experience that?

See, this was after the war and shellac was available. We had no problem getting material, and subsequent to that we had no problem getting vinyl. Because we started out with shellac, and then vinyl came in and we would press records on vinyl.

I'm curious about the compound, the shellac for the 78s. What actually went into that, do you have any idea?

No—just shellac. To the best of my knowledge, it was just shellac.

Somebody told me that they used to use chimney soot, to make the records black.

They might have done that at the plant that created the shellac. The company that we got most of our material from was called Biddy and Smith. And they were in Pennsylvania. And they used to supply our shellac—and then subsequently the vinyl. And we used to test the vinyl because there were some batches that were not quite as good as others. And the office of that plant was in an old building behind my father's factory. And the office was on the second floor. So, when we were testing it, we'd throw our record down the steps, if it didn't break, then we thought the batch was good. [*Laughs.*] That's how it happened.

Was it a hazardous job to work a record press in terms of inhaling what came out of the press when he heated that stuff?

No, it never became a problem. It was never considered a problem. The only thing that came out was steam.

Did they trim the excess off the outside?

As you opened the mold, these fell off.

Then where did the platter go? What did you do with it?

Into a sleeve, a paper sleeve—a normal paper sleeve. And then it got stacked and put it in a box. It was a manual job, as opposed to what you have now, which is done on injection molding. We had six presses, and they were pretty much busy most of the time with local record companies and occasionally, somebody from another part of the country, if another label when their record got real hot and they had to get them out to distributors real quickly, would send us masters and the labels to press for them. Those days, remember, we didn't have FedEx or UPS or anything like that. So, what we would do as a label owner, we would send the masters and labels to various pressing plants around the country. Like I remember Buster Williams had a plant in Memphis. And so, he did most of our pressing to our distributors in New Orleans, Memphis, Baton Rouge, Nashville. And he would just drop ship from there.

Shellac was never translucent was it?

No, it was the vinyl who became translucent. Shellac wasn't.

You could make like green, red, blue, translucent records. That was sort of a novelty item.

Yes, I remember those days. Yes.

Did you make vinyl 78s?

Yes.

For how long?

Till I got out of the business.

Well, I bet those were a bit more durable than the shellac things.

Without a doubt—we never threw shellac down the stairs. [*Laughs.*] But we would test vinyl that way.

You talked about Abner, did you have other Black employees?

Probably half the staff were Black. I had press operators and you hired people that were capable of operating the press. We didn't think in terms of black and white. Growing up in Chicago, you don't think of those things. You get exposed to it when you're in that business and you listen to the stories and then when you travel. You know, I remember traveling in the south. Sometimes I would travel with a fellow named Ernie Leaner, who owned United Records. And we'd go, for example, to Memphis and to the pressing plant. And Buster would pick us up at the airport and I'd have to sit in the back of his car. Ernie sat up front with him. And we used to tease him at that time because we walked in the plant and I remember Buster had two water fountains. One was refrigerated with "Whites Only" on it and the other was negros only. And Ernie and I both got really PO'ed at him. Don't we give you enough business that you could have two refrigerated water coolers? And in Kansas City, Ernie and I would go to visit a big disc jockey in Memphis. He was on the mezzanine or the second floor of the Gayoso Hotel, a historic hotel in Memphis. And I walked down the streets, he was called Visit Phillips, he was a disc jockey, there was the brother of Sam Phillips. I walk into the lobby, and I'd start heading for the elevator. And Ernie said, "No, I'll have to walk up and meet you there." Those are things we never think about in Chicago. "Let's stop and get a cup of coffee." "Well, I can't go in that place." Things that were a little different in Chicago.

Did you hang out at clubs? Were you listening to music? How was it that you were exposed to the music?

Simply by being involved in pressing the records. Getting accustomed to the Aristocrat people, subsequently the Chess Brothers, and then ultimately married Evelyn Aron, who was a producer of Aristocrat Records. And so, it just seemed to be a natural thing that I understood the business people came to us to do recordings. And it just evolved from that. It seemed to be kind of a natural thing. First club I saw was the Chess Brothers' club, the Macomba. And that was located at 39th Street and Cottage Grove, as I recall.

So, prior to that you weren't a jazz fan.

No, I wasn't any kind of fan at that time. Remember that we're talking back in the late '40s. I had just gotten out of the army in 1945, or 1946, just kind of finding my way in life and wound up operating this plant, albeit next to my father's plant, but I became the president of Armour, Plastics. And in that plant, of course, we made a couple of other things that were used in my father's plant like the Bakelite switches, as you find in appliances, and things like that. And then subsequent we also had a plant in Dubuque, Iowa, that I farmed out the manufacturer of electric switches.

How did you decide to start Chance Records? You tell me that artists came to you. When did you make the decision?

Somebody sent me something on Chance Records, and according to this history, from Wikipedia, I started Chance Records in September of 1950. Now, that's probably as close as we can remember. But it's simply because being involved with Evelyn, I was not uncomfortable with starting a record label. And being involved to some degree with Bill and Bernie at Universal Recording. Well, I just started doing that. And Doo-wop became somewhat of an interesting thing at that time. So, Leonard would turn down an artist and the artist would come down the street and knock on my door. Or if I didn't like an artist, they may go to Leonard. Just simply that way.

Do you remember who your first artist was?

No, as a matter of fact, I had difficulty remembering at one time, who my artists were—I still do, but this article had a list—a list with all my records that came out.

How about if I run the names by you, and maybe you can tell me what you remember? There was a tenor man from Gary Indiana. John Porter?

Yeah. Yeah. School Boy Porter. Yeah.

How did that connection happen? You have any recollection of that?

I don't recall how I met him. But at that time, I thought many of the jukebox operators would want to have instrumentals. Remember, through our distribution company, we would sell records to jukebox operators. And so, I figured, well, that's a good thing to do. And he sounded extremely good. So, I would cover popular tunes with instrumentals by School Boy Porter. Like the Tennessee Waltz sticks out my mind. I liked the tune and let's do one. So, we provided that sort of thing that we could sell to jukebox operators and occasionally, radio stations would like it.

Could you make a profit by selling strictly to jukebox operators?

No. No, but they were a means of promoting your material. You wanted the operators to be buying your material to put in the boxes because that was the way to promote it. Between that and disc jockeys, that's about it.

You've got a new record that you're issuing, and you want them to take it. How many would a jukebox operator take?

Usually, it depended on how many jukeboxes they ran—somewhere, usually maybe fifty, sometimes eighty, depending on the boxes.

Do you recall? Who was it that ran the boxes? What were their specific companies?

Yeah, but I don't remember the companies anymore. Those are the people that also sometimes ran gaming machines in those days.

Another one that they seem to talk about, the Chanceteers?

That's probably just a group we picked up and we simply had to name. I don't really recall. And please understand that I don't mean to offend any artists that might still be around? I don't remember specific things. It's been a long time. I've done many other things since.

Let's talk about you as a record producer. What was your policy? Did you try to advise the musicians? Or you just say, no, that sounds good. Yeah, we'll go with that.

No, I would try to advise what I would hear in the studio, I pretty much involved I'd like what I liked. And I didn't like what I didn't like. And I would try to ask or cajole the musician to do something a little different. And I would also talk to the recording engineer, if I needed more bass or more something, or whatever, you know, either do it again, or tell the engineer would you bring that track up? Remember, we only had four tracks in those years. I don't recall anything really unique. Because that's the way it was done, you go into a studio, or sometimes you do it in a nightclub. I remember many times; you would maybe only have three tunes. And under the union rules, you could do four, and you had a three-hour session under the license to record. Many of those blues artists when they did things with Joe Brown and other people didn't have a license or union. But if you were doing a union session, you'd sit there maybe and dream up the fourth tune, you know, blues are not difficult. Like "I Woke Up This Morning and my baby, she left me," You know, that goes on and on. So, you just put it together. And then if you were the producer, you might get credited as a writer just to put on the label. You know, but keep in mind, I'm thinking of it as it was, and I don't find it unique.

How did you record Jojo Adams?

Jojo probably came to me through one of the other people who had recorded him. A lot of the people who were doing recordings on the side would bring us the masters and we put them out. But then they'd get a royalty—again, an advance *and* a royalty. I kind of remember, there was one guy, Joe Brown. He used to bring us quite a few artists. Yeah, JOB record label—he was quite a guy.

You took artists into the studio. Do you have any recollections, any clear memories? What stands out to you among the Chicago, the downhome artists, the blues artists, that you did? Do you still remember some of the names of the guys that were here in Chicago?

No.

Well, how about Homesick James or Sunnyland Slim?

I don't recall that we actually recorded Sunnyland. Those might have come from Joe Brown. Because Sunnyland was on anybody's label. Sunnyland would record for almost anybody. And then you'd get a master and that was Sunnyland Slim, and you knew he would sell. So, you put it out. Once you were sure that you got the rights from either Joe Brown or whoever gave it to you.

You've got one of the big names in Little Walter, the genius of the harmonica. You actually had a Little Walter title in your catalog that apparently you got from Abrams?

Could well be . . .

Do you remember Abrams? He had Maxwell Street Radio . . .

I don't remember.

Do you remember Willie Nix, the drummer? Where did Willie Nix come from?

I think he came originally from Joe Brown, and then sat in on some of our recordings.

JB Lenoir?

I don't recall it.

You probably wouldn't have had any personal exposure to him if you bought the master from Joe Brown.

Oh, sometimes he'd bring the artists along. Yeah, because we want to make sure that he had the right to lease it to us. I think I probably saw 80 percent of the artists because we wanted to meet them. We wanted to know that if we got a license from the producer that we really had the authority to have it. And so, we would try to meet them. Sometimes we'd sit in on a rehearsal that somebody else was having, but just to become familiar with the artist.

Somebody that I think that you must have done—not Joe Brown. Do you remember an artist Big Boy Spires?

I remember the name, but I can't remember if I did it or somebody else did. I just can't remember. I'm sorry. I'm just not doing a good job, but a lot of years—what forty or fifty years have gone by.

How did you come to wrap up your label?

I just got tired of it. I had financial problems with some of the stuff we were putting out, and then I got more involved with Vee-Jay. And then the nightclubs. And that was it.

I think I was reading this in the Red Saunders Research that there was some dispute with the union about certain artists.

I don't remember the specifics of it. I read about it in Wikipedia on Chance Records, that when we did Schoolboy Porter, in one session, one of his artists was not union, which we didn't know. And so, we got censored for that. I don't remember that incident at all. Then I got more involved in Vee-Jay with Jimmy and Vivian and Abner. I thought one of the interesting things was we had—both in Chance, and then in Vee-Jay—we had good distribution throughout the country, which is the key. So, a lot of artists would come to us, particularly Vee-Jay over the years. We were in London, Abner, myself, Jimmy and a lawyer that we had in New York, who was pretty familiar with the entertainment business. We went there to establish some distribution. We had a meeting with Jay Arthur Reich. By that time Abner was, by and large, running Vee-Jay. We had some interest in an acquiring an Australian artist, I don't remember his name. But the deal was, "If you want Artist X [the artist that we were thinking about], we have a group of young people here who are beginning to make some noise. Would you take this group too?" kind of a package deal. And that group was the Beatles. So that's how the Beatles were first released in the United States on Vee-Jay Records. There was an LP, in fact, I have a copy of it, probably the only record I kept. Unfortunately, the album sold only 3,200 copies, so it didn't mean a great deal to us, and we didn't understand it. Then Ed Sullivan had the Beatles on his program and they took off like a ton of bricks. By that time, people who owned the masters decided that the Capitol Label could do a much better job. So, we lost them and that was a very stupid thing. But we would get other artists on Vee-Jay like the Four Seasons, when they first came out simply because we had distribution. We knew how to get a record exposed, had relationships with disc jockeys so that we could get a record played. That helped grow the label. And it did very well plus we had a fellow there, Calvin Carter, who was the "A&R man," and Calvin got on very well with the artists to do some very good recording work. So that worked out very well over the years.

Then we went off on a different tangent, we decided that we'd like to have a place to have our artists play and expose them or—we really just wanted to have a nightclub. So, we tried to put a nightclub in a hotel in downtown Chicago on the near Northside where there wasn't a nightclub. We thought about buying it. Ramsey Lewis started playing it and then couldn't do that. So, then we opened the club on Dearborn and Division, called the Birdhouse. That was Charlie Bird. That was a pretty large place. It sat about 400 people and we brought in jazz artists from all over the world. Then Jimmy and Ab said, "You know, we'd like to have a place on the south side," and they were my partners. The Sutherland Lounge had closed. You've heard about the Sutherland Lounge—that's at 47th Street and Drexel in the Sutherland Hotel. So, then I was tasked with going over there and trying to see if we could rent the place, get some acts. And the owner was a gentleman who owned the hotel, and he owned all the equipment in the bar, the furniture, everything else. We had run the Birdhouse for a while and made some noise with that place. Somebody else wanted to rent the Sutherland but the owner said, "No, I think you guys seem to have a good reputation." And he agreed to let us lease that place. So, we reopened the Sutherland Lounge and brought in all kinds of acts—jazz and people like Nancy Wilson, Slappy White, Miles Davis, all of which played in both of those clubs. Then I decided I'd like to do Dixieland. So, I opened another club called the Basin Street, in what was the old French Village in Chicago. Are you familiar with that? My recollection is it was on Clark Street, and probably 400 North of Ohio Street, to the best of my recollection. There was a little enclave there that had several different kinds of clubs. We had a store there that became Basin Street. It was a Dixieland club and we'd bring in Dixieland—and jazz customers are much different than Dixieland customers. The jazz club people are very attentive to modern jazz and very quiet from an audience point of view. Not so in a Dixieland club. A whole different atmosphere. The music itself was much more raucous, people enjoyed it, and drank more. So, it did well. When we opened the Birdhouse, we were originally going to have a kid's nightclub. Our first partner was Al Grossman, who had the Gate of Horn. Are you familiar with that at all? It was a folk club and we were going to have a young people's club. We weren't going to have liquor, everything we served would come from vending machines. As a matter of fact, we had the first dollar changer in the city. And that didn't work that way. So ultimately, we got a liquor license and had many trials with that situation. But we split the room. It was a huge room and had been a playhouse before that. And so, we split the room. On one side, you can get in without ID and liquor was served on the other side, but you had to prove your age. We had a narrow area in the middle, so you couldn't hand things across. That was split like the velvet ropes you would have lining people up. That was the Birdhouse. And we brought in the major acts that you would find in jazz and it did well for a while. It was on the second floor, the space itself, I understand, had originally been a gambling casino. And then it was empty. Then it became a playhouse and then it was empty and then we rented it. So that was kind of an interesting thing and from that group we did Basin Street and the Sutherland Lounge.

The Sutherland Lounge—you're talking about the late '50s and early '60s—was pretty interesting. The Sutherland Lounge was a pretty large room—it had about seven bars. It had a central bar, which the acts played in the center of that and the bar rang it and then there were bars in different corners of the place. It was quite interesting. Our acts were pretty good. Miles Davis was always kind of a kick because he started playing and then he'd walk off the stand but the band would still play. So, people loved him. I don't know if they loved him particularly because what he played but the way he acted.

I remember one time when we were in London working on what we accidentally wound up was the Beatles, got a call from Ramsey. He was going to work in the Birdhouse. But I had bought a new piano, a Yamaha, and I got a call from the manager saying "Ramsey says he doesn't want to go on." I said, "Why?" When we bought a new piano, it only had eighty-seven keys—not eighty-eight. Those are the early Yamahas you know we're talking about the late '40s and '50s. I finally talked to Ramsey, and he did go on. But I see him occasionally now and we still joke about eighty-seven keys. Another funny incident when we were opening Basin Street. I think that was my third club. So, by that time, I became a little used to running nightclubs and things like that. I went in there in the afternoon, late afternoon, the opening night, and the manager there was a young man I found, Tom, I don't remember his last name, but he had worked somewhere else. And they were putting in the last finishing touches. They painted a couple of things and it had a screen that made it look like the New Orleans garden type thing. They were securing the fixtures and so on. Doctors said, "Everything's okay. You've got stock, you're ready." So, my opening act was Jimmy McPartland and his band. I knew Jimmy from Universal Recording because I'd been there when we did his recordings there. Here it is opening night. So, I drove home, got dressed, tried to catch a little nap. And all of a sudden, I realized I didn't see the piano. I bought a new piano for that place. I put in an upright, because that's typical at that kind of a club. So, I called Tom. I said, "You know, I didn't see the piano there." He said, "Oh my god, I forgot to have it delivered." So, I'm figuring I got a problem here. I get to the club. And Jimmy and his band come in. He has his wife Marian with him—the pianist, yeah, but she wasn't playing in the band. She was an artist in her own right—okay? Jimmy had his four-piece band. So, I tell Jimmy, "I'm sorry, I screwed up somehow. We didn't get the piano here. But, would you guys go on?" "Oh, not a problem. We'll go on. I'll just have my piano player sit over there." Marian said, "You know, I'm a Wurlitzer artist." She said, "Let me call them." At that time, Wurlitzer had a store on Wabash Avenue, under the El at Jackson or Adams. So, she came back and said, "Look, if you can get some guys in a truck, they'll lend you a piano for the night." So, I talked to Tom the manager, and in the middle of the second set, four of the scruffiest guys you ever want to see walked in carrying his piano, over the top of their heads. They come in set it down on the stage, the band is playing. And the piano player without a missing a note, gets up, walks over, and just starts playing with them. If I had planned that it would have been a great publicity stunt. You know, it happens you kind of get along with it after a time.

What were the headaches of running a nightclub, running a record label?

Oh, well, dealing with people. You know, sometimes that was very difficult in the record business because so many artists had different people involved that hung around them and so on. And often times an artist or somebody would think they weren't being fairly treated and become a problem and remember, when you have a good artist, you become the mother and father, you know, you got somebody who comes in to record with you, that sounds good and kind of might be ragtag, and you're going to give them a start and he signed your standard contract. And then he begins to make noise. So, you got to get him out on the road for exposure, and he wants to be on the road. So, you wind up buying them a wardrobe, you buy him a car. And when they get a little bigger, you have to hire a guy to make sure they get from date to date, because they may not make it if they don't have somebody in charge of them. So, all that comes out of their record royalties. And when they got their accounting, sometime people would feel cheated. They forgot that all this comes out of their money. And so, it becomes a problem.

From what you said, though, you sound as though you actually were a talent manager? Did you manage talent at some point?

No, I just had to deal with them in the sense that they were there and if they didn't have a manager, then you became unofficially called the manager because you had to make sure they would get there, both for their sake, and for the sake of your label. And you wanted your artists to get exposure. Nightclubs are a whole different ballgame in the sense that you have outside people you have to be concerned with and you have the lobby to be concerned with. And you also have to make sure that you are on your toes all the time, because of your exposure or your place's exposure to all kinds of people, you know, a real drunk could cause you a big problem. A bartender who's stealing can cause you a problem. Those kinds of things. And the act, usually the acts are really the least problem. You know, you'd hire a musician, if they were union, you'd deposit their fee with the union. They'd show up on time, they play. Occasionally one wouldn't show up on time, something like that, you know, but they were pretty well-disciplined people. It was just the physical operation that bothered you. I got out of the entertainment business, primarily when Vee-Jay went to California. You know, it's like, I've had enough. I didn't want any more. I didn't want to own another nightclub, you know, didn't want to own another act. I just wanted to go someplace, be entertained and buy my drinks. I learned to fly after I got out of the army, which is what I originally wanted to do. But I had a colorblind problem. And they wouldn't let you fly in the army at that time. So, the two things I did when I got discharged was; first thing was to buy a blue suit. And the second thing was learned to fly. And I got my license in 1946. And I'd been flying up until two years ago. I just was getting old enough that I felt I wasn't as sharp as I wanted to be. Since then, I've taken up parachuting and I find that quite interesting. It keeps the circulation going—particularly when you're standing in the doorway of the plane and you're saying, "Why in the heck am I doing this?"

Johnny Parth

Johnny Parth is a German record collector, a fan of both jazz and blues. His main claim to fame is that he was responsible for the Document reissue series. The Document series reissued 99 percent of sides listed in the Prewar Blues discography on a series of more than 800 CDs and made it possible for blues collectors to hear and own CD copies of what were previously rare and prohibitively expensive prewar Blues recordings, originally issued as 78 RPM records. In an hour-long phone interview from 2007, Johnny tells his story.

I was born in Vienna, on the eleventh of January 1930. I went to school in Vienna. My father was a clerk and my mother was at home all the time. There were three kids, I was the oldest. My brother is ten years younger and my sister is twelve years younger. During the war, when I was fourteen, I had some friends from the underground and this was the first time I came in contact with jazz music. And this changed all my education, you see, this music fascinated me so much. I ran in this circle and we came together once a week. And I was not allowed to tell anybody that we listened to the BBC from London, you see that was prohibited. This was the first time that I heard jazz music. In German radio, you could only hear operas or Wagner or marching music or folk music, things like that. And then I visited a friend of mine from school. "You must listen to something," and he played "St. Louis Blues" by Louis Armstrong. This was the first time in my life that I heard a jazz record and was so fascinated that I wanted to hear more of this kind of music. He said, "Yes, you can. But you must promise that you won't tell anybody, even not your parents—nobody at all, because somebody will get the information that we come together. They will lock us in jail." And so, I had to swear that I wouldn't tell anybody. And so, we met once a week and they played BBC London, and there was jazz on the radio. And that was strictly prohibited during Hitler's time. And every half hour, there was a break and they read the news in the German language.

And then I heard for the very first time in my life of the concentration camps and all these things. I couldn't believe it, but they told me that even relatives of my school friends were in the concentration camp. And so, it was a very hard situation for me that I was not allowed to tell my parents. I couldn't believe that they sympathized with it—it was so political. You see, I couldn't even ask if they knew about this. This was very hard for me because I was fourteen years of age. My father was in war, he was not at home and our house was bombed. So, my mother, my little brother and I had to leave Vienna. We walked about 300 kilometers, walking and living in the countryside, you see, because everything was bombed. For a short time before the war was over, where we lived there was a Nazi. A poor peasant stayed with him, a foreign laborer, he was Polish. He slept on the floor in the stable with the horses, you see. And they gave him only enough food to stay alive—he was always hungry. So, I made friends with this guy. I went to the kitchen, took a lot of bread and meat from there and brought it to him in the stable. Also, when I lived in the countryside, another friend, the son of an important person, told me that at the post office there was a letter for me from the army. They wanted to take me at fourteen years old in to the army. So, I left my mother—I didn't even tell her. And I was gone. I lived a month and a half in the woods. Because if they found me, they might have killed me or something like that. During the daytime I was always in the woods and in the evenings, I went to the peasants and asked them if they had something for me to eat. That lasted about one week—and then the war was over. I saw people in the woods close to the city. They wore clothes with stripes and they were from the concentration camps. They were free now. And then I could go among other people again. This was the hardest time of my life, believe me. But the war was over. And then I promised that jazz music was, for me, the most important thing in my life, and I promised that I would, all my life, work to promote this kind of music. And this was the beginning of everything for me, but it was not my profession at that time.

After the war, I went to art school, because I was a very good painter. So, when my father came back from the war, he sent me to art school. First, I went to high school, and from there to the art school. And then I became a portrait painter. Most of my life I painted portraits. I loved music more, but I wasn't a musician. You see, I learned a little bit of trumpet playing—but I was an amateur. But I was a very good painter. And so, for a long time, that was my profession. And I also began to collect records, by the end of the 1940s. And it was very hard to get records, because no records were available at that time—only a few from private people. And in the early 1950s, 1952 or 1953, there was a club in Vienna, a private club called Hot Club, DVM. I went there and I could hear some recitals about jazz music and blues music. And the third time I came there, many people were standing on the street in front of the café. I said, "What happened?" They said the rent wasn't paid, so they wouldn't let us in. When they said that, I went downstairs, because I had just come from a company for which I made a portrait. And I had some money in my pocket. And I went to the owner of the café and said, "If I pay the rent for the club, can we come in?" She said, "Yes." So, I paid it. Then, I went upstairs and said, "We can go down to the club, and I'm your new president." [*Laughs.*] So, the first time, it was not democratic but we carried on with the club, but no live music. The next year, they loved this and then sometimes also live musicians came. One of them was Joe Zawinul, who is very famous in America. He died in Vienna a few weeks ago. You probably know the group he played with, Weather Report—but he was also with Miles Davis. Blues came later in my life, you see, but first came jazz. Blues music that was in the 1950s when I first heard that. Blues fascinated me even more than jazz. During the time when I had the jazz club, I had a lot of ideas. I thought we could change the Blue Danube River to the Mississippi. So, I asked the people who manage the ships on the Danube if it would be possible to rent a ship for people, for jazz fans on board and make riverboats out of them like in America. They quoted a price and I said, "Okay, let's try it." So, I borrowed money from all my friends and we got enough to rent the ship and this was the first riverboat tour. This was in 1956, I think—exactly fifty-one years ago. So, I made a few jazz riverboat tours. Then I had the idea to ask a priest if they would like to hold services on the riverboat and then we arranged the first Catholic mass on the river in Austria. The first time there were problems with Catholic religion higher-ups, but after the first tour, there were no more problems and from then on, the tours were successful over and over again. And then I made arrangements to promote concerts with jazz music. And I met many jazz musicians, like Lionel Hampton—many, many—too many musicians to list.

How did you make the transition from a jazz fan to blues?

The first blues record I heard was Blind Lemon Jefferson. It was on a little LP that came out in America on the Riverside label and in Europe on a ten-inch record on the London label. This was around 1957 or 1958. It fascinated me and I tried to listen to more of the same kind of material. I found people who had records and they sent them to me and I taped them. That was the beginning of my blues interest. When I was the president of the Hot Club of Vienna, I made the first private recordings. These were releases of early 78s. King Oliver's

Creole Jazz Band and Louis Armstrong's Hot Five and Hot Seven. They were long-playing records, thirty copies each [*laughs*]. I made everything myself, the covers and everything. I sold them only in the club. Then I put out the first blues album—it was a three-volume set, *Anthology of the Blues*, also on the Jazz Perspective label. Later came the Roots label—I believe that was at the end of the 1960s.

Did you actually own any 78s?

I had a big collection, and a friend of mine in London, Pete Segal, he was in the fish market—he sold my whole collection. I needed money one day and I decided to sell my complete 78 collection—first my favorite records, then it was easier to sell the others [*laughs*]. So, I began with my favorites and I got rid of them. Then I started with LPs. Then I sold my LP collection and had no money. So, I put everything on cassettes. I wasn't happy with cassettes so I started with LPs again. Then I had no money again—and then I went with CDs.

How many Roots LPs did you issue?

Let me think—about sixty.

And what was a press run for a Roots LP?

One hundred—and if it sold all one hundred, then I pressed another one hundred—but that only happened very few times. At the same time, I made the blues records, I also recorded Austrian folk music—also early recordings of Viennese folk music, which I got from collectors here in Vienna.

I married the first time when I was twenty-one. That was in 1951. I was married six years and divorced in 1957. A few months later I married my second wife Evelyn—and we were together twelve years. Then, she met a friend of mine and left me! [*Laughs.*] Then, about six months later I met my third wife. She was twenty-five years younger than I—very beautiful—and we were married thirty-two years. She left me two years ago . . .

Now, from the Roots label to the Document label, there was a long period of time when I issued no records. I started painting again. I made my money with painting. This was a very hard life. Sometimes we didn't have enough to eat. We'd go to the neighbors and ask them to loan us money so we could buy bread. After that, I had the idea to start issuing LPs again—and that was the beginning of the Document label. It seemed that the same 78s were reissued again and again on LP but there were many original sides that had never been reissued—all that duplication made me crazy. So, I said, "What I want to do is reissue everything, by every artist, in complete chronological order." So, I started to do that on LP—and continued for two years, and then in August 1990, I switched to CDs. I finished the project in July of 1999, issuing 880 CDs.

How many copies of each LP did you press?

Three hundred copies of each LP.

How many of each catalog item when you switched to CDs?

Five hundred—with one hundred copies when re-pressing each catalog item.

Collectors who have items from the Document project know that you reissued better than 99 percent of the records listed in the Prewar discography. How did you manage to get copies of all those records?

[*Laughs.*] I actually called all the different record collectors—and many, when they heard about the project, many collectors actually called me. There was a collector in Canada, Roger Misiewicz, he had lists of contact information for many collectors, worldwide. He got the collectors in touch with me—and me in touch with the collectors. He was very, very helpful.

Were there any collectors who were reluctant to participate?

A very few. There were also collectors I had to pay for use of their recording—most didn't ask very much, some simply wanted a copy of the CD that included the records they had made available, but then, a few wanted quite a bit of money, as well. Most didn't want anything—they just wanted me to put all the records out. They all sent copies of their records on tape. Some sent their records on reel-to-reel, many on cassettes. A few even provided copies on DAT [digital audio tape]. I would take them into the recording studios and we would try to improve the sound quality. I have a long list of collectors who made their records available—but no record of who contributed what artists or titles. I took the tapes to a recording engineer, Hans Klement. He was a heavy drinker—an alcoholic. And then I changed and worked with a friend of mine Gerhard Wessely at the Soundborn Studios in Vienna.

Let me ask about the tape copies that you received from collectors around the world. I suppose in many cases, you had duplicate copies. For instance, if you had three copies of a song by Tampa Red, how would you choose which copy to use?

I would compare them in the studio—which one sounds best. You simply use the best available copy. And, if only a very bad copy was available, no other could be found, then I'd hate to use it but, to put out the complete works, I sometimes had to use very bad copies. It's not always easy to make a complete collection.

Are there still any titles that are missing today?

No, not many. Absolutely not. No. That's what I've done. And there is all the material which we found later, which came out during the years after I've stopped producing the Document issues.

I have made private issues of this later material. So, they are for myself and my friends. But they are homemade.

Each Document CD came with a set of liner notes, compiled by one of a variety of writers. Who assigned the liner notes to the various writers?

At the start, the people who knew what I was doing would sometimes ask to write liner notes and we discussed it mostly. Also, they would recommend writer/collectors who had strong knowledge of a particular artist or particular genre of the blues and I would ask them to write liner notes. The liner note assignments were all very democratic and generated a great deal of cooperation—otherwise, I would never have been able to finish the project without the help of so many people.

And, who did the cover art for the Document label CDs?

I did. You know, I'm a graphic artist. Before I made portraits, I did a lot of work for companies in Vienna—posters and things. So, it was no problem for me—I made the covers. A computer friend of mine would put them into the computer, and that was all.

There were some CDs which didn't sell at all—but I knew this when I produced them. I knew nobody would buy nine volumes of Rev. J.M. Gates just talking and preaching, you see—but I had to do that because it's a part of the entire project. There were other items which sold very well, and whenever I had a "good run" it allowed me to issue other things that would not sell. There were certain artists that had already been reissued in complete chronological order by other labels—Bessie Smith and Robert Johnson were issued by the Columbia label—so I didn't include them in the Document project—but I pledged that I *would* reissue these items if they were ever deleted by Columbia.

After you finished the Document Blues series, you started a series of white string bands. How did that happen—and, with prewar blues you had a discography to guide you. How were you able to decide what to include in the white string band series?

It was Tony Russell's idea that I should do the white country and string band series, and many of the collectors of the Blues series liked the idea. So, I decided to do it. Tony sent me all the material and the information because I didn't know much about that music. He did the compilations and wrote all the liner notes. He did all the work—I just spent the money. But—at the end of the blues series I was almost seventy years old, and getting tired, so we did this next series with the understanding that, if I said I'd had enough, the series would end.

How did you decide to sell the label as a whole?

The problem was my wife. She liked blues but she would always say, "You have no time for the family. You work sixteen hours every day, even on Saturday and Sunday." And so, she wanted me to have more time for her. That was when I turned seventy years old. And I said okay, this is the time to finish. I'm seventy-eight now but when I was seventy, I finished the project and sold the whole thing. There were two or three American producers who were interested in buying it from me but they wouldn't agree that when current stocks of items in the catalog ran out, they would agree to have it repressed so it would stay in print. I wanted to sell it with the condition that nothing in the catalog could be deleted—that was my condition. That's why I wouldn't sell it to them. But there was a guy in England, Gary Atkinson, who said, "Alright—I'll do that . . . " I would continue to work for him. I would compile them for him. I would get the material from the collectors and he just had to put them out. For me, that was a better contract and he bought all the rights and everything from me. But, after he paid ten percent of the whole amount, he said he couldn't pay anymore and he had no money. So, everything was stolen. It was terrible for me that he stopped paying. He had all my stocks—a few hundred thousand CDs—and I don't have the money to take him to court in Scotland.

I love the Document project; you could say it was my life. The most important thing in my life, more than the Hot Club and all the other things. In 2001, I received the "Keeping the Blues Alive" award from the folks who do the W.C. Handy Awards in Memphis, Tennessee. They flew me and my family to Memphis to attend the awards ceremony. The next year I received a gold medal from the folks in Vienna for my Document label project. The Library of Congress has copies of the entire catalog, so it's not lost to future generations.

Franz Jackson

Franz Jackson was an acclaimed tenor veteran around Chicago who made a name for himself with stints in the bands of Fletcher Henderson, Roy Eldridge, and Earl Hines—pretty impressive credentials. I was surprised to get a phone call from him early one morning on the program. He was calling to take issue with my on-air description of Frankie Half-Pint Jaxon as a female impersonator. It turns out that Franz actually worked on a regular basis in Frankie's band back in the late 1920s/early 1930s. I was fascinated talking with anyone who actually knew Half-Pint in person and we made arrangements to talk at length about his time in Jaxon's band. We met at a very popular Sunday morning jazz brunch in the northern suburbs and, unfortunately, I was unable to use any of the interview due to the crowded room ambience. The crowd noise shouldn't bother us here in print.

■ ■ ■

There was a fellow, Dave Kapp. He was the brother of Jack Kapp who did Decca Records. He was around Chicago here. Somehow, he got Frankie Half-Pint Jaxon a radio show. Frankie was accompanied by a studio band—a white band. He used to go on every day, sometime around supper time. The program was fifteen minutes long and his hit record, "Fan It," was his theme song. He would do that song—and other numbers, all arranged by the white band. And they did fairly well here around Chicago because that was the range of the radio station. But, the white band was strictly for the radio broadcast and nothing else. So, they organized another band, a Black band to play live dates. When they booked Frankie on live dates, it was always with a Black band. I was a part of the band and we got a lot of work out of that in theaters. That came in handy because the depression was on and there weren't too many jobs, you know. And we could make as much from one night in a theater as we could make in a week on a club date. The theater band was led by the piano player—Eddie King was his name. We had eight pieces. The tenor man was a fellow named

Fred Brown, and he and I used to always work jobs together. We'd go from one band to another. The band had Fred—and Bob Schoffner on trumpet. There was a banjo player, James Thomas. Harry Gray was the bass player. The band played gigs behind Half-Pint but it wasn't any special setup, it just sort of happened, you know. "Okay, we'll pick him and him . . ." I think Eddie King took the band over after we left Half-Pint Jaxon and they did some dates after that. But it wasn't enough work for me. I was young and adventurous. I left the band and went out of town somewhere. Later in life, Fred King became a school teacher. James Thomas committed suicide, and Harry Gray got to be the president of the Musicians Union, the Black union local 208. I believe they used Bob Schoffner when they recorded Half-Pint. I believe it was a big band. He took that band over after I left. Most of the theater dates that we played with Half-Pint were out in the suburbs. It was a "cold stage"—we played behind a white screen. They'd just pull the curtain, the band would get up on the stand, and we'd start playing. They pushed him just that much. It was a neighborhood, a local thing. Sometimes it would be us—and a movie. We got a lot of nice work out of that. Frankie was unique as a performer. He was very small. Five feet, or four foot something—very short. He wore a little skull cap. He had a high voice and was very light on his feet. Frankie wasn't a dancer but he would prance the stage and talk to the band, particularly when the various players would solo. He tried to learn saxophone . . . [*Laughs.*] I bought a saxophone from him—the saxophone had buttons on it, and I traded it to Roy Eldridge for a trumpet. Frankie was unique as a performer, but the songs he sang—they weren't soft wrist—you know, limp wristed. That's the reason I called you. You mentioned that some critics regarded Frankie as a female impersonator—but I never saw that. He was married and had a family. In fact, he had a son and he was trying to get him to take up the saxophone. But as far as Half-Pint being a female impersonator, I never got that impression at all—and I had been working around female impersonators. There were a lot of places like that. They usually started about eleven or twelve o'clock at night and they'd go on until four or five o'clock in the morning—an after-hours place. At that time, they had a place called Pleasure's Inn, definitely a female impersonator club, owned by a guy, she called herself Gloria Swanson—down on 31st Street.

Joel Dorn

I met Dick LaPalm through my old buddy, veteran jazz jock Dick Buckley. LaPalm gave me a wonderful interview about his days working for Nat King Cole—and it turns out LaPalm and I were both fans of jazz vocalist Joe Williams. Dick suggested that if I wanted to hear stories about Joe Williams, the fellow to talk with was jazz jock/record producer/label owner Joel Dorn. Joel was kind enough to share several stories about Joe Williams. What follows is one of them . . .

■ ■ ■

When I was twenty-five I worked at a station, WHAT-FM, it was Jazz at 96.5—and it was Philadelphia's version of a radio phenomenon that was happening all over the country at that time, a twenty-four-hour-a-day, seven-days-a-week jazz station. There was one in each major city—and sometimes two. That was when jazz was kind of a hipper music for people going from high school to college to young adulthood. They would listen to jazz because it was music of that time. There were giants roaming the earth. You had Horace Silver and Miles Davis and John Coltrane and Cannonball Adderley and Art Blakey and along with all of the modern jazz guys, you still had Louis Armstrong and Duke Ellington and Count Basie and people like that. And Joe Williams had kind of single-handedly revived the Count Basie band. The Big Band era was over at the end of the '40s. In the '50s there were just some bands hanging on—Basie and Ellington among them and even they had rough spots. So, when Joe hooked up with Basie in '55, they had a string of hits—"Alright, Okay—You Win," "Every Day I Have the Blues," "The Comeback." Basie had a spectacular band at that time, and Joe was at the absolute height of his powers, so he was a big star in jazz—and he also had some crossover attraction. He left Basie in '61 and went on the road with a trio—Junior Mance, Bob Cranshaw, and Mickey Roker. And off of the strength of his years with Basie—he was exposed to audiences all over the world, and the fact that he had made a few hit albums, most notably *A Man*

Ain't Supposed to Cry, his ballad album on Roulette, Joe was a big star. I met him when I was disc jockey in those days—and I was on a station that was one of the top jazz stations in the country. If you got your records played on WHAT in Philly, your records would sell. And I was a big Joe Williams fan—and so were all the other guys at our station. So, he got a lot of air play. Consequently, he played at one of the two jazz clubs in Philly twice a year. He played a club called Pep's—the other club was the Showboat—and he always did business. You know, Joe drew the jazz crowd but he drew that crowd outside of jazz that came in for certain acts. He was a very bright, well-spoken, well-traveled, savvy kind of guy—very charming. And he could sing anything. He could go from Cole Porter or Gershwin ballad right into a Muddy Waters song. He could do both things, and he could do them equally well. He could swing—and he could scat—and he was great on stage. And he was very smart when it came to radio. He came to town and he would come by the radio station. He would do interviews. He would invite you to the club as his guest. He would introduce you from the bandstand. He'd been on the road for years, so he knew the game. I met him the year before. I was buying his records—and now he's a guest on my radio show. We would hang out—we would have breakfast after the gig and go different places. He was very, very nice to me—very kind. I was nineteen or twenty and Joe was already forty, and had been through all the show business wars before he landed with Basie. He was very kind, he would say, "Here's what you do, young man . . ." He always called me "young man." "Be careful of this . . ." or "Be wary of that . . ." or "This is something you should get better at . . ." He was a very good guy—I was thrilled to know him. I was a punk kid with a deep voice—and he was Joe Williams and we're having breakfast. It was great and I remained a fan, obviously, during his entire career.

Joe was playing Pep's. And another guy—a connected guy, wanted Joe to come by his club. He had a club that was not far from Pep's. He had these two juke boxes that he was extremely proud of. They were mostly Sinatra. It was mostly Sinatra on the juke box but he was a tough guy—and he pretty much got what he wanted to. He called Pep's and he told the owner there, Jack Goldenberg, he said, "I want Joe Williams to come by. I want to buy him a drink and I want to show him my juke boxes." Well, Jack didn't really want to do it—and I owed Jack a lot of favors—because he was another guy who was very nice to me. I was a kid and he'd let me in the club, even though I was underage. He connected me with a lot of people that I wanted to meet. So, he ropes me into taking Joe to this guy's club after the final set from 1:20 until 2 in the morning. Joe didn't want to go—he was through with that stuff. So, he goes there. It's after the clubs in Philly were supposed to close because of the liquor law but the club is full of people, so Joe and I walk in. He sees Joe and he clears the joint. It's just Joe and me and him and a pretty chick—and a guy that looks like a refrigerator, a big guy—not a guy to mess with. He gives us one-hundred-year-old brandy and tells Joe how great he is, and how much he's loved and honored that Joe would come by and everything. We're sitting there and we're looking to get out. Joe's thanking him and telling him we have to get out. And the guy says, "Just a minute, Joe . . ."— and I knew someone just threw one low and inside. He showed us the juke boxes and he was so proud of them. One box was all Sinatra. The other box was half Sinatra with Tony Bennett and Nat Cole—and Joe Williams—all quality stuff. So, he says to me, "Kid, we're gonna play something from Joe's album *A Man Ain't Supposed To Cry*—it's on the juke box. You introduce it and then Joe will sing along with it." Joe looked at me—he didn't like doing this junk. His days of doing that were over when he had to do it in front of mob guys in Chicago and they would make him tap dance and things he didn't want to do. So, they played the song and the song comes on, and I kinda mumbled "Here's Joe Williams from his album, *A Man Ain't Supposed To Cry*." The song comes on and the strings start playing and Joe's not singing—he kinda going "Da-da-da-da-da—say it isn't so . . ." And about thirty or forty seconds into it this guy, Big Bill, freaks. He tells the other guy to go over and stop the juke box. He starts shrieking at me, "What's wrong with you? Don't you have any respect for this man?" And—I'm not using the language he's using because we're on radio. "Didn't I tell you to introduce the guy!?" And veins are popping out of the side of his head—and he's got his thumb jammed into the part of my body I now know is called the clavicle, and he's twisting it—and I'm seeing rainbows. He says, "Now we're gonna do it again." He said, "You introduce it like you do on the radio, you understand?" I say, "Yes, sir." And they start the juke box again and the string introduction comes up and as it comes up [*laughs*] and in the best radio voice I could muster, I go, "From his classic album on the Roulette Label, the great Joe Williams. The album is *A Man Ain't Supposed To Cry*, and this is his version of 'Say It Isn't So.'" And I timed it just right—the strings were ending and Joe comes in, "Say it isn't so . . .," and he's singing—and snarling at me [*laughs*]. We finally got out of there. He didn't even talk in the car on the way home. He was mad, man. I wrote him a note and he called me the next day and he said, "Alright—don't worry. You were paying your dues last night. I remember when I had to do that kind of stuff." He said, "Just remember, someday you're going to have an opportunity to help somebody like I helped you last night. Remember last night." And then he paused and said, "You want to have some breakfast after the gig?" I thought that was so cool. Inadvertently, I put him in a mortifying position and after he got over being pissed off, he was really good to me. We always laughed about that.

Index

STEVE CUSHING has hosted *Blues Before Sunrise* for more than forty years. He is the author of *Blues Before Sunrise: The Radio Interviews*, *Blues Before Sunrise 2: Interviews from the Chicago Scene*, and *Pioneers of the Blue Revival.*

The University of Illinois Press
is a founding member of the
Association of University Presses.

Composed in 10/13.25 Minion Pro
with Univers LT Std display
by Lisa Connery
at the University of Illinois Press
Manufactured by Sheridan Books, Inc.

University of Illinois Press
1325 South Oak Street
Champaign, IL 61820-6903
www.press.uillinois.edu